Greene & Greene Furniture
Poems of Wood & Light

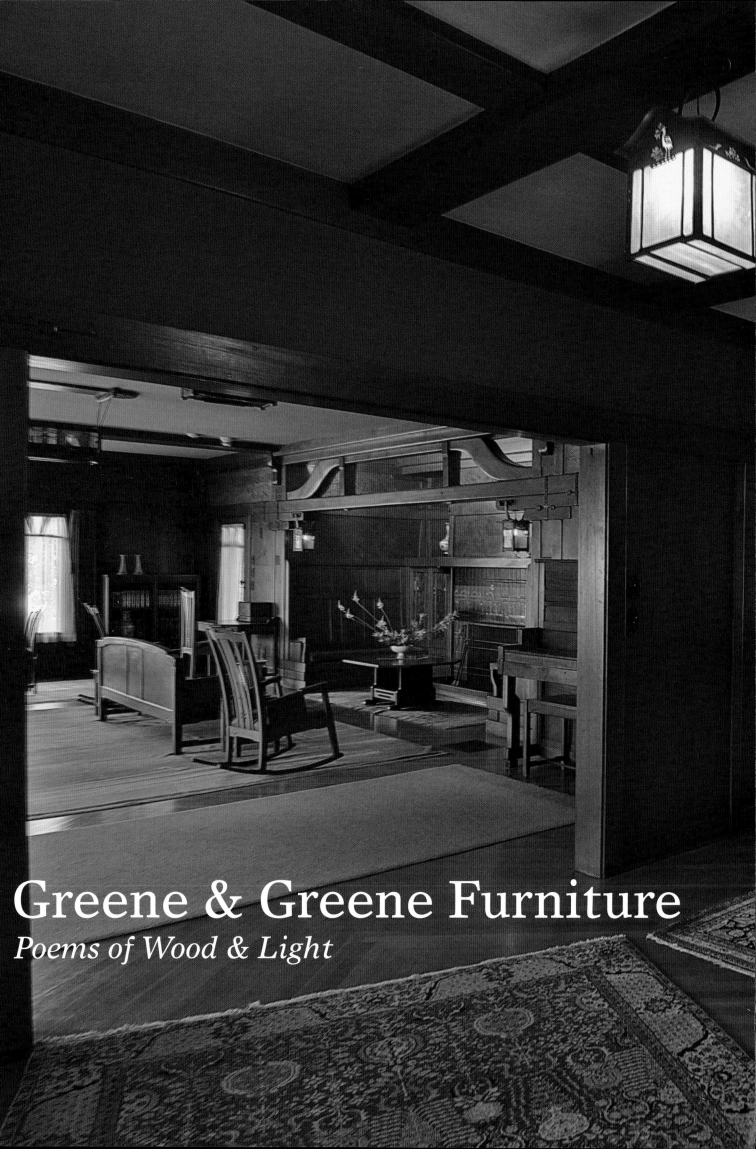

Greene & Greene Furniture

Poems of Wood & Light

David Mathias

BETTERWAY HOME
CINCINNATI, OHIO
www.popularwoodworking.com

METRIC CONVERSION CHART

TO CONVERT	TO	MULTIPLY BY
Inches	Centimeters	2.54
Centimeters	Inches	0.4
Feet	Centimeters	30.5
Centimeters	Feet	0.03
Yards	Meters	0.9
Meters	Yards	1.1

GREENE & GREENE FURNITURE. Copyright © 2010
by David Mathias. Printed and bound in China.
All rights reserved. No part of this book may be
reproduced in any form or by any electronic or
mechanical means including information storage
and retrieval systems without permission in writing
from the publisher, except by a reviewer, who may
quote brief passages in a review. Published by
Popular Woodworking Books, an imprint of F+W
Media, Inc., 4700 East Galbraith Road, Cincinnati,
Ohio, 45236. (800) 289-0963. First edition.

Distributed in Canada by Fraser Direct
100 Armstrong Avenue
Georgetown, Ontario L7G 5S4
Canada

Distributed in the U.K. and Europe by David & Charles
Brunel House
Newton Abbot
Devon TQ12 4PU
England
Tel: (+44) 1626 323200
Fax: (+44) 1626 323319
E-mail: postmaster@davidandcharles.co.uk

Distributed in Australia by Capricorn Link
P.O. Box 704
Windsor, NSW 2756
Australia

Visit our Web site at www.popularwoodworking.com.

Other fine Popular Woodworking Books are available
from your local bookstore or direct from the
publisher.

14   13   12   11   10   5   4   3   2   1

Library of Congress Cataloging-in-Publication Data

Mathias, David.
   Greene & Greene furniture : poems of wood & light /
by David Mathias.
      p. cm.
   Includes index.
   ISBN 978-1-4403-0299-2 (hardcover : alk. paper)
   1. Greene & Greene. 2. Arts and crafts movement-
-California. 3. Furniture design--California--History-
-20th century. I. Title. II. Title: Greene & Greene
furniture : poems of wood & light.
   NK2439.G76M38 2010
   728'.370922794--dc22
                                        2010008546

Acquisitions Editor: David Thiel
Senior Editor: Jim Stack
Designer: Brian Roeth
Production Coordinator: Mark Griffin

About the Author

David Mathias (pictured at left with the original entry mirror from the Blacker house) recently abandoned computer science for the full-time pursuit of writing and photography. His interests include woodworking which led him to the Arts & Crafts movement in general and Greene & Greene in particular. He has built a number of furniture pieces inspired by the Greenes and Gustav Stickley. David's magazine articles on Greene & Greene gave him the opportunity to visit and study many Greene & Greene homes including the Gamble, Blacker, Robinson, Ford and Thorsen houses. His photos and articles were the seed for this book. David lives near Vevey, Switzerland, with his wife Patty and sons Dylan and Zachary.

Acknowledgements

Researching and writing this book have been a tremendous privilege and, perhaps, the best experience of my professional life. The work of Charles and Henry Greene has been a great source of pleasure for me, as it has for many others. This project has allowed me to see and to experience many of their houses and much of their furniture. I am happy to say that my sense of awe and wonder never subsided. Every time I enter a Greene & Greene house I experience the same feeling of history, of being in the presence of genius, and I am acutely aware of the privilege being afforded me due to the generosity of others.

Generosity has been a constant throughout the past two years, for no project such as this is possible without the generous assistance of many people. I have wondered often how I came to be the beneficiary of so much kindness from so many but have failed to find an explanation. All I can offer, tongue in cheek, is that the stars must have aligned in my favor. My purpose here is to give my humble thanks to all who have given their assistance, opened their homes to me, and shared their knowledge and experiences. I sincerely hope that the accounting is complete but offer apologies to anyone I neglect to mention. Any such omission is due only to the large numbers and my addled brain, certainly not to any lack of gratitude.

For many reasons, I am very grateful to the staff of the Gamble house. Because of its significance in the Greene & Greene canon and because it stands today nearly as it did a century ago, the Gamble house must figure prominently in almost any book on this subject. The time I have been afforded in the Gamble house (a place to which I often refer as "the cathedral" or "the happiest place on Earth") has been substantial and enlightening. Kori Capaldi has been very accom-

modating in allowing me as much time as I needed for study and photography. She has also become a good friend. Anne Mallek has helped greatly with approving use of photographs. In addition, she had the Thorsen living room table uncrated so that I could photograph it. Bobbi Mapstone has been very supportive in allowing access to the house. Finally, Ted Bosley has been exceptionally helpful. He has done everything from coordinate contacts with homeowners to answer numerous questions and provide encouragement. And, of course, he graciously agreed to write the foreword. I will never understand why Ted gave so much of himself, but this book is much improved because he did.

I have never lived in an historic home so I can't imagine what it must be like to be bothered constantly by guys like me who want to invade, to take photographs, to ask questions. Fortunately for all of us, the owners of Greene & Greene houses understand the historic significance of their homes. Most seem to see themselves as stewards and to feel some obligation to posterity. My most sincere thanks to all of those who so graciously invited me in: Judy and David Brown, Roxanne Hampton and Brian Kabateck, Jan Hurff, Lyn Boyd-Judson and David Judson, Ellen and Harvey Knell, Phaedra and Mark Ledbetter, Susan and Derek Pippert, Nancy and Tom Reitze, Bev and John Richardson, Mark Sailor, the Brothers of Sigma Phi. Special thanks to Matt Bierman, Scott Earnest and Bryce Kellogg, Kathleen Thorne-Thomsen, Tim Toohey and David Liu, and Gwen and Robert Whitson.

Several individuals were instrumental in helping gain access to houses that were vacant or are not currently used as residences. Thanks to Alyssa Bellew, Lee LaPlante, Peter Martocchio, Elizabeth McGregor, Gretchen Reed and Brian Williams.

During the course of working on this book, I visited a number of museums to see and photograph Greene & Greene pieces. Staff at the museums were very generous with their time. My gratitude to: Jason Busch and Laurel Mitchell at the Carnegie Museum of Art; Stephen Harrison, Carol Ciulla and Elizabeth Saluk at the Cleveland Museum of Art; Jim Tottis and Sylvia Inwood at the Detroit Institute of Arts; Ron Labaco and Sara Hindmarch at the High Museum of Art; Thomas Michie, Alexandra Moran, Piper Severance and Cheryle Robertson at the Los Angeles County Museum of Art; DeAnn Dankowski at the Minneapolis Institute of Arts; Nonie Gadsden and Jennifer Riley at the Museum of Fine Arts, Boston; Catherine Futter, Karin Jones and Stacey Sherman at the Nelson-Atkins Museum of Art; and Rachel Swiston, Patricia Woods and Kendra Baker at the Saint Louis Art Museum. I am especially grateful to Jacqueline Dugas, Susan Colletta, Jessica Smith and Sydney Moritz at the Huntington Library, Art Collections and Botanical Gardens.

The Guardian Trust is doing fantastic work in enhancing the Greene & Greene legacy by making pieces available for public view and by preserving and restoring several structures. I am very grateful to Ted Wells for his work and for his assistance with photographs, permissions, access and questions.

I would like to thank Miranda Rectenwald at the Washington University Archives; Jim Gerencser at the Dickinson College Library; Linda McCurdy at the Duke University Rare Book, Manuscript, and Special Collections Library; William Fischetti at the Western Historical Manuscript Collection at the University of Missouri-St. Louis; Ann Scheid at the Greene & Greene Archives; Carrie McDade and Miranda Hambro at the Environmental Design Archives; Stuart Feld and Alexandra Neville at Hirschl-Adler Gallery; Lauren Fresco at Christie's; Sarah Kaplan and James Zemaitis at Sotheby's; Dominick Bruno, Julie Horton, Ronnie Wexler, Jon Gilbert and Stacey Hoppe at Warner Bros. Studios; Rick Porter; Paul Holbrook at the Warwick Foundation; Kazuo Hozumi; Ayako Akaogi at Kodansha International; Alice Siempelkamp at House Beautiful; Susan Barell at Dover Publications; David Young; George Walker; Michael Whittington; Geoffrey Goldberg; Andre Chaves; and Bill Evans and Steve Pelzer at the Evans Hotel Group.

This book grew out of a series of articles for *Popular Woodworking* magazine. I have written several articles for the magazine and have always had great experiences because of the wonderful staff. I am grateful to Bob Lang; Chris Schwarz; Megan Fitzpatrick, Linda Watts and Glen Huey for their assistance and support. At a lunch meeting one day with Bob and Chris, I was stunned when Chris transformed a planned Greene & Greene design article into a three-part series. It was a great opportunity for which I am very thankful.

A number of friends and acquaintances were very helpful in many ways. Thank you to Darrell Peart, John Hamm, Jim Ipekjian, John Ipekjian, Randell Makinson, Gary and Betsy Hall, Bruce Smith, Juan de la Cruz, Rich Muller, Tom Stangeland and Tom Volz. Even among this elite group, one person stands out. He accompanied me to almost every Greene & Greene site I visited. He helped with arrangements and logistics. He proofread rough drafts. He offered advice and answered questions. He provided me with several photographs for publication. He and his wife, Jenny, allowed me to stay at their home. Most importantly, he was a great friend. Very special thanks to Tom Moore for sharing this journey.

From the very outset, my editor at F+W Media, David Thiel, has been a pleasure to work with. David was enthusiastic about the project from the first time we spoke. He guided me through the process quite patiently, answering every trivial question I posed. He was constantly encouraging and supportive. There really has not been an anxious moment in all of this and that is due entirely to David. Designer Brian Roeth did excellent work with the layout and look of the book. Early in the proposal stage, David Thiel sent me another book Brian had designed. Seeing that helped seal the deal for me. Finally, Bob Lang makes an appearance here as well. Bob recommended me to David — a favor that was instrumental in helping get things moving for a first-time book author.

Fourteen years ago, at the conclusion of graduate school, I dedicated my dissertation to the person most responsible for my success. I have had the honor of spending my entire adult life with a remarkable woman. It is not an exaggeration to say that anything I have accomplished is due to her. Her love and support are the great constant in my life. We now have two wonderful sons, Dylan and Zachary. Patty and the boys have been very supportive during this process. Patty has encouraged me to do everything necessary to complete this project including significant investment in travel and equipment with no guarantee of a return. My sons have sacrificed as well. Time I should have spent with them, time that was rightfully theirs, was surrendered with little complaint. While all of the homeowners, curators, directors, friends and editors have been essential, I humbly dedicate this work to Patty, Dylan and Zachary. Without them this book would not have been possible. More importantly, if I couldn't share it with them, then it simply wouldn't have been worth doing.

DAVID MATHIAS

Contents

Foreword

Sudden seduction is sometimes the unintended by-product of genius. When David Mathias first encountered the work of Greene & Greene he was transported to a state of being akin to falling in love. Nor is it uncommon for an epiphany to occur in the presence of Greene & Greene's artistic architecture and decorative arts. One realizes that the Greenes' bold designs, sublime materials, satin finishes and sensuous craftsmanship signal a level of creative care far beyond that which the majority of architects — including the "greats" — have typically been able to muster. Charles and Henry Greene's confident control over design and execution fills us with awe for their objects: light fixtures, rugs, picture frames, piano benches and much more. Ultimately, it is humbling to realize that a structure and its contents can provoke the emotional response that can come over a visitor to a Greene & Greene house. But this is surely the hyperbole of the over zealous, the reader will object. I can only offer that Greene & Greene had the same effect on me.

As an incoming freshman looking for a place to live at the University of California at Berkeley, I found myself standing across from the William R. Thorsen house designed by the Greenes in 1909. I learned that it had been the local chapter of the Sigma Phi fraternity since 1943, and, smitten by the splendor of the place — a truly seductive combination of Asian elegance and Western rusticity — I asked how I could become one of the guys of Sigma Phi. This bit of serendipity, and the subsequent experience of living in a Greene & Greene house for four years, had a life-altering effect. I have since observed this to be true of others who have also come into close contact with the Greenes' work. David Mathias, author of this richly-personal appreciation of the Greenes, stands out among these. David comes to Greene & Greene from the perspective of an amateur woodworker with a fine aesthetic sense. Through his writing we are able to appreciate the Greenes' houses and furnishings almost as if we were hearing from one of their builders. Through stunning and perceptive new photography, the illustrated spaces and furnishings illuminate the genius of the Greenes' designs, material selection and craft, which has caused so many to celebrate and be seduced by their work. Within a narrative that describes the personal impact of the Greenes on the author, the power of the Greenes' creative output is persuasively communicated. We can also understand how that particular brand of creativity might have been appreciated by clients of the turn of the last century. Being a woodworker, Mathias also pays due homage to John and Peter Hall, the Swedish brothers who worked closely with the Greenes on their finest houses. Mathias correctly grasps how without the Halls, the Greenes would lack a significant measure of the reputation that they enjoy today. Relatively few writers have focused exclusively on Greene & Greene, and so it is a privilege whenever a talented one such as Mr. Mathias comes along. Be forewarned that through this book his seduction may become yours, too.

Edward R. Bosley
James N. Gamble Director
The Gamble House, Pasadena
School of Architecture
University of Southern California

Preface

"Any fool can write a book but it takes a man to make a dovetail door."
CHARLES FLETCHER LUMMIS

On a beautiful Southern California evening a couple of years ago, I had one of the more surreal experiences of my life. At about sunset, I found myself standing at the front door of the Gamble house, the best-known of a series of significant and wonderful residences designed by Charles and Henry Greene in the first decade of the 20th century. Having rung the doorbell, I waited for someone to answer, to open the door to the most beautiful man-made place I had ever been.

My first visit to the Gamble house was in September 2000. I had pored over photographs of that house and others, but located in the Midwest, I had only daydreamed of experiencing the beauty firsthand. The visit was a revelation — even with my very tired six-month-old son in tow. While the exterior of the

house is a work of art, inside one experiences sensory overload. Incredible views in every direction make it difficult to focus on any one object or detail for long. Normally patient, I suddenly had the attention span of a gnat. The one-hour tour passed far too quickly.

In subsequent years, I became increasingly enamored of the work of Greene & Greene. Their style began to dominate my woodworking designs and implementations. I continued to pore over books and magazine articles, and I continued to daydream, this time of a second visit to Pasadena, the center of the Greene & Greene universe.

It wasn't until October 2007 that I had the opportunity to return. By that time, I was beginning work on a series of articles about Greene & Greene designs for *Popular Woodworking Magazine*. A chance meeting with Kori Capaldi, Operations Manager at the Gamble house, led to an invitation to a reception at the house for a speaker in the Sidney D. Gamble lecture series. Which brings us back to the remarkable art glass paneled front door on that remarkable Southern California evening.

The Gamble house is a magical place at night. Perhaps only a poet could describe the glow that seems to emanate from every wooden surface in the dim light provided by the fixtures designed by Greene & Greene. It is truly extraordinary. The combination of this

unusual light and the shadowy darkness present in corners and recesses, gives the 8,000-square-foot house a comforting, homey quality that is both unexpected and immediate. Beyond any of my Midwestern daydreams, those couple of hours amplified my already considerable respect for the artistry of Charles and Henry Greene.

In *Inventing the Dream: California Through the Progressive Era*, Kevin Starr refers to Greene & Greene, writing that their "…Pasadena homes were poems of wood and light." When reading that, I immediately recalled the wonderful light in the house at night and knew that I had found the title for this book. Since that evening, I have had the good fortune to visit numerous Greene & Greene houses. Each one, whether modest or masterpiece, is a wonder. In fact, each time I enter one, I am acutely aware of the privilege being granted me, of the opportunity to witness history and further understand the talented men who designed and built this incredible body of work.

At about the time that I began writing this book, my wife and I took a brief vacation to the Lodge at Torrey Pines in La Jolla, California. Perched on a prime piece of real estate overlooking the famed Torrey Pines golf courses and the Pacific Ocean, the lodge is likely the most substantial Greene & Greene-inspired structure ever built. While some purists might complain about compromises, one must bear in mind that this is not a private residence but a modern hotel that must meet strict building codes and accommodate guests in addition to presenting a beautiful reference to historic architecture.

While at the lodge, I met with Bill Evans, President of Evans Hotels, the lodge's owner. The Lodge at Torrey Pines exists solely because of Bill Evans. It is a

OPPOSITE Greene & Greene achieved a rustic elegance even when working with modest materials. Dining room, Josephine van Rossem house, No. 1, Pasadena, 1903 (altered 1906).

ABOVE Wood glows and shadows entice in the twilight. Detail, entry hall, David B. Gamble house, Pasadena, 1907-09.

The garage didn't receive the same attention as the house, but it certainly wasn't an afterthought. Like all things, it can, and should, be made beautiful. Thus, the garage is unified in design with the house. The door is functional but exhibits typical Greene & Greene elements. Garage, David B. Gamble house, Pasadena, 1907-09.

testament to his passion, energy and desire to create something exceptional. One of the first things Bill said to me was, "Does the world really need another Greene & Greene book?" He was joking. Mostly. I think. But it's a valid question that deserves an answer.

In the past couple of decades a number of books about Charles and Henry Greene, and their work, have appeared. Among them are volumes by those responsible for the Greene & Greene renaissance and the continued resurgence of their legacy. Anyone with an interest in this topic owes a debt of gratitude to Randell Makinson for helping to rescue their legacy and bring the Greenes' work back from the brink of obscurity. Randell has authored several volumes including *The Passion and the Legacy*.

Randell discovered Greene & Greene while an architecture student at USC. One day he went to see the Gamble house (when Gambles still lived there). As Randell stood outside the house admiring the design, the front door opened, and a man demanded to know what Randell was doing. That man was Cecil Gamble, son of David and Mary Gamble who built the house. After an impromptu tour, Randell was hooked. He went on to help engineer the transfer of the house from the Gamble family to USC and the city of Pasadena and to be the house's director for a couple of decades.

Current director of the Gamble House, Edward (Ted) Bosley has an equally compelling story. As an undergraduate at the University of California at Berkeley, Ted one day saw a house that intrigued him. It was the home of the local chapter of the Sigma Phi fraternity. It is also known as the Thorsen House, the last of the Greenes' "Ultimate Bungalows." Built in 1910 for lumber baron William Thorsen, the house and its furnishings are among the Greenes' greatest accomplishments. Remarkably, those accomplishments are still visible even though it has been a fraternity house for more than 60 years.

Ted pledged Sigma Phi and lived in the house for four years. That he went on to become director of the Gamble House is one of those great American stories, like the kid who meets Babe Ruth and then grows up to play for the Yankees. *Greene & Greene* is Ted's history of the brothers and their work. It is the definitive volume on the topic and a stunning achievement.

There are, of course, other excellent books on the subject of the Greenes and/or their commissions. *Greene & Greene: Masterworks* by Bruce Smith and Alexander Vertikoff is, in my opinion, the most notable. Bruce's Greene & Greene scholarship is among the very best. His upcoming book on the Duncan-Irwin house is highly anticipated. Alexander Vertikoff is an outstanding architectural photographer, well known in the Arts & Crafts world. He is my photographic hero. His photos in *Masterworks* are beautiful.

This brings us back to the question that Bill Evans asked me, "Does the world really need another Greene & Greene book?" The unspoken subtext of that question goes something like this: "There are already many excellent books on the topic. Do you have anything new to add?" I believe that the answer to that question is "yes." I submit that there is something new in these pages.

I have not tried to reinvent the wheel by writing a definitive history. Any such attempt would be doomed to failure by comparison. Makinson, Bosley and Smith have set a very high bar. Unlike the others, I came to Greene & Greene through woodworking. I was drawn to their spectacular designs: spare and graceful, with subtle details that define many pieces and, more generally, their style. Woodworkers, even hobbyists like me, develop an eye for details and a curiosity about how those details are implemented. It's a blessing and a curse (go to a furniture store with a woodworker and you'll see what I mean).

Greene & Greene took great care with seemingly minor details, such as doors. Patio doors, William R. Thorsen house, Berkeley, 1908-10.

Think of this book as a guided tour through the Greene & Greene store. There are many photos here of exteriors or entire rooms. What makes this book different, however, is that there are also many photos that focus on details. While the best books on the topic are filled with photos of pieces of furniture, the reader is often left wanting to see more, to see close-ups of inlays, pegs and joinery, the beautiful details that help define what we know as the Greene & Greene vocabulary. In these pages the reader will find those close-up shots along with discussion of the broader themes of the designs.

The topic of this book then is Greene & Greene design with a focus on the details that distinguish their work. Pegs and lifts are obvious and often used by designers to make a piece "Greene-ish." Of course, there is much more variety, and subtlety, in the Greene canon. We explore that here. Additionally, it is best to examine Greene & Greene pieces in context. Every piece of furniture was designed to occupy a particular place in a particular house. Though much of the furniture no longer resides in the houses for which it was designed, we can consider the recurring, unifying themes that are an important aspect of the design philosophy, one that merits closer examination.

Only you can judge if this work has, in fact, contributed anything new to your enjoyment of and appreciation for the incredible output of Charles and Henry Greene. I sincerely hope that to be the case.

David Mathias
December 2009

Greene & Greene:
An Introduction

"A designer knows he has attained perfection not when there is nothing left to add, but when there is nothing left to take away."
Antoine de Saint-Exupery

One hundred years ago, in Pasadena, California, two young brothers were in the midst of an astonishing period of creative success. Fueled by the artistic genius of the elder brother and the wealthy clients willing to provide a great deal of freedom, they created a new and distinctive architectural style that is instantly recognizable still. The brothers were Charles and Henry Greene. Their style, a synthesis of the Arts & Crafts with Asian influences, a casual, California sensibility and obsessive attention to detail. They uniquely combined these elements to create an

A single piece that contains many trademark details, this table may be a perfect piece of furniture. Hall table and armchair, David B. Gamble house, Pasadena, 1907-09.

innovative style, a "new and native architecture."[1] An architecture well suited to the lifestyle in Southern California at the dawn of the 20th century.

One often reads of "the Greene & Greene style" as if it was static, constant. Such references are almost certainly to the fully mature forms represented in their best-known commissions, those from 1907-1910. That style, of course, was the culmination of a period of development, of an evolutionary process that resulted in many lesser known but beautiful houses and decorative arts objects. Even during their most productive period, a brief four-year span, the style was not static. Their designs continued to evolve, the vocabulary growing with each new project.

Interestingly, despite this continued development, one thing remained constant: Greene & Greene applied their style, whatever the current iteration, equally to houses large or small. Materials would vary, as would the degree to which they designed furniture and decorative objects, but the basic vocabulary was used without regard for the size of the commission. In this sense they were creators of a form of "democratic art" with architecture as their medium. In fact, they have been credited with creating "…the type form from which sprang the most delightful little houses we have ever had."[2]

To describe a complex object is difficult. One might easily express the idea of a simple geometric shape, such as a square (though imagine trying to do so for someone completely unfamiliar with the vocabulary of geometry). However, to convey the intricacies of an object of beauty could be impossible. Consider the Chrysler Building or a 1962 Ferrari 250 GTO. Now put one of them into words. Both are iconic and familiar. Yet neither can be easily described. Certainly, the exercise is no less demanding when speaking instead of the work of Greene & Greene. There are, however, a number of factors that help distinguish the designs of the Greenes, factors that might aid in our descriptive task. These include graceful forms, unifying themes and attention to detail.

Graceful Forms

Decorative arts objects of the Arts & Crafts period, including furniture, are noted for their clean lines and

TOP Beautiful under any circumstances, The Gamble House is magical at night. View of east façade, David B. Gamble house.

ABOVE Representative of the fully developed Greene & Greene style. Detail, dining-room armchair, 1909-10, William R. Thorsen house, Berkeley, 1908-10.

functional quality, eliminating excess ornamentation in favor of an existential purity. One result of this move, particularly at the outset, was the loss of a sense of grace in many designs. Arts & Crafts furniture can appear overly spartan, rectilinear, plain. That is not to say that some of these designs aren't appealing, even beautiful, but many cannot be described as graceful. Graceful, however, is exactly the right term to describe most Greene & Greene designs. Subtlety and the harmonious interplay of numerous elements are largely responsible. Lifts, tapers, almost imperceptible curves, all contribute to the effect if only in the viewer's subconscious. Variation in planes is another important factor, as when two components meet offset by $\frac{1}{8}$", or in pegs or inlays that stand proud of the surface. Grace absent the ornate, or perhaps, grace resulting from that absence.

Unifying Themes

During the decidedly ornate Victorian era, it was common to decorate a room by filling it, seemingly at random, with as much unrelated clutter as possible. Greene & Greene, and more generally proponents of the Arts & Crafts movement, rebelled against this trend. The Greenes, however, went much further than simply reducing clutter and promoting use of complementary decorative objects. They merged various aspects of a house — exterior, interior, furniture and objets d'art — through commonality of design

elements. These unifying themes were incorporated at the outset of the design process. No mere add-ons or appliqués, the motifs were established with the elevations of the house. English Arts & Crafts designer M.H. Baillie Scott expressed this idea in 1897.

"For it is not enough that furniture should possess intrinsic beauty, unless it also possesses this further quality of exquisite appropriateness to its position and to its use. It should appear almost to be a piece of the room in which it is placed and in absolute harmony with its surroundings.

"It is in this respect that the various kinds of fixed furnishings become of especial value in the effect of a room, filling the gap between the house and its furniture, and thus giving an appearance of unity and harmony. The fixed seats to the inglenook, the mantelpieces and bedroom fitments, all appear as part of the structure itself and so form a connecting link between the movable furniture and the house.

"The essential point then in the choice of furniture may be said to be not so much the individual merit of a particular thing as its relation to everything else in the room. The furniture should appear to grow out of the requirements of the room, to represent the finishing touches of a scheme which had its inception when the

Keys for the Culbertson secretary are representative of the Greenes' extreme attention to detail. Keys for secretary, c. 1911, Cordelia A. Culbertson house, Pasadena, 1911-13.

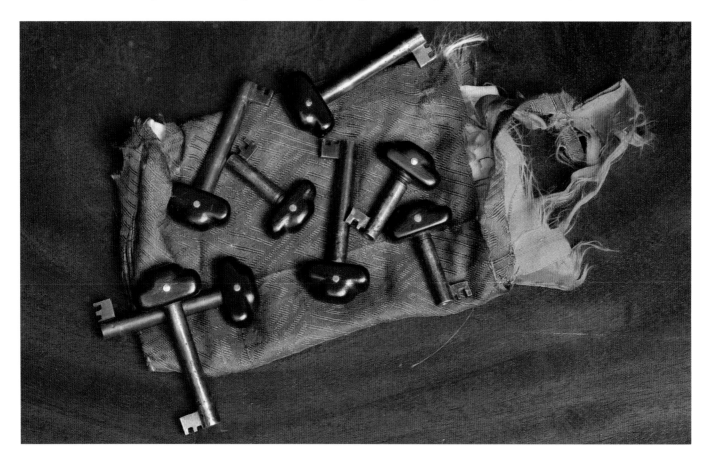

first stone of the house was laid, and not an alien impor-
tation from the upholsterer's of spick and span suites,
at war with themselves and their surroundings."[3]

That is, the concept of the room and the furniture should be one and the same, indistinguishable
in design and implementation. It is worth noting that
Greene & Greene saw fit to ensure that not only did
each piece relate properly to all else in the room, but
also that it stood on its own merit, thus going beyond
Scott's thesis. Fifty years later, author Jean Murray
Bangs, who helped rediscover the Greenes in the middle of the 20th century, wrote eloquently about this
aspect of their work:

"The imaginative flights of Maybeck, his superb
handling of historic form; the plastic quality so desired
by Wright and the mastery of it which gives his work
its characteristic quality, were lacking in the work of
Greene and Greene. To a greater degree, however, than
was achieved by Wright, Greene and Greene houses were
beautifully integrated structures in which the interior
and exterior of the house, the furniture and the garden
were all parts of one harmonious and beautiful whole."[4]

Attention to Detail

Integrating various aspects of a home through use of
a common vocabulary is certainly one hallmark of

the unique Greene & Greene style and is one aspect of
attention to detail. In both design and implementation, however, the Greenes' attention to detail went
well beyond. Henry Greene once noted, "…the whole
construction was carefully thought out and there was
a reason for every detail. The idea was to eliminate
everything unnecessary, to make the whole as direct
and simple as possible, but always with the beautiful
in mind as the final goal."[5] No object was too trivial to
receive the architects' attention — "a reason for every
detail." Doors and stairs were transformed into features of extreme beauty. Switch plates and escutcheons
were treated creatively and with care. Even the pins
assigned the task of aligning the halves of the dining
room table were, in some cases, elevated to art.

Charles Greene wrote of his firm's principles for
domestic architecture, that they strove "…to make
these necessary and useful things pleasurable."[6]
Charles was not alone in this sentiment. As Anne
Mallek notes, Charles Greene and William Morris
were kindred spirits.[7] Morris famously said, "Have
nothing in your house that you do not know to be

useful or believe to be beautiful."[8] A social philosopher as well as poet and entrepreneur, he expressed this idea at much greater length. In a later-published lecture to the Society for the Protection of Ancient Buildings on the topic of the lesser arts of life, he said:

"You understand that our ground is, that not only is it possible to make the matters needful to our daily life works of art, but that there is something wrong in the civilisation that does not do this: if our houses, our clothes, our household furniture and utensils are not works of art, they are either wretched make-shifts, or what is worse, degrading shams of better things."[9]

ABOVE Interesting details are not limited to the interiors. Post and beam elements with metal strapping are part of the iconic style. Detail, northeast corner, Robert R. Blacker house, Pasadena, 1907-09.

OPPOSITE The Robinson house is not as wooden as is typical for Greene & Greene but it is a wonderful example of their versatility. Detail, south façade, Laurabelle A. Robinson house, Pasadena, 1905-06.

Adherence to this principle,[10] as much as any other factor, propelled the Greenes' work to levels of refinement in design and quality in implementation far beyond what was common and helps explain their continued legacy. The idea that even the simplest objects in a house, such as stairs, can be artful and the source of pleasure is likely more alien today, when low prices are the sole enticement for our largest retailers, than it was a century ago. A quote attributed to John Ruskin addresses this point with amazing prescience. Ruskin, a proponent of social change in 19th century England, and an inspiration to Morris and others in the English Arts & Crafts movement, is often quoted thus: "There is nothing in the world that some man cannot make a little worse and sell a little cheaper, and he who considers only price is that man's lawful prey."[11]

An article in the August 1912 issue of *The Craftsman* highlighted the work of Greene & Greene. In concluding, the author addresses the attention to detail in their work, particularly with respect to construction. "… the quality of materials and workmanship that goes into the houses built by Messrs. Greene & Greene renders them of necessity expensive. The construction is always of the best and includes much hand labor — which obviously cannot compete with machinery as to price, though the results, of course, far surpass machine work, both in durability and taste. In every instance, the dominant note of their work is sincerity…"[12]

The Style in Brief

The well-known Greene & Greene exterior style is familiar, probably even iconic. Walls are often, though not always, shingled and stained in various hues of green and brown, colors found in the surrounding natural landscape. Eaves are deep to provide shade. Rafter tails are exposed and protrude resulting in wonderful shadows. Charles Greene, on at least one occasion, cited the lovely shadows as the reason for this well recognized feature.[13] Arroyo stones, or boulders in some cases, are given numerous tasks. Most frequently they are mingled with clinker bricks in retaining walls or stout fences. They also appear in chimneys and occasionally support wooden posts as in the Japanese idiom. Posts and beams are both structural and decorative, often sculpturally shaped and creatively joined with iron straps and wedges. Main entry doors are always interesting and often stunningly beautiful, incorporating custom art glass.

The well-known exterior vocabulary is not, however, the only one used by the Greenes. A number of their houses add elements to the common recipe while others deviate more significantly. The Ware house (1913) provides an example of the former with the

second story finished in stucco while the first story retains the familiar wood shakes. The James Culbertson house (1902) which, in original form, predates the familiar style, is an example in the English country idiom. It was a triumph, its English stylings not alone in the Greene annals.[14] The Robinson house (1905) is a commanding *Gunite*-coated structure that is simultaneously quite distinct from the Greenes' trademark style and sufficiently similar to give clues as to its heritage. It stands as wonderful testament to the firm's versatility.

Interiors of Greene & Greene houses vary considerably, correlating with time frame and budget, though some elements are used throughout their canon without regard to such distinctions. Rich woods (mahogany, teak, Port Orford cedar, redwood) are used liberally for paneling and wainscoting. Stairways include a landing with a window to provide light and a perch from which to admire nature, particularly when a window seat is incorporated. Stair railings and posts are taken as an opportunity for creativity and unexpected beauty. In some homes even lowly stair risers are a decorative element. Windows are used generously, providing for ample natural light and circulation of fresh air. An added benefit is that it brings the outdoors in, helping blur the distinction between the typically delineated spaces.

Interior trim is custom-made and integral to the design. Typically finger-jointed and pegged at outside corners, it serves to unify architecture and furniture as described by M.H. Baillie Scott. Picture rails are ubiquitous and functional but also provide a break in the wall, an opportunity to distinguish the frieze level and prepare it for decoration in the form of murals or carved panels. Lighting is, after 1903, typically custom designed to suit a house's interior (or exterior in the case of lighting outside the house). Unifying themes and attention to detail revisited.

Greene & Greene furniture is among the most beautiful ever designed. That is a bold statement. And given that there is no universal scale for beauty, it's a statement that can be neither proven nor disproven. Ultimately, it is best to allow the designs to make their own argument, to speak for themselves as it were — which is precisely the strategy employed in Chapter 4.

TOP LEFT   Perhaps the ultimate implementation of the Greene & Greene aesthetic; a perfect space. Living room, Robert R. Blacker house.

LEFT   A wonderful green light peeks through the perforated ebony pegs on this sconce. Living-room sconce, 1907-08, Freeman A. Ford house, Pasadena, 1906-08.

Much Greene & Greene furniture is constructed of mahogany though woods such as teak and walnut are used as well; quality materials, as noted in *The Craftsman*. Finishes are simple leaving a close-to-the-wood look and feel that well suits the expertly prepared surfaces. Subtle decorative elements are used to stunning effect: ebony pegs, inlays, carvings, heavily eased edges and surprising details all serve to stamp pieces as unmistakably Greene & Greene. As with the architecture, mundane elements are used as an opportunity to introduce unexpected beauty. Breadboard ends are more than functional necessities, they are wonderful design features. Drawer joinery becomes the dominant visual theme of some pieces. Table extensions are functional as they should be, but also quite beautiful and inventive. Variations in these details serve to enhance the surprise and draw one into the designs. Once there, the lucky onlooker can consider for himself the claim above. The most beautiful furniture ever created? In the end, it doesn't matter. For those with the good fortune to experience the genius of Greene & Greene, the question is rendered moot.

TOP With the Robinson dining room, Greene & Greene demonstrated a new sophistication in their furniture designs. Dining room furniture, 1906-07, Laurabelle A. Robinson house.

ABOVE Good things in small packages — this curio cabinet has an extraordinary number of details for a diminutive piece. Cabinet for Belle Barlow Bush, 1907, William T. Bolton house, Pasadena, 1906-07.

A Brief History

"History is a kind of introduction to more interesting people than we can possibly meet in our restricted lives; let us not neglect the opportunity."
DEXTER PERKINS

The Early Years

Genius is fascinating. Not the mere possession of a high intelligence quotient, but the gift of an innate talent to create something entirely new, something that has not existed previously. This capacity is exhibited in vastly diverse ways. Consider: Mozart, Einstein, Michelangelo, Newton, Ramanujan. One common factor among most creative geniuses, whether in the arts or sciences, is that their primary contributions occur when they are young. Wisdom may come with age, but genius is innate and typically manifests itself early.

Charles Sumner Greene was a genius. He and his brother, Henry Mather Greene, didn't set out to be among America's most accomplished designers. They trained as architects and set about the practice of that profession. Henry, the more logical of the two, may have been well pleased with this career choice. However for Charles, an artist at heart, it was a concession to his father. Like many fathers before and since, Thomas Greene wanted proper professions for his sons. Bohemian artist didn't fit that bill. For an artisti-

The house for James Culbertson signaled the arrival of Arts & Crafts in the Greene & Greene office including the first use of Stickley furniture by the firm. Southeast façade, James A. Culbertson house, Pasadena, 1902-14.

cally minded young man, however, architecture would at least provide an outlet for creative energies.

Thomas Greene, a Civil War veteran, married Lelia Mather of West Virginia in 1867. The young couple settled in a working-class section of Thomas' native Cincinnati. They were joined, in short order, by Charles on October 12, 1868. Henry followed little over a year later on January 23, 1870. In 1874 the family moved to St. Louis where they remained, aside from a three-year return East while Thomas attended medical school, until Charles and Henry graduated college. The family enjoyed a comfortable lifestyle during the boys' childhoods.[1]

By the last decade of the 19th century, the industrial revolution had been gaining momentum for roughly 100 years. The effects were far-reaching, influencing every aspect of human life. The move toward manufacturing resulted in a significant reduction in the traditional trades. For centuries, trades had been passed from master to apprentice or father to son. In the industrialized world, this was often no longer the case. Thus, many young men outside of agricultural areas might receive no training in the use of tools. Supporters of the manual training movement[2] sought to remedy this through a curriculum that included classical academic subjects, such as English and physics, along with drafting and shop training in both wood and metal.[3]

Calvin Woodward, first Dean of Engineering at Washington University in St. Louis, was a proponent of technical education. In particular, he believed that it was important for boys to be skilled in the use of tools in preparation for a career in an industrial society. In 1879 he opened the Manual Training School of Washington University. The purpose of the three-

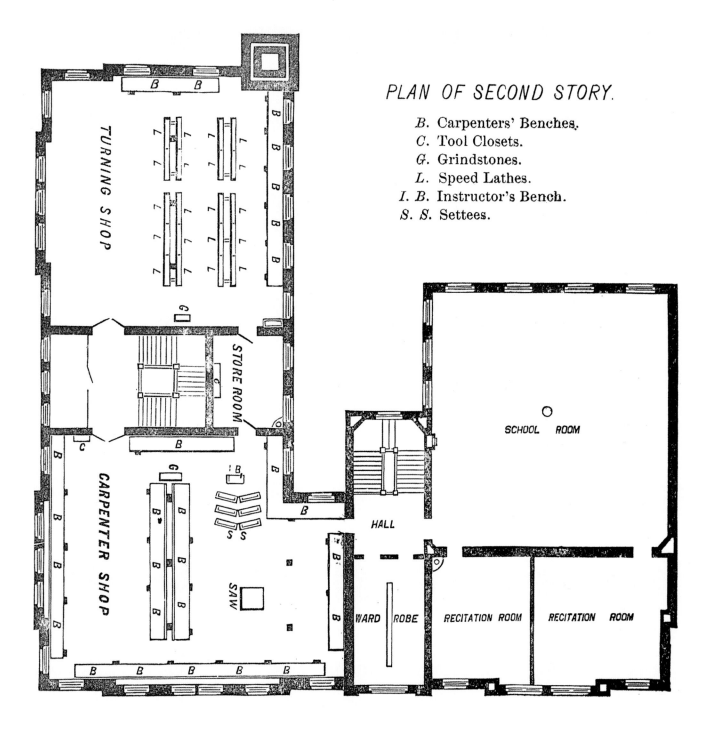

PLAN OF SECOND STORY.

B. Carpenters' Benches.
C. Tool Closets.
G. Grindstones.
L. Speed Lathes.
I. B. Instructor's Bench.
S. S. Settees.

year curriculum was, as Woodward put it, to train the head, heart, and hand — "The cunning mind, the skillful hand"[4] in the words of the school's motto. It was not the goal of the school to create craftsmen or tradesmen. Fitting with Woodward's beliefs, the program strove to prepare boys for the varied activities of careers in a quickly evolving society, particularly careers in engineering and related fields. Charles entered the Manual Training School in 1884 and was followed a year later by Henry.[5]

Though the boys could not have known it, their education at the Manual Training School would figure quite prominently in their architectural careers. The first-year woodworking curriculum included courses in woodcarving, carpentry and joinery.[6] Furniture

The Manual Training School of Washington University provided sound fundamental training that would prove valuable to Charles and Henry during their careers.

designs by architects are often visually striking, but are not always well-designed with respect to function and construction requirements. Greene & Greene furniture is an exception. Their pieces are typically quite functional and well-engineered. Their knowledge of woodworking certainly plays a role in this regard.

The curriculum of the Manual Training School of Washington University required students to achieve proficiency in making a number of woodworking joints ranging from simple mortise and tenon to standard dovetails to complex mitered double mortise and tenon. Even

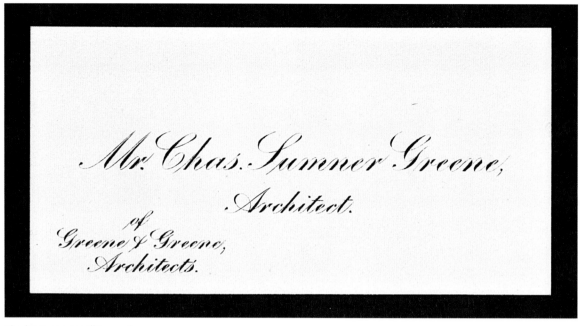

Charles Greene's calling card.

a rafter joint is covered.[7] Though Charles and Henry certainly would not have gained skills nearly as advanced as the craftsmen who would later implement their designs, their knowledge of joinery would allow effective communication with the craftsmen. More importantly, effective joinery is the key to well-constructed furniture. Thus, Greene & Greene proved to be case studies for the intended purpose of manual training.

From St. Louis, the brothers moved to Boston to pursue the study of architecture at the Massachusetts Institute of Technology. MIT offered two- and four-year programs — Charles and Henry enrolled in the more typical, for that time, two-year course of study which they completed in 1891, a year later than planned. During and after their time at MIT, each engaged in internships and apprenticeships with prominent local firms.[8]

In 1892 Thomas and Lelia Greene moved to California with the hope that the climate would improve Mrs. Greene's asthmatic condition. That the area was a healthful oasis is part of the Southern California mythology. Begun in 1857 with the publication of *Climatology of the United States,* by Lorin Blodget, the legend could do little more than taunt the Eastern populace as California must have seemed impossibly remote. In the 1880s however, the advent of relatively inexpensive rail travel made it possible for many infirm to make the pilgrimage. While some did recover their health, many others were less fortunate.[9] Who can say how many of the success stories accrue to beneficial effects of climate?

The Greenes settled in Pasadena, drawn by the warm, dry climate that also attracted many wealthy families from the East and Midwest. The climate was not the only draw. Located at the foot of the San Gabriel mountains, Pasadena was, and is, a place of surpassing beauty. An arroyo seco — Spanish for dry river bed — nestled between the mountains and the town provided recreation for inhabitants as well as ample land for livestock and citrus groves. Very much a part of the frontier, Pasadena provided an appealing, even tempting, mix of climate, topography, nature and seemingly boundless possibilities. In short, the California dream.

Charles and Henry arranged in 1893 to follow their parents to Pasadena, arriving late that year. Pasadena at that time was a very small city quite distinct from Los Angeles and already home to several architects. It was not obvious that there was need of another architectural office to serve the limited population that existed there at that time. It is even less obvious that two young men with very little experience would be able to compete. Despite these apparent obstacles, in January 1894, Charles, 24 years of age, and Henry, 23, established their practice, Greene & Greene Architects.[10] In September of that year they secured their first commission.

Houses for the firm's earliest clients were modest though size and expense increased over the course of their first decade in practice. Designed in a variety of styles, these jobs constitute an eclectic set. Some designs had an English flavor with timbering and leaded windows. Others bore elements of the California Mission style. Many are easily identifiable as Victorian, though somewhat subdued for that form. Their first house, for Martha Flynn, is not unlike the chalet style to which they would return in the next decade.[11]

There is, of course, no vice in the use of various styles. Nor is there virtue in uniformity merely for

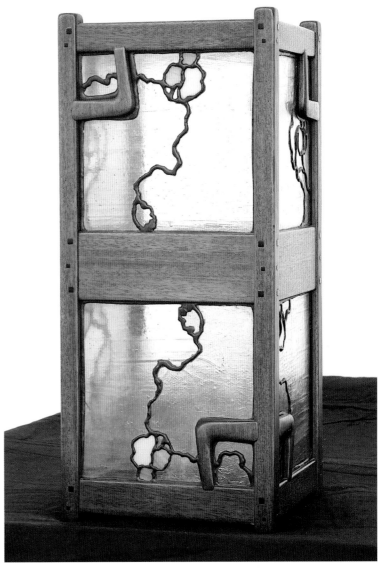

LEFT The Glory of… Panels carved with natural scenes and quaint sayings were an important aspect of the Culbertson house. Carved panel, c. 1907, James A. Culbertson house.

ABOVE James Culbertson continued to engage the Greenes for years. This wall lantern demonstrates the evolution that occurred between 1902 and 1907. Lantern, c. 1907, James A. Culbertson house.

uniformity's sake. In the Greenes' case, the diversity they displayed early on is indicative that they had not yet discovered a philosophy with which they were at ease. At this stage of their nascent careers, the young architects were exploring, searching, learning about themselves and the strange surroundings that would play a significant role in shaping them and their aesthetic. It may also be that, due to their tender years, they were not yet comfortable suggesting the unanticipated to their clients. Perhaps they were simply designing what they thought, or were told, was expected of them.[12] At the dawn of the 20th century, however, the Greenes found their own voice, a voice in harmony with their environment and an emerging philosophy, a voice that would define them for posterity.

A New Direction

By 1902, when Charles undertook the design and construction of his own home on a desirable site overlooking the arroyo, the Greenes' aesthetic had become distinctly simpler than during the eclectic period comprised of the eight years since opening their practice. Oakholm, as the house was known, was in constant flux during the 13 years that Charles shared it with his wife, Alice, and their ever-growing family. It expanded with the family and evolved with Charles' style, serving as a canvas on which Charles would test his evolving ideas. From the outset though, it was a departure from their earlier work.

In another project dating to 1902, the Greenes demonstrated their versatility in a house design for James Culbertson. Sited on a corner lot very near Charles' own home and even nearer the arroyo seco, the English-style house was quite lovely.[13] Beauty, however, is not the reason for the significant position of the Culbertson house in the firm's progression. In James Culbertson, Charles found an enlightened client, one willing to indulge artistic excursions into new territory. In this case, the territory was that of the "Morris movement" including the first use of Stickley furniture in a Greene & Greene commission.[14] Culbertson remained committed to artistry and growth, returning to the Greenes often for additions and modifications. In this way, by the close of the decade, the house would contain many elements of the Greenes' mature style — a style that found the genesis of expression in this house.

The house designed for Mary Darling in 1903 continued Greene & Greene's movement to an Arts & Crafts aethetic. Though not one of their grand commissions, it is clear in the Darling house that the trade-mark Greene & Greene style was beginning to emerge. Certainly many of the elements we associate with their work are absent, but enough others are present to make the structure recognizable as theirs: stained wood shingles, deeply overhanging eaves, a broad front door and numerous windows. Two large bays on the front of the house are supported by large rocks[15] presaging use of the Japanese technique of anchoring posts on stones more directly adopted for the Arturo Bandini house later in the same year.

In the interior, an oversize brick fireplace, built-in cases and wooden sconce lighting mark the arrival in earnest of the Arts & Crafts sensibility begun during work for James Culbertson. Perhaps most significantly, for the Darling house Charles sketched complete roomscapes, incorporating Stickley furniture and standard Arts & Crafts decorative elements.[16] This event is significant in that it signals Charles' move into the realm of the gestalt. Henceforth, Greene & Greene would be increasingly involved in providing fixtures, decorative elements and furniture, rather than simply the structure.

If one were to create a genealogy of Greene & Greene clients, complete with all relationships, it might be natural to conclude that, were it not for referrals from earlier clients, the architects would have had a meager existence. Mary Pratt was a Vassar classmate of Caroline Thorsen. Caroline Thorsen's sister was Nellie Blacker. Freeman Ford was a friend of Henry Robinson. Adelaide Tichenor was a close friend of Jennie Reeve. Jennie Reeve was Mary Darling's mother. If this were truly a family tree, there would be a number of marriages between cousins. While the names Blacker, Thorsen and Pratt are associated with some of the Greenes' greatest achievements, the last two relationships on the list are among the most significant.

Jennie Reeve was a pivotal client for Greene & Greene. She commissioned three houses in a span of four years, but volume was not the primary reason for her importance to the Greenes. She came to the firm at the dawn of their move toward designing complete environments and provided them the resources and freedom to move further along that path. For the Reeve house the Greenes designed 139 decorative objects including furniture, numerous lighting fixtures and built-in cabinets in addition to a well-documented living room inglenook.[17] The Reeve furniture is quite simple compared to later pieces, even so it is indicative of developing trends. Architect Ted Wells has characterized the Reeve furniture as looking at the work of Gustav Stickley through a Japanese prism, a very apt description.[18] Unusual for that time, the inglenook and stairs form a central island that can be circumnavi-

Though less polished than later pieces, this double sconce from the Jennie Reeve house is a wonderful example of decorative arts in early Greene & Greene houses. Sconce, 1903-04, Jennie A. Reeve house, Long Beach, 1903-04.

gated via the living room, dining room and entry hall. The overall result was a wonderful success. One of the most significant aspects of the Greenes' relationship with Jennie Reeve, however, was that she introduced the architects to Adelaide Tichenor.

In the pantheon of Greene & Greene clients, Adelaide Tichenor occupies a distinguished position. Mrs. Tichenor was a strong-willed, wealthy widow when she contracted Greene & Greene to design a large oceanfront house in Long Beach. The combination of her desire for a complete environment — even more so than Jennie Reeve she wanted an all-encompassing design including house, landscape, furniture, lighting and decorative arts — and her insistence on exploring a new aesthetic played a significant role in Charles' artistic development. The relationship was not entirely pleasant for Charles, as Mrs. Tichenor did not allow him absolute freedom to implement the design according to his vision.[19]

In 1905, Greene & Greene Architects were presented with an opportunity to advance their practice by taking on a project of greater scope than any they had undertaken thus far. The previous several years had prepared Charles and Henry for the challenges of a project of a greater magnitude, for the design of a substantial

TOP Hanging dining room cabinets appear in a number of Greene & Greene houses. Dining-room cabinet, 1903-04, Jennie A. Reeve house.

ABOVE Adelaide Tichenor provided Charles Greene with the opportunity to design furniture for much of the house. The results provide a glimpse of what was to come. Bench, 1904-05, Adelaide M. Tichenor house, Long Beach, 1904-05.

landscape rather than smaller gardens, for the application on a grand scale of their new skills in the design of furniture and decorative arts. This opportunity came to them in the person of Laurabelle A. Robinson.

For the Robinson project, the Greenes were provided a beautiful parcel of land, a large budget and the charge to create completed interiors.[20] In the hands of an artist, such as Charles, this happy set of conditions was sure to yield a very special result. And indeed it did. Given the distinct style of recent commissions, the Robinson house is something of an anomaly with its *Gunite* exterior bearing no resemblance to wood shingles. Though the exterior materials are distinct, many elements of their new and still emerging style remain: deep eaves with exposed rafter tails, integra-

tion of exterior spaces with the interior, a broad main entry door with decorative art glass, numerous windows, particularly on the West elevation to provide views of the arroyo below. Stylistically, the Robinson house defies easy categorization. The cementitious exterior evokes the California missions, but the house is clearly not mission; half-timbering recalls English forms, but the house is clearly not English; Asian elements abound but the overall effect is clearly not Asian. Despite this lack of identity, the whole is undoubtedly greater than the sum of its parts; the result is stunning.

For the interior, Charles designed a number of remarkable pieces of furniture. Best known are the dining room table and chairs and the spectacular,

height-adjustable chandelier. The table introduces a form to which they would return for the Gamble house. The Robinson dining chairs evoke a Chinese design. The low-armed host and hostess chairs are particularly dramatic, a study in sublime, simple elegance. (This is a perfect example of the Japanese concept of shibusa. See Chapter 3 for more discussion of this topic.)

The importance of the Robinson house derives not solely from the scale, which is imposing, but from what it demonstrates about the abilities and direction of Greene & Greene. In this house we see a new philosophy as, for the first time, rooms are distinguished by different themes. Uncharacteristic curves and low, broad forms in the living room. Asian-inspired themes in the dining room. A rather traditional Arts & Crafts

Set at the edge of the arroyo seco, the Robinson house makes a strong argument for the genius of Greene & Greene. At night, the *Gunite* exterior exudes a warmth and almost seems to glow. View of east façade, Laurabelle A. Robinson house, Pasadena, 1905-06.

influence in the den. A lighter, more characteristic Arts & Crafts feel in the entry hall. Yet the whole is cohesive and harmonious. While the Greenes were already known for attention to detail, the Robinson house presages the arrival of their near obsession in this regard and serves as an introduction to the firm's most productive period, soon to come.

It is generally agreed that the increasingly rapid development of the Greenes' trademark style from

In the Robinson interior, we see details that are unusual for Greene & Greene, as in the curves on the front of this cabinet and the mantle across the room. Living-room cabinet, 1905-06, Laurabelle A. Robinson house.

1905 onward was enabled, in part, by a shop of talented craftsmen able to implement their designs. Not coincidentally, during 1904 their firm began working with contractor Peter Hall and, soon thereafter, his brother John Hall.[21] The Halls, Scandinavian-born woodworkers, came to Pasadena in the late 19th century. By the time they began collaborating with the Greenes, they had significant experience in construction and cabinetmaking. This provided the Greene firm with consistent, high-quality, one-stop shopping — the Halls and their craftsmen could implement almost every aspect of the ever more complex commissions. This included general construction, intricate finish carpentry and exquisite furniture.

The relationship between the Greenes and Halls was highly interactive. Examining original drawings, one can see evidence of this. One drawing, for a Pratt house desk, bears the notation, "Layout shelves and submit to architects."[22] Trust and mutual respect had

fostered a synergy that benefited both the Greenes and the Halls but more significantly, the clients as well. By the time construction began on the Pratt house in 1909, Charles Greene and John Hall could likely read each other's minds. Charles was known to visit the Halls' shop almost daily to inspect, change and even help construct his works in progress. This collegial rapport continued through, and beyond, the timeframe of the Greenes' most industrious phase.

That the Halls were significant in the success of the Greenes is neither hyperbole nor revisionist. To understand why, one need only look at Greene & Greene furniture constructed prior to the Greene-Hall collaboration. Pieces designed for the Tichenor house

serve as examples. Tichenor pieces are interesting — they lack the grace and refinement of later work, but the designs are successful, their heritage identifiable. In particular, lifts and pegs are conspicuous if not yet fully developed. In execution, however, these pieces are clearly inferior to the Halls' work. Stock selection is particularly suspect with wild, unattractive grain dominating and detracting from the result. Even the best designs can be diminished, or worse, by poor implementation. An improvement in craftsmanship was a matter of necessity in order for Greene & Greene to realize fully their goal of furnishings as art.

The quality of work exiting the Halls' shop was first rate. Joinery is expertly executed, seamless. Pieces are shaped beautifully, giving an organic impression. Surfaces are silky, begging to be touched. Inlays are particularly impressive — incorporating a vast variety of materials from exotic woods to mother-of-pearl, semi-precious stones, copper and silver. Complex designs are masterfully executed. Given that the quality of the furniture and interiors improved significantly when this association began, one can't help but wonder what course the Greenes' practice would have taken had fate not brought them together with the Halls. We are fortunate not to know the answer to that question.

ABOVE In the year leading up to the Blacker house commission, Greene & Greene created several superb houses in which iconic elements first appeared. The Cole house makes a statement with its porte cochere and boulder chimney. View of southeast corner, Mary E. Cole house, Pasadena, 1906-07.

BELOW Graceful and refined, with more than a hint of Chinese influence, this table for the William Bolton house is evidence of another step in the development of Greene & Greene decorative arts. Hall table, c. 1907, William T. Bolton house, Pasadena, 1906.

Following the Robinson commission, Greene & Greene returned, for a while, to designing less grand residences. Homes such as those for Caroline DeForest, William Bolton, John Bentz, John Cole, John Phillips and Robert Pitcairn, all from 1906,[23] were substantial, but not on the scale (in size nor scope) of the Robinson. What these homes provided Charles, though he likely didn't realize it, was an opportunity to further refine his style in preparation for what was to come. The Bolton house is particularly significant in this regard.

The Bolton house was actually the third designed for Dr. William Bolton. The plan included many pieces of furniture in addition to a number of wonderful built-ins. Unfortunately, Bolton died shortly before the house was completed. His widow rented the house to Belle Barlow Bush who continued production of the furniture and commissioned additional pieces from Greene & Greene. The Bolton/Bush pieces demonstrate progress toward the Blacker and Gamble furniture.

It has been well documented that furniture for the Bolton house was the first to include square ebony pegs. While significant, particularly given the importance of this detail in later pieces, it is not the most noteworthy development. The most significant change is, perhaps, less concrete. Bolton/Bush furniture exhibits an elegance and grace of form that is well beyond the brothers' earlier work. The well-known hall table serves as an example. Lifts on the stretchers

The Pitcairn house is a nearly forgotten Greene & Greene gem. Sleeping porches, very deep eaves, an inviting patio and a cantilevered second story are all recognizable features. View of north façade, Robert Pitcairn, Jr. house, Pasadena, 1906.

are more sculptural and organic than those on previous pieces. A subtle, almost subliminal, arc on the stretchers juxtaposes the primarily rectilinear form. A superb gateleg library table is similarly elegant. The side stretchers and aprons are molded to accommodate the gates when closed. The effect is that of a lift, but in the horizontal plane. It is a fantastic detail that is both functional and stunning. A fern stand includes a form of Greene & Greene finger joints and includes cutouts that presage a Thorsen side table. Pieces in the dining suite are wonderfully unified by use of struts adjacent to the legs. This is an early example of reserving a detail for use in only one room of a house. Dining room furniture also includes inlays that begin a trend of very successful and innovative uses of this design element.

Perhaps the most important legacy of the houses from this era is that they demonstrate the Greenes' mastery of creating "livable" houses, houses suited to the needs of the occupants and the environment in which they existed. Features such as sleeping porches, great rooms, patios, and 36-inch high kitchen counters all served to enhance the lives of the families who were

Charles and Henry Greene reached the architectural pinnacle very quickly. The Gamble House appeared only six years after the James Culbertson house. Detail, west façade, David B. Gamble house, Pasadena, 1907-09.

the firm's clients. Even careful siting of the structure had a role to play in enhancing the homeowners' experience. Not all of these characteristics were present in every house, but Greene & Greene developed a repertoire that allowed them to choose appropriately to meet the clients' practical and aesthetic requirements.

The Legacy Years

By 1907 the Greenes' synthesized Arts & Crafts/Asian/California style was fully developed. It would evolve still, but more incrementally than during the preceding years. The result is a series of houses known today as the "Ultimate Bungalows." The Blacker, Ford, Gam-

ble, Pratt and Thorsen houses, all built between 1907 and 1910, constitute an amazing body of work. Designing these homes and hundreds of furnishings in such a short period must have taxed the Greenes' practice. However, the extreme workload did not detract from the results as it was for these homes that Greene & Greene designed the iconic furniture, and interior and exterior elevations revered today.

What is an Ultimate Bungalow? How do these houses differ from others in the Greene & Greene canon? Merriam-Webster defines a bungalow as, "a house having one-and-a-half stories and usually a front porch."[24] In common usage the term typically implies, in addition, a house of modest size with some built-in cabinetry and generous use of unpainted wood in the interior.[25] While some of that definition applies to the Ultimates, these homes are certainly not modest. All are substantial with generously proportioned rooms. Some have entrance halls larger than most modern family rooms. "Ultimate" does not, however, refer only, or even primarily, to size. The materials chosen were the finest available: mahogany, teak, ebony, Port Orford cedar and redwood. The smallest details, such as switch plates and doors, were given significant attention and incorporated into the meta-level design. An overarching artistic vision permeated each project and guided every detail. Thus, in the end, what makes these homes ultimate is that they embody the fully mature vision of a creative genius at his peak.

Much of the last several paragraphs certainly applies not only to the Ultimates but also to the Robinson house. In scale, detail and execution, it is surely on par with the others. Why then is it not a member of the club? There are several possible explanations for exclusion. Clearly, Charles was still, at the time of designing the Robinson, defining his style. The house is in this sense transitional — distinct from that which came before, but not yet completely in the style we associate with Greene & Greene.[26] Another possible factor is timing. While the Ultimates were designed more or less consecutively, the Robinson preceded the Blacker, the first Ultimate, by roughly two years.

The term "Ultimate Bungalows" was coined by Randell Makinson and Robert Judson Clark as a way to distinguish the Greenes' greatest work from the rest of their output. (Makinson no longer favors use of this phrase, thinking it inappropriate.[27]) At that time, the Robinson was in a state of disrepair. This might also have played a role. Now fully restored, however, the house makes a strong argument on its own behalf.

Finally, the Robinson is less "woody" than the others, perhaps less bungalow-like. As we've seen, however, none of the Ultimates truly fit the definition of a bungalow. In the end these arguments are unconvincing. With due respect to the well-considered opinions of esteemed members of the Greene & Greene community, the Robinson is included here as an Ultimate Bungalow simply by virtue of the end result.

The Ultimate Bungalows have been widely documented and will be more so later in this volume. There is no need to go into great detail here, though some discussion of the firm's best work is called for. The Greenes considered the Blacker house to be their masterpiece. Touring the Gamble house can make one somewhat skeptical about this fact. However, even a brief time inside the magnificent Blacker makes clear that the Greenes' choice was correct. The entry hall and stairway alone could constitute a life's work. The living room is sheer genius, incorporating many elements yet yielding a result that is soothing with an appearance of simplicity. Barring the privilege of a

The Blacker house presents a dramatic visage. This massive porte cochere is one of the best conceived exterior elements on a Greene & Greene house. View of north façade, Robert R. Blacker house, Pasadena, 1907-09.

visit, Randell Makinson's excellent book dedicated to the house is the best available substitute.[28]

The only Ultimate to have undergone significant structural changes,[29] the Freeman Ford house is an underappreciated gem. Like the Robinson house, it's exterior is cementious — each of the other Ultimates is clad in wood shakes. Furniture designed for this house is likely less known than that for the other Ultimates, as very little is on public display. One iconic piece, a serving table, is quite well known and on loan to the Huntington Library, Art Collections and Botanical Gardens, where it is available for view. Other dining room pieces are as lovely but in private hands.

The Gamble house is surely Greene & Greene's best-known work. The house remained in the Gamble family from its completion in 1909 until it was

donated to the University of Southern California in 1966. For 57 years the house was maintained essentially as built, even the original furniture remained intact save for a couple of minor pieces in the possession of family members. Thus, visitors are able to see the house largely as intended by Charles and Henry. Recall that each piece of Greene & Greene furniture was designed for a particular location. While beautiful when viewed in any context, viewing the pieces in the original setting certainly enhances the experience.

Built on more than 40 acres in the foothills of the Ojai valley, the Pratt house sits in a more rustic setting than the other Ultimates (or most Greene & Greene houses). Always one to carefully consider siting, Charles was especially attentive in this case, even allowing the site to dictate the footprint of the structure. The resulting obliquely-angled design maximizes mountain views. Furniture for the Pratt house may be the most sophisticated designed by the Greenes. Inlays, in particular, are at another level, beyond any done previously.

Berkeley's Thorsen house is the last of the Ultimates and the only one outside Southern California.

The house for Freeman Ford has been substantially altered. However, the courtyard still invites one outdoors into the California sunshine. View east from courtyard, Freeman A. Ford house, Pasadena, 1906-08.

A compact mansion in an urban setting, the Thorsen announces its pedigree with the magnificent clinker brick work visible from the street. Painted friezes in the living and dining rooms are a highlight as is the elegant dining room suite.[30] Despite the small lot, the Greenes created a wonderfully private yard through use of an L-shaped plan. Even in this setting they successfully blurred the distinction between indoors and out with numerous windows and patio doors. Even some interior doors are leaded providing an open feel.

From 1905 to 1910 the Greenes designed and oversaw construction of these six masterpieces. The duration of their architectural nirvana was brief indeed. Each project included a substantial house, numerous pieces (in some cases, dozens) of exquisite furniture, lighting fixtures, andirons and fire screens (as well as the fireplaces) and enough fantastic interior woodwork to deplete a rain forest. Architectural trim is given the

same careful attention as fine furniture, blurring the line between structure and furnishings. Stairways are especially beautiful perhaps because the Halls had particular expertise in this area.

Of course, there were many other jobs moving through the firm during this time including additions or alterations for a number of earlier clients. It's small wonder then that in 1909 Charles, on whom the bulk of the design work fell, and whose obsessive nature made such a quantity of work doubly difficult, was in need of a break. He took his family to England for an extended stay while Henry oversaw the business. Charles returned later that year resuming work on several of the larger commissions, particularly the Thorsen house in Berkeley. For all practical purposes, however, this was the end of the heyday of Greene & Greene. Charles and Henry Greene had been able to enjoy, if only for a brief time, the artist's dream of enlightened clients with nearly limitless budgets.

The brothers continued to work together for several more years, most notably on the Mortimer Fleishhacker estate in Woodside, California, and the Cordelia Culbertson house, built by three maiden sisters of James Culbertson on the same Oak Knoll street as the Blacker house, but the firm was winding down.

Furniture designs for the Pratt house, the penultimate Ultimate Bungalow, illustrate the Greene & Greene style at the evolutionary zenith. The whimsical wave motif appears in several forms. Living room armchairs, 1908-11, Charles M. Pratt house, Ojai, 1908-11.

In 1916 Charles moved his family north to Carmel-by-the-Sea. Though Greene & Greene Architects wasn't officially dissolved until 1922, the brothers worked independently save for some projects for past clients.

After relocating, Charles was mostly content to pursue the life of the Bohemian artist he had always wanted to be. He undertook a handful of new commissions, such as the D.L. James house — a stone masterpiece on the cliffs of Carmel — but was more interested in writing, painting and working on his studio. He was not yet 50 years of age.

Henry remained in Pasadena and continued a solo practice for a number of years. New commissions were much more scarce than during the heyday though he did design a number of houses. He also continued to design additions and alterations for earlier clients. Unfortunately, he was never again able to attain the level of success he and Charles had found in that remarkable period during the first decade of the 20th century. [31]

ABOVE An example of extreme grace, this table combines a perfect form with incredible detailing such as carved scrolls and fantastic inlay. Living-room table, c. 1910, William R. Thorsen house, Berkeley, 1908-10.

LEFT Charles Greene's studio in Carmel may be the ultimate expression of his personality. Note the scrolled brickwork at the upper right. Fence and gate, Charles S. Greene studio, Carmel, 1923-24.

OPPOSITE This inglenook represents a career in microcosm. The elements work together in a way that only a genius could have foreseen. Detail, living-room inglenook, David B. Gamble house.

Of England, New York, Japan and California

"Without tradition, art is a flock of sheep without a shepherd. Without innovation, it is a corpse."

Sir Winston Churchill

Charles and Henry Greene's rise to prominence was rapid, their stay at the summit of the architectural world short-lived. The time from the opening of their practice in 1894 until its informal dissolution in 1916 encompassed 22 years, a span remarkable for its brevity. Nearly all of the work for which they are remembered today was created in a period of only about a dozen years. Time, in the short term, was not kind to the Greenes. Their work fell out of fashion and they were largely forgotten. Many of their houses suffered unspeakable abuse ranging from routine "brightening" of interior surfaces to ill-conceived modernization.[1] Worst of all, many were simply demolished in the

Stepping into this room is like stepping back in time. No other Greene & Greene house is as intact. Living room, David B. Gamble house, Pasadena, 1907-09.

name of progress. We are all poorer for the disappearance of masterpieces such as the Arturo Bandini and Dr. Arthur Libby houses.

By the late 1940s, a small number of architects had begun to rediscover Greene & Greene. Drawn perhaps by the anti-modern (and ante-modern) yet timeless aesthetic, several took it upon themselves to reintroduce the Greenes to a wide audience. L. Morgan Yost, a disciple of Frank Lloyd Wright, was one of the first to reexamine Greene & Greene. He began researching their work at a fortuitous time — both Charles and Henry were still alive and most of their biggest commissions were still intact.[2] Henry, in fact, took Yost on a tour of the Blacker house when Mrs. Blacker still lived there. Yost notes, "This was an experience never to be repeated as Mrs. Blacker died the next year, the property was sold, divided and disfigured, and the furniture dispersed."[3] What a thrill it must have been for a residential architect to see that masterpiece through the eyes of one of its creators and his enlightened client, to experience it intact and untouched by the indignities held in its future.

Yost's architectural practice was in Chicago. In 1985 he was interviewed by Betty J. Blum for the Chicago Architects Oral History Project.[4] In a wide-rang-

The wood and gold-leaf of the Blacker living room glow in the warm light from the art glass lanterns. Due to furniture by Jim Ipekjian and the hard work of the current owners, the room appears today much as it did 100 years ago. Living room, Robert R. Blacker house, Pasadena, 1907-09.

ing discussion, over the course of several days, Blum and Yost covered many topics. More than once, the conversation turned to Greene & Greene. When asked what message the Greenes' work held for him, he replied, "The message of perfection, of course, which is unattainable. They did. If anybody ever attained perfection, they did. They had tremendous ability in form, materials and putting things together. It's an architecture that has to be seen and felt, including their furniture. They were able at that time to do a house for a wealthy family that would be complete right down to the last table cover and throw, all the furnishings. It was amazing to see such complete perfection."[5]

Later, when asked what pre-war (World War II) house he considers most influential, Yost answered, "The residence that influenced me or my work perhaps it's very difficult to answer because I've studied so many and looked at so many built in the last 400 years that I can't narrow it down particularly. If I had

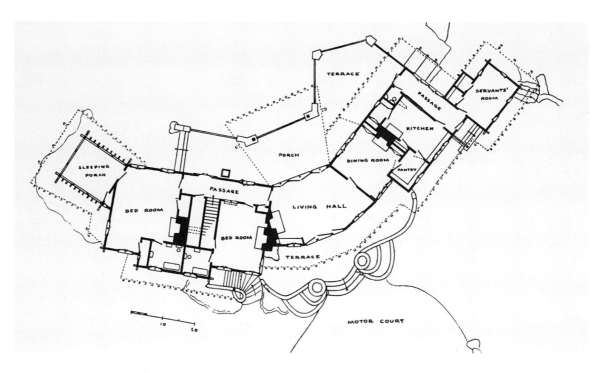

The Pratt house is an exceptional example of the fusion, by Greene & Greene, of varied influences. The California influence is particularly evident. Plan view, Charles M. Pratt house, Ojai, 1908-11.

to name any, which is no chore really, I would say the Blacker house by Greene and Greene."[6]

Perfection is a difficult mistress, perhaps an impossible one as Yost implies. Genius is a heavy mantle. It may be that the short duration of Greene & Greene Architects was inevitable — victims of their own genius and pursuit of perfection. It's worth noting that Yost's opinion was not one clouded by the passing of decades and fond recollection. He expressed the same thought in 1950, soon after having encountered the Greenes and their work firsthand: "Every detail was obviously supervised in execution after having been individually designed. These are the most perfect houses, I believe, that have ever been built."[7]

One must ask what allowed Greene & Greene to attain the unattainable, to achieve perfection in domestic architecture. Of course, even while asking, it is obvious that there is no clear answer to the question. In the Greenes' work, as in any masterpiece, there are many elements, both tangible and not, working harmoniously to create a whole that exceeds the sum of its parts. Were it otherwise, were we able to easily dissect and understand creative genius, such inspired works would be commonplace rather than rarities. It is precisely that there is no boilerplate, no recipe to follow, that makes these masterworks the lightning strikes of creative endeavors. Certain artists, however, such as Charles and Henry Greene, appeared able to make lightning strike at will.

Though impossible to reduce to a template, we can identify some of the reasons for their success. Not least among these was their ability to synthesize a new, iconic style by drawing on their training and experience as well as a set of quite varied influences.

Architect and historian Clay Lancaster recognized the variety of influence in the development of the California bungalow. "The bungalow movement differed from earlier revivals in the indefiniteness of its source of inspiration, which allowed the architect's imagination free play, thereby sanctioning originality in a roundabout way."[8]

This is, perhaps, the great triumph of their careers — the sensitive fusion of elements of the Arts & Crafts movement, an Asian aesthetic and the requirements of their adopted California in a way to appear entirely rational and natural, even inevitable. Of course, it was anything but inevitable at the dawn of the 20th century. Only a visionary could have anticipated the result of this integration; of incorporating such seemingly disparate aesthetics.

Arts & Crafts

Viewed through the lens of more than a century, the Victorian era can seem rather quaint. Popular perception is of a time of extreme formality, fussy ornamentation and a strict moral code. It was also a time, however, in which prostitution and child labor were rampant, social classes were rigid (leaving many in abject poverty) and technology, in the form of the industrial revolution, was changing the nature of work for many.

It is against this backdrop, indeed in response to it, that the Arts & Crafts movement was born. A reaction against elements of the Victorian world, the Arts

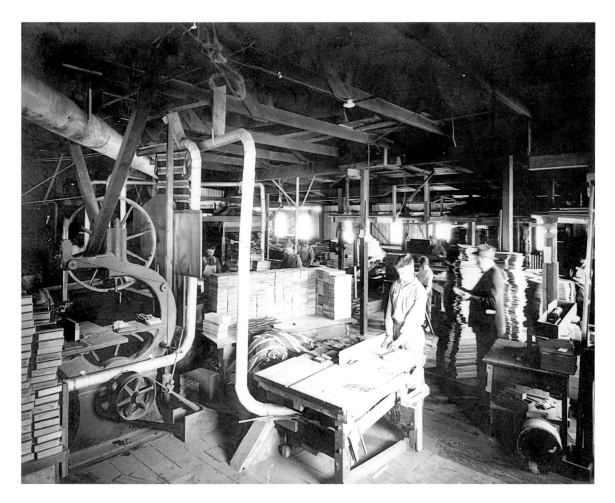

& Crafts movement was much more than a simple design philosophy; it was a social movement. Early proponents in England, such as John Ruskin and William Morris, were social philosophers, in point of fact, socialist philosophers. They encouraged a return to craft rather than a continued move toward assembly, arguing that it dehumanizes a man to repeatedly perform the same task rather than to create an object, such as a piece of furniture, from beginning to end.

It is noteworthy that Charles and Henry Greene were not social philosophers. They did not publicly advocate social or political change. One can only speculate as to the reason but one rational candidate is that there was little need. In England, Ruskin and Morris had a well established society against which to rebel, an established hierarchical class structure to overthrow. In California, the ultimate land of opportunity, on the other hand, the Greenes were not presented with this tempting target for reform. There a man, any man, could make his way and hope, with some reason, to be successful. Charles Greene himself addressed this notion in a 1905 article: "California, with its climate, so wonderful in possibility, is only beginning to be dreamed of, hardly thought of yet."[9]

Ruskin, Morris and other founders of the movement also railed against overly ornate Victorian design with excessively applied decorative flourishes, often poorly

If Greene & Greene did, in fact, attain perfection, it was due in no small part to Peter and John Hall. Their alliance was essential to the Greenes' legacy. Peter Hall transitioned to making boxes for fruit and candy companies when work for Greene & Greene decreased.

constructed. They argued instead for far simpler, more functional designs, honestly made so that construction details were often apparent, as with exposed joinery.

Thus, the Arts & Crafts movement had two primary goals: the improvement of working conditions, particularly for those employed in the manufacture of goods; and a fundamental change in the style and utility of objects people would choose to have in their homes. Indeed, it was hoped that there could be improvement in what people perceived as beautiful.[10] There was some success on both fronts, at least for a time. However, even many of those closely associated with the movement were not in lockstep. This was a big tent with many proponents holding views at varied points along a broad spectrum.

Aesthetic differences among individuals with common philosophies are not surprising. That a Frank Lloyd Wright chair differs from one by Charles Rennie Mackintosh is, in fact, to be expected. Highly creative artists will always try to distinguish themselves. What may be more surprising, given the emphasis by the originators of the movement on a return to artisanship, is the degree to which followers disagreed on the use of machinery in production.

To fully understand the place of the machine in the Arts & Crafts movement, one must first understand the manufacturing practices of the time. While it is true that the industrial revolution brought about a dramatic increase in the use of machinery in the manufacture of goods, another complementary development was likely more troubling because it was more dehumanizing. That development was the increased use of assembly lines.

There is a correlation between increased reliance on machines and increased use of assembly lines. However, the former does not necessitate the latter. The assembly line (not to be confused with the moving assembly line) had been in use, in some form, for centuries. The result of assembly line use is an increase in repetitive tasks by the worker and a concomitant decreased role in the artistic creative process. This is

This chair from the Tichenor house is not very well constructed, but the design includes lifts and brackets that are recognizable to any fan of Greene & Greene. Desk chair, 1904-05, Adelaide M. Tichenor house, Long Beach, 1904-05.

the dehumanization the founders of the movement sought to eliminate. To be sure, machinery played a role as well, particularly in those cases in which the worker was reduced to a mere machine operator.

Many proponents of Arts & Crafts sought a true return to the pre-Renaissance guild system, complete with a total lack of machinery. However well-intentioned, this absolutist viewpoint was largely unrealistic. Social economist Thorstein Veblen addressed this point, "Therefore, any movement for the reform of industrial art or the inculcation of aesthetic ideals must fall into line with the technological exigencies of the machine process, unless it choose to hang as an anemic fad upon the fringe of modern industry."[11]

Between these two extreme views, one finds many practitioners, those who, unlike the academics and socially-minded wealthy, made their living producing goods for public consumption. Forced perhaps, as Veblen suggests, to be practical, they may adopt modern machinery where necessary. Certainly this is the case for many producers of Arts & Crafts furniture in the United States. Even William Morris was willing to use machines "to relieve drudgery" provided that the product did not suffer.[12]

Peter Hall was sympathetic to this view. In his shop one would find many machines to increase efficiency and relieve drudgery. One would also find, however, numerous benches at which artisans performed handwork of great finesse and high quality. This form of woodworking will be familiar to many modern woodworkers who recognize the utility of both hand tools and machines. Why spend time setting up a machine to perform an operation when a few swipes with a hand plane will do the job? Conversely, why spend hours dimensioning a stack of lumber by hand when machines can do it in a fraction of the time?

This eminently reasonable approach is entirely consistent with the Arts & Crafts philosophy. Ernest Batchelder is today most famous for his beautiful decorative tiles. During the first decade of the 20th century, however, he was a well-known and respected designer and educator. From 1902 until 1909 he taught design theory and manual arts at Pasadena's Throop Polytechnic Institute (precursor to the current California Institute of Technology). Batchelder addressed the point at hand quite eloquently, arguing that the use of machines is not inherently immoral: "The evil of machinery is largely a question of whether machinery shall use men or men shall use machinery."[13]

An important aspect of the Arts & Crafts philosophy is the unification of mental and manual processes. While traditional academic study was seen as critically important, the view was that it should not be to the exclusion of manual abilities such as wood and metal-working. A proper balance was seen as necessary for the development of a man. Charles Robert Ashbee, founder of Britain's Guild and School of Handicraft (1888), saw the man as the end product: "The real thing is the life; and it doesn't matter so very much if their metalwork is second rate."[14]

This same view was the genesis of the Manual Training Movement that spread through the United States in the second half of the 19th century. Charles and Henry Greene attended the Manual Training School of Washington University where they gained experience in the use of both hand tools and machinery. Similarly, William Morris "learned to dye, weave, embroider, and print in order to design for the peculiarities of each craft."[15] Ashbee included a manual training school in his guild after he relocated to Chipping Campden and transformed it into a Utopian colony. In this way, part of the Craftsman ideal was introduced to segments of the public who may have been unaware of Arts & Crafts or, perhaps, knew it only as a style of furniture.

In the spring of 1901, Charles Greene married Alice White, formerly of England, and the couple departed for a honeymoon of several months in Europe, where they visited both the Continent and Great Britain. Charles and Henry had been aware of the Arts & Crafts movement prior to this time, but Charles' time in England and Scotland clearly had an impact. There Charles would have had the opportunity to see work by leaders of the movement such as C.F.A. Voysey, Charles Rennie Mackintosh and M.H. Baillie Scott. It is not known precisely which works Charles did or did not see. What is known is that soon after his return Greene & Greene designs began to change rapidly.[16]

In America, Gustav Stickley is all but synonymous with Arts & Crafts. While he is best remembered today for his furniture designs, he was also a publisher. His magazine, *The Craftsman*, gave him a forum for expressing his ideas and spreading the Arts & Crafts gospel. While it also gave him a vehicle for selling his furniture, Stickley published his furniture plans in *The Craftsman* so that anyone could, with Stickley's explicit encouragement, implement his designs themselves. Rehumanization for the masses through woodworking.

Stickley was, for a while, quite successful. His designs and manufactured furniture were ubiquitous and often copied. His shop (or was it a factory?) churned out many pieces of Mission-style furniture that are coveted today. Typically quite spartan, even severe, they were true to the principles of the movement, particularly as practiced in America: wonderfully straightforward and well constructed.

A house should be one with its environment rather than simply sit on it. No Greene & Greene house adheres to this principle more fully than for Walter Richardson. Adobe and rocks are from the site, giving the impression that the house grows out of the ground. Detail, west façade, Walter L. Richardson house, Porterville, 1929.

In a brief essay, entitled "An Argument for Simplicity in Household Furnishings," in the first issue of *The Craftsman*, Stickley articulates the Arts & Crafts approach to design. "In all that concerns household furnishings and decoration, present tendencies are toward a simplicity unknown in the past. The form of any object is made to express the structural idea directly, frankly, often almost with baldness. The materials employed are chosen no longer solely for their intrinsic value, but with a great consideration for their potential beauty."[17] He later adds, "We are no longer tortured by

exaggerated lines the reasons for which are past divining … We are, first of all, met by plain shapes which not only declare, but emphasize their purpose."[18]

Greene & Greene certainly shared this view though whether that was the case before reading Stickley is difficult to determine. For an article in the *Pasadena Daily News*, Charles wrote, "Consciously or unconsciously we admire things that are true to themselves…"[19] This is a concise statement of the same principle: that objects should be well designed, suit their purpose and be constructed with sensitivity to the materials used. This sense of honesty or integrity was perhaps the dominant theme of Arts & Crafts designs since there was no definable style, no rulebook for determining the Arts & Crafts pedigree of a piece.

In practice, this led to an interesting conclusion: that construction details could themselves serve a decorative purpose. We see this in the carefully wedged or pegged joints in furniture of the period. We see it in the beautifully expressed post-and-beam construction in the homes. We see it in the attention paid to finishing wood in a way that enhances, rather than hides, its grain and natural character. Wood was sometimes abraded with a wire brush to make the grain more visible, a more prominent part of the design. "No ceiling ornament can equal the charm of visible floor joists and girders, or of the rafters. They are not there merely to break up the monotony of a flat surface, but primarily to keep the upper stories from falling on our heads.

Incidentally, they are a most effective decoration with their parallel lines and shadows."[20]

Charles and Henry Greene were not the only architects working in Pasadena to hold views in accord with this philosophy. At least one wrote about these ideas quite eloquently. Elmer Grey demonstrated his sensitivity, "…all commoner forms of deception that would disguise the natural expression of a building's character are immediately discernible as defects in style."[21] The Greenes were quite successful in applying this principle in their work. Such judgments were made contemporaneously by critics. "…and above all things to have all construction and materials true to their own nature, believing that brick treated simply as brick, stone as stone or wood as wood, is better than any disguise that can be put upon them."[22]

In addition to using materials in a way sympathetic to their character, there was a desire to use, to the extent possible, local materials. The argument is that a house should not sit on the landscape but rather should be a part of the landscape. Use of locally sourced materials, or even better, materials from the home site, certainly helps accomplish this. Greene & Greene practiced this often. A number of their homes along the arroyo include arroyo stones in the con-

struction, appearing in fireplaces, chimneys, retaining walls, etc. In one particularly interesting case, the bricks used in construction of the Richardson house in Porterville were made by hand on site from clay derived on site. Many other materials, mahogany for example, were not local but Greene & Greene clearly demonstrated their commitment to this principle in significant ways.

In America, Gustav Stickley was the public face of Arts & Crafts. Charles saw Stickley's furniture in 1901 during the return trip from his European honeymoon when he and Alice visited the Pan-American Exposition in Buffalo. There Stickley displayed his line of United Crafts furniture.[23] This was the first significant exposure for pieces that would soon become part of the public consciousness. The first issue of *The Craftsman* appeared later that year. Charles and Henry were readers from very early on.

Viewing the well-known designs of the mature Greene & Greene style, it can be difficult to believe that Stickley's work influenced them. The Greenes

Simple, natural beauty is integral to the concept of *shibusa*. The garden is as necessary as any other part of the home.

never publicly promoted the political ideals of the movement nor did they adhere as strictly to the design tenets. Their pieces appear lighter, more graceful than most Arts & Crafts pieces, particularly Stickley's, with significantly more ornamentation. We know, however, that Stickley was an influence as Charles' notebook is littered with clippings from *The Craftsman*. Charles frequently suggested Stickley pieces to furnish homes for which he did not design furniture. Ultimately though, the Arts & Crafts influence was merely a point of departure, a genesis that the Greenes would use in the synthesis of their own style.

The Call of the East

Perhaps no culture has codified aesthetics as thoroughly as the Japanese. In Japan, no object is considered too trivial to be made beautiful. Beauty is essential, as necessary as food and shelter. It is integral to the Japanese psyche.[24] Such thinking goes well beyond mere stylistic conventions, which are numerous. It extends to material selection and methods of construction. It is a nearly religious devotion to not only the final result but to the practices employed as well. The ends do not justify the means. The means are, in fact, an end unto themselves. The journey is as important as the destination.

Recall the famous quote by William Morris, discussed in Chapter 1, "Have nothing in your house that you do not know to be useful or believe to be beautiful." Perhaps the best-known quote to arise from the Arts & Crafts movement, this seems to share the Japanese sentiment regarding beauty. However, on closer inspection, we see that Morris was not sufficiently restrictive to rise to the level of the Japanese aesthetic. In Japan, Morris' "or" would be replaced with "and" so that only useful objects that were also beautiful would meet the standard. This distinction is significant and helps emphasize the place of beauty in Japanese culture. The work of Greene & Greene, particularly during the height of their careers, is certainly more in line with the Japanese view. To repeat the quote from Charles Greene, it was their goal, "…to make these necessary and useful things pleasurable."

Such an attitude inevitably leads to a quest for perfection. In this regard, the Japanese may have surpassed all other cultures. In Japan, artistic traditions persist for centuries, their forms and practices refined and codified. Think of the formal tea ceremony or haiku. Each is a rather mundane concept elevated to high art by an insistence on perfection. In his seminal work *Impressions of Japanese Architecture*, architect Ralph Adams Cram addresses this point: "In a way, Greek and Japanese art are closely akin: each represents the exquisite perfecting in every minutest detail of a primary conception neither notably exalted nor highly evolved, yet the result is, in plain words, final perfection." He notes that in the West this does not occur, as Westerners move on to new art forms of the day: "…each was supreme as a radiant, almost divine conception, but none, not even thirteenth century Gothic, nor fifteenth century Italian painting, was suffered to develop to its highest point: each was abandoned when hardly more than sketched in…"[25]

A relevant illustration of this Japanese viewpoint comes from an 11th century book on gardening. *Sakuteiki*, written by a Japanese court noble, is the earliest known book to describe Japanese garden design principles. Discussing the use of stones in landscape, the author writes, "The placement of the stone must follow the stone's request."[26] Thus, synthesis of method and design has a long history in Japan, a country in which history is revered. This quote also reveals another aspect of Japanese design — sensitivity to materials.

It seems natural in a society that codifies and adheres to principle to such a high degree that particular attention is paid to use of materials. Wood is an exceptionally important material and is treated with a respect, a reverence, quite uncommon in the West. A Japanese woodworker is much more in tune with the material than most of his Western counterparts. This is partly a cultural phenomenon but also likely

Charles Greene's admiration of Japanese architecture is evident in Greene & Greene designs after 1903, though the effect is often not literal.

stems in part from the way in which the Japanese woodworker interacts with the material, which is quite intimately given the nature of the low benches used. The attention is not limited to wood, however, as all of the materials used in architecture are treated with respect. Writing of Japanese buildings in *House Beautiful,* author Curtis Besinger writes, "The beauty of their buildup depends to a great degree upon the materials used and the thoughtful and careful manner in which they are put together."[27]

One obvious application of this principle is the use of materials appropriate to their intended purpose. This is a crucial, and long recognized, aspect of Greene & Greene architecture, "…it is beautiful, it is contemporary, and for some reason or other it seems to fit California. Structurally it is a blessing; only too often the exigencies of our assumed precedents lead us into the wide and easy road of structural duplicity, but in this sort of thing there is only an honesty that is sometimes almost brazen. It is a wooden style built woodenly, and it has the force and integrity of Japanese architecture."[28] Perhaps as apt a description

of the idiomatic Greene & Greene style as exists, "a wooden style built woodenly" and "an honesty that is sometimes almost brazen" are high praise from Ralph Adams Cram who was something of an idealist.

A less obvious interpretation, though one that is no less important in an analysis of Greene & Greene commissions, derives from the extreme attention to detail required to solicit a stone's intent when placing it in a design. Charles Greene's propensity for very direct involvement in the implementation of his designs is well-known. In some cases Charles insisted that workers dismantle portions of projects and redo them, possibly under his direct supervision. Charles is said to have chosen stones for placement, presumably at the stone's request. He understood that stones and bricks could not be placed at random, that sometimes the decision belongs to the material.

That the Greenes, Charles in particular, were influenced by Japan is indisputable. One must be careful, however, not to be overly aggressive, not to confuse merely sympathetic philosophies with influence. That two events occur does not establish a causal

ABOVE The server from the Ford dining room is both simple and dramatic. The overhangs at each end mirror the broad eaves of the firm's architecture. Dining room server, c. 1908, Freeman A. Ford house, Pasadena, 1906-08.

LEFT Closer inspection of the Ford server reveals subtle details. The legs are slightly concave, lightening the look. The lift on the upper rail is actually an unusual, more complex segmented shape than is typical. Detail, dining-room server, c. 1908, Freeman A. Ford house.

relationship. There are many features present in both Japanese art and architecture and the work of Greene & Greene, and there are many concepts that apply well to both. Given that the Japanese work and concepts predate Greene & Greene, often by many centuries, it is tempting to conclude that direct influence occurred. While we know some of the venues by which Charles and Henry encountered Japanese forms, there is also much that we do not know. Charles was likely drawn to Japanese designs when he encountered them because they resonated with something innate within him. It is possible, even probable, that he developed some detail, or designed in sympathy with an Eastern design philosophy, without having encountered the original. We should not, however, allow this fact to quell our curiosity or prevent us from investigating the similarities and wondering about the degree to which Japan is responsible.

In Japanese there is a term that expresses the ultimate in beautiful design: *shibusa* (*shibusa* is the noun form while *shibui* is the adjectival form). Not surpris-

Scrolls are a theme in the Blacker house entry. They appear on beams and on numerous pieces of furniture. Note the two distinct scroll forms in this scene. Detail, stair, Robert R. Blacker house.

ingly, it is a term that doesn't translate uniquely or easily as attested to by the broad range of English definitions. Described variously as calm understatement;[29] quiet, sober refinement;[30] severe exquisiteness;[31] and interesting beauty,[32] it is an important concept in Japanese aesthetics for it is intrinsically Japanese.

The August 1960 issue of *House Beautiful* was devoted to an introduction to and examination of *shibusa*. In one brief article, the editors consider the idea of beauty in Japan. They present a hierarchy of four terms and definitions that shed light on the concept in Japanese culture. The terms are *Hade, Iki, Jimi* and *Shibui*.[33] The list is presented in order by increasing level of sophistication and decreasing level of ostentation with *shibui* described as the essence of Japanese culture and the ultimate in taste.[34] While neither description does much to fix the meaning for one not already familiar, they do underscore the importance of the concept in analysis of Japanese art and architecture ("art" is used here in the broadest sense).

Fortunately, more descriptive definitions are available to help those without the intuitive grasp that can be achieved only through immersion. Jiro Harada wrote, "It is that quality which is quiet and subdued. It is natural and has depth, but avoids being too apparent, or ostentatious. It is simple without being crude, austere without being severe. It is that refinement that gives spiritual joy."[35]

There is no evidence that Charles or Henry Greene were familiar with the concept of *shibusa*. It does not, for example, appear in Edward Morse's *Japanese*

Homes and Their Surroundings, a book Charles Greene owned. It is possible that they had encountered it; however, what seems more likely is that they understood the idea, were sympathetic to the view, without having been exposed to it. While we may never be able to know, one thing of which we can be certain is that much of the work of Greene & Greene is *shibui*. When viewing the server from the Freeman Ford house or the dining table from the Gamble house, phrases such as, "simple without being crude, austere without being severe" certainly come to mind. The entire Blacker house is a study in "refinement that gives spiritual joy." Thus, whether Greene & Greene were actually influenced by knowledge of *shibusa* is a moot point, for their work demonstrates a sensitivity to the concept and, by extension, to Japanese aesthetics.

While Greene & Greene are not mentioned in any of the numerous articles in the *House Beautiful shibusa* issue, several contain passages that describe their work quite aptly (these passages also apply very well to the work of others, of course). One example, that seems particularly relevant to the Greenes' commissions after 1905, addresses integrated design: "The most notable thing is the serenity of the houses, the gardens and the domestic works of art. This characteristic is quite frequently mistaken for simplicity or denial. But upon deeper analysis, it clearly stems from a highly controlled, highly developed complexity. The illusion of simplicity comes from the fact that they have put their

The Japanese Pavilion at the Louisiana Purchase Exposition (the 1904 World's Fair) in St. Louis was a source of inspiration for Charles Greene.

development effort where it will count most: the making of an integrated whole."[36]

Integrated design is also a familiar theme in the Arts & Crafts movement. This is but one example of values common to both Japanese design philosophies and the Arts & Crafts movement. As discussed above, a strong interest in, or even devotion to, the selection and use of materials was a key element in both schools of thought. While there is no notion similar to *shibusa* in Europe or the United States, Arts & Crafts designers typically strove for a level of simplicity and commonly used themes from nature, both of which are *shibui* attributes. Further, elements drawn from nature were often used in highly stylized form as in the Japanese/Chinese cloud scrolls[37] and mist symbol and in many Stickley inlays as well as those in much of the furniture in the Blacker house. Finally, in both philosophies, there is a deep respect, perhaps a reverence, for labor and the process of creation. While more formal in Japan, this idea was one of the cornerstones for the founders of Arts & Crafts in England. This should not be surprising since in England this was seen as a return to the medieval guild system while in Japan there was no need for a return as the system had changed very little over time.

One needn't have formal training in design to detect Asian elements in the work of Greene & Greene. They are numerous, as are the sources from which the Greenes may have borrowed them. One of the best known examples occurred during their trip west to California in 1893 when Charles and Henry made a detour to Chicago, host of the World's Columbian Exposition. Physically the largest world's fair to that time (and second in attendance only to the 1889 Paris International Exposition), the Expo consisted of 630 acres of science, technology, amusements and architecture.[38] Most of the architecture, particularly on the central Midway, was in the classical style. However, the grounds also included a large number of other buildings, contributed by U.S. states and other countries. The styles of these outlying buildings varied greatly from the uniformity found in the Midway.

Much has been made of the Columbian Exposition as a pivotal event for the Greenes, particularly with respect to the influence of the *Ho-o-den* Japanese exhibit. However, as Greene & Greene scholar Bruce Smith argues, there was no significant incorporation of Japanese elements in their work for about a decade after the Columbian Exposition.[39] This makes a compelling case that there were other, more seminal, Asian influences. One such influence came to the Greenes courtesy of a determined, perhaps strong-willed, client.

Most architect-client relationships are rather one-sided. While the architect may take cues from the client, the flow of real ideas is largely unidirectional. Once in a while a fortunate architect might find a special client who pushes them to new places, encourages them to expand, to experiment with new ideas. The Greenes found such a client in Adelaide Tichenor. In 1904, prior to the design of her house,[40] Mrs. Tichenor attended the Louisiana Purchase Exposition in St. Louis. So struck was she by what she saw that she wrote Charles imploring him to travel immediately to St. Louis. "… the more I see of it, the more I feel that I do not want to go on with my home until you see it." She continued several lines later, "I really think that you will never regret it if you arrange your affairs to come at once. I think it must be as hard for you to leave one time as another — and you will be able to get so many ideas of woods and other things for finishing what you now have on."[41]

Despite a heavy workload, Charles did journey to St. Louis, persuaded not only by his very insistent client but also by a desire to see the firm's, and his own, entries in the architectural exhibits at the fair. What Charles saw at the fair, the display that had so excited his client, was the impressive Japanese Pavilion. Consisting of eight buildings and surrounding gardens, the

The Van Rossem house (the first of three) is the site of an amazing clinker brick wall. This gate, with Chinese tiles, clearly shows the Asian influence on the Greenes' work. Detail, wall and north façade, Josephine Van Rossem house #1, Pasadena, 1903.

Japanese exhibit provided a significant and authentic view of both temple and imperial architecture.[42] The gardens and Main Hall, a scaled near-replica of the *Shishin-den*,[43] sometimes described as the heart of Kyoto's Imperial Palace, particularly appear to have impacted Charles. Though some Japanese forms had emerged in the firm's work previously, the trend accelerated from 1904 onward.

While visits to the 1893 and 1904 World's Fairs were undoubtedly significant, one must be careful

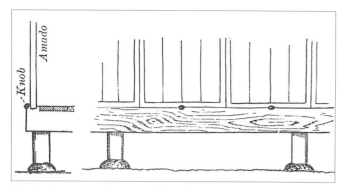

Charles Greene owned a copy of Edward Morse's *Japanese Homes and their Surroundings*, likely his source for the practice of setting posts on stones or rocks.

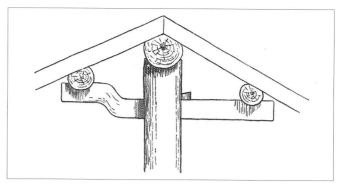

Morse depicted and described many aspects of the Japanese house. In some cases, the influence of the images on Greene & Greene was indirect.

Though first used by Greene & Greene in the house for Arturo Bandini, the firm often returned to the practice of setting posts on stones. View of courtyard, Cora C. Hollister house, Hollywood, 1904-05.

to place them in proper context. Both Greenes had been exposed to Japanese forms prior to 1904 while in Boston. Beginning in the late 1870s and through the 1880s, Boston was in the grip of a craze of Japonism. At the 1876 Centennial Exposition in Philadelphia, Japan had ignited the public's imagination with the first display of (supposedly) authentic Japanese forms in the United States. During this time, the Museum of Fine Arts in Boston prominently featured their large collection of Japanese and Chinese objects. Charles and Henry almost certainly viewed the collection as students at MIT were granted free access to the museum.[44]

Even without leaving Pasadena, Charles and Henry Greene had access to decorative objects from the Orient courtesy of client John Bentz. Charles and Henry visited, and patronized, the shop regularly.[45] In addition, Charles owned a copy of *Japanese Homes and Their Surroundings* by Edward S. Morse. In this book, Morse gives a detailed, firsthand account of Japanese

residential architecture in the mid-19th century. Thus, Charles was ready for a move toward increased use of Japanese themes. Perhaps the most noteworthy aspect then of his trip to St. Louis was that he knew he had found a client eager to help him make that move.

In some cases the Japanese influence in Greene & Greene designs is obvious. The exposed timber construction in their houses is also common in Japanese architecture, particularly Imperial buildings and temples.[46] For the Arturo Bandini house (1903), Charles borrowed another traditional Japanese form. Posts, supporting the roof over the broad walkway around the perimeter of the courtyard that forms the focal point of that house, rest on carefully placed stones as in the Japanese idiom.[47] Though the effect is not overtly Asian in the context of the rustic Bandini house, the influence is plain to see. Broad eaves, a standard feature on the firm's houses, beginning around the time of the Culbertson house, are another Japanese form (a detail mirrored in wide overhangs on furniture — recall the discussion of integrated design).

Less known examples abound as well. One is the scroll detail — a Chinese element — best known for its use in the Blacker house. In that house, the scroll is omnipresent in the entry hall furniture. It also appears in both interior and exterior architectural details. Sometimes called "cloud scrolls" in Chinese design,[48] the Greenes also used this detail more subtly. One instance is at the base of the stairs in the Gamble house, as well as in some Gamble furniture. Another is in the carvings on the legs of the beautiful Thorsen living room table. Scrolls also appear throughout the exquisite Robinson house. Sometimes nearly hidden, seeking the scrolls there makes for something of a sport, for those obsessed with such things.

The cloud form is nearly ubiquitous in Chinese furniture for a period of nearly 2,000 years. The shape and meanings evolved through the dynasties from the Han (roughly 200 BC to 200 AD) to the Qing (into the 20th century). Author Sarah Handler writes: "As far

Chinese cloud scrolls appear in a number of Greene & Greene houses including the Blacker, Gamble and Robinson. In the Robinson house they are scattered throughout the house and are sometimes subtle, as in this chandelier. Hall chandelier, 1906-07, Laurabelle A. Robinson house, Pasadena, 1905-06.

back as the Han dynasty, clouds are depicted as long scrolling lines with curled flourishes, which sometimes resemble birds' heads or dragons' claws and are thus endowed with animistic powers. They are associated with the life-giving power of rain and were vehicles on which the immortals rode above the earth. In the Tang dynasty billowing clouds with lobed heads were added to the repertoire. Song dynasty furniture often had cloud-shaped leg flanges and cloud-shaped feet… During the twelfth and thirteenth centuries. The motif came to symbolize many blessings, particularly good fortune and long life."[49] Given Charles' affinity for Eastern philosophies, it seems likely that he was aware of the symbolism.

While one often reads of Japanese influence in the work of Greene & Greene, the Chinese influence is sometimes overlooked. One possible reason for this is that it can be difficult to distinguish the two. Many aspects of Japanese culture can be traced to China, though only by traveling through many centuries of history. That is not to say that the sources are interchangeable — after appearing in Japan the forms followed independent evolutionary paths in the two

The chairs for the Robinson dining room are heavily influenced by Chinese furniture. The concave crest rail and arms are particularly obvious. Dining-room armchair, 1906-07, Laurabelle A. Robinson house.

countries. The most commonly made distinction is that the Greenes were influenced by Japanese architecture and Chinese furniture. While likely a simplification, there is enough truth in that statement to allow it to stand as a reasonable explanation.

Chinese furniture is viewed as small-scale architecture. Sarah Handler: "Each piece of furniture is a form of architecture in miniature with walls, joinery, and an implicit duty to serve human activity. Each example is made from wood, has a rhythm in its harmonious parts, and is an act of beauty by its presence. The architecture of furniture fits into and lives within the architecture of the building. The two art forms grace and enhance each other."[50] In Chinese, the words for building framing (da muzuo, or large carpentry) and furniture making (xiao muzuo, or small carpentry) are quite similar, further illustrating the connection between structures and furniture. This is a similar concept to the Greene & Greene approach of creating furniture and interior woodwork that is in harmony with the overall structure of the house.[51]

California: A New Land

Both the Arts & Crafts movement and Asian forms clearly affected the Greenes, particularly Charles. Another seminal influence, however, may have super-

Designed by Henry Greene and built on a working citrus ranch, the Richardson house is in a setting unlike any other in the Greene & Greene canon. View to the north, Walter L. Richardson house.

seded England and Japan: California. With its unique climate, and topography, Southern California suggested, perhaps even imposed, a lifestyle. It was the Southern California lifestyle that captured the imagination of the country. It was the Southern California lifestyle that lured the wealthy to Pasadena. Ultimately, it was the Southern California lifestyle that dictated the fundamentals of the California Bungalow developed by Greene & Greene.

M.H. Baillie Scott wrote, "The most reasonable basis from which to start in furnishing is obviously the actual practical requirements of the particular family…"[52] Charles Greene shared that sentiment writing, "The style of a house should be as far as possible determined by four conditions: First — Climate. Second — Environment. Third — Kinds of materials available. Fourth — Habits and tastes i.e., life of the owner."[53] California puts its imprint on each of these factors. The dry warm climate, with several hundred days of sunshine annually, requires that the design protect the interior from heat caused by direct sunlight, hence broadly overhanging eaves and sleeping porches. The Greenes were masters of using local materials such as arroyo boulders in walls and foundations. California clearly influenced the habits of the firm's clients, many of whom were Midwesterners seeking the Southern California lifestyle, including escape from the months-long incarceration imposed by harsh Midwestern winters. The Greenes responded with residences that blur the distinction between inside and out, allowing seamless movement between the two.

This idea was neither new nor particularly Western. Chinese-born American architect I.M. Pei has expressed it this way: "The indoors and outdoors are always one … A study for a scholar without a small garden in front of it is not a study. You have to talk of the two as one."[54] Pei implies a total interdependence between indoors and out. Perhaps more philosophical than practical, his approach, common in China and Japan, is one with which the Greenes were entirely sympathetic.

That clients of the firm would desire outdoor living is little surprise. Aside from the ideal Pasadena climate they were seduced by the arroyo seco, bordering Pasadena to the West, near which many of their houses were built. In the August 1912 issue of *The Craftsman*, devoted to the American West (which is to say, California), an article entitled "Parks for the People" waxes poetic about the arroyo.

"In winter and spring, the seasons of rain in the Southwest, and the time when the snow is melting and flowing down from the mountain tops, the stream widens into a broad rushing torrent that tugs at the boulders and tree trunks on the banks. In the upper end of the Arroyo the stream-bed holds water the year round, and trout are found in the deeper quiet places; but on the lower levels summer finds the path of the stream empty, huge boulders and small stones gleaming white and clean from their winter flood polishing. In winter, spring and early summer there are luxuriant beds of wild ferns of many varieties hiding in shadow of trees and crags, or delicate maidenhair and fluffy mosses cling to precipitous rock walls, and the wild-flower beds are radiant with Nature's loveliest offerings of color, perfume and flower textures."[55]

The arroyo was far more than simply a beautiful natural resource, it provided the basis for a sub-culture quite distinct from the more traditionally formal society of the wealthy whose houses lined Orange Grove Avenue. The arroyo culture was an Arts & Crafts culture, one steeped in the traditions of Morris and Stickley. Alice Batchelder, wife of Ernest Batchelder of tile-making fame, described the culture this way: "The house, the home, music, art, self-expression, love,

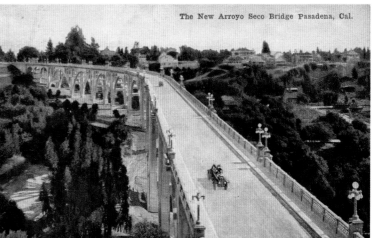

TOP Another successful use of the U-shaped form, the Richardson house courtyard provides an oasis in the arid Central Valley Summer landscape. Detail, west side of courtyard, Walter L. Richardson house.

ABOVE The arroyo seco played a significant role in the development and life of Pasadena. Rather than destroying the landscape, the beautiful Colorado Street Bridge (1913) became a man-made highlight.

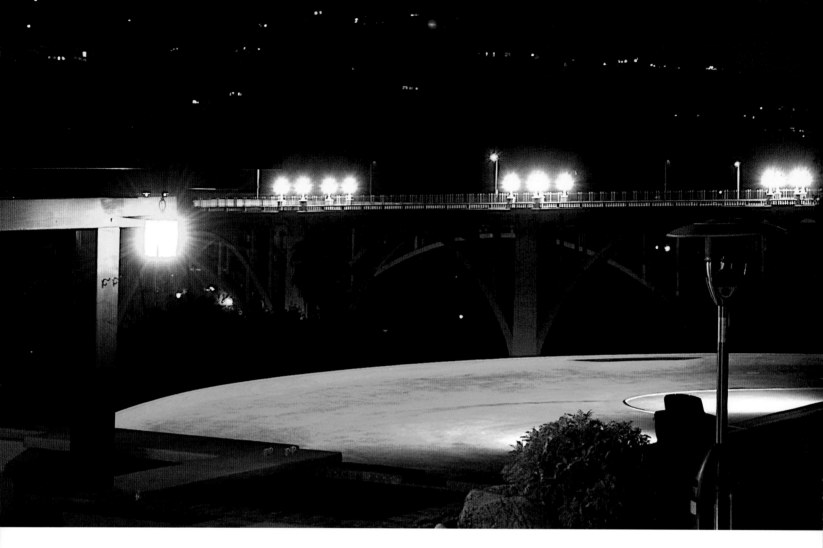

understanding, and work blended in a manner to create a complete, well-rounded pattern of living."[56] It was a culture centered on an informal moral code tied to nature, learning, handwork, artistry and local materials. Fifty years later it might have taken the form of a commune had anyone with such intentions at that time the means to afford real estate in that rarified location.

Though a largely informal group of similarly minded individuals, there was some degree of organization in the form of several people who strongly espoused the lifestyle. Much of what we know today about the arroyoans is due to Southern California's proselytizer-in-chief, Charles Fletcher Lummis, who through his magazine *Land of Sunshine* (later *Out West*) promoted arroyo culture in particular and the Arts & Crafts philosophy in general. No mere snake oil salesman, Lummis lived the life as well. His own home on the arroyo was a meeting place for intellectuals and the artistically inclined. That home, built largely by Lummis with additional labor provided by local Native Americans, was a 13-room, arroyo-boulder-clad testament to the Southwestern traditions Lummis so loved. Any advocate of the American Arts & Crafts movement would certainly have felt at home there as well.[57]

Another important figure in promoting the arroyo culture was George Wharton James whose very short-lived journal *The Arroyo Craftsman* (only one issue was published, in October 1909) was intended as the voice of the Arroyo Guild of Craftsmen. James wrote repeatedly about the arroyo for Stickley's *The Craftsman*, where he was an associate editor. Little is known about the Guild except that its purpose appears to have been to provide homes designed and fully furnished in the Arts & Crafts manner.[58] The membership is, unfortunately, not known. Nor do we know if Greene & Greene were involved with the Guild. It seems unlikely that they would have been actively involved at the time that *The Arroyo Craftsman* appeared due to the volume of work in their office and Charles Greene's decreasing interest in the full-time practice of architecture.

In an article he wrote in 1908, Charles Greene describes Arroyo Terrace, a street perched above the arroyo offering inspiring views. A street that by that time included half a dozen Greene & Greene homes including Charles' own. "From one side of the street the land drops steeply. The slope is covered with live oaks down to the valley below, and in the distance in

LEFT Perched at the edge of the arroyo, the Robinson house looks over the once natural landscape and the Colorado Street Bridge. View to the west, Laurabelle A. Robinson house.

BELOW Despite a modest budget, the Arturo Bandini house was a significant commission for Greene & Greene. It was in this house that the California influence first asserted itself in a significant manner. Isometric sketch, Arturo Bandini house, Pasadena, 1903.

DINING-ROOM IN THE HOME OF ARTURO BANDINI, ESQ.

one broad view rise the mountains. It is unlikely that this land will ever be built upon, — probably it will be a park." [59] The arroyo had more important proponents than the Greenes. During a 1903 visit to Pasadena, President Theodore Roosevelt, known for his outdoorsman tendencies, spoke glowingly of the arroyo: "What a splendid natural park you have right here! O, Mr. Mayor, don't let them spoil that! Keep it just as it is!" [60] He reiterated his admiration in a post-presidential visit in 1911. At that time, he remarked to friend Charles Fletcher Lummis that, "The arroyo would make one of the greatest parks in the world." [61]

Charles Greene was, unfortunately, incorrect about the arroyo's prospects for development, his prediction somewhat naïve in hindsight, as President Roosevelt's advice was not heeded. While the city of Pasadena acquired significant parcels of the land, much fell into private hands. Houses began to appear, not just on the edges of the arroyo but in the arroyo proper. Certainly not as disastrous as full-scale commercial development, this encroachment did alter the character of wilderness the arroyo had possessed.

ABOVE AND RIGHT Charles Greene wrote that "Habits and tastes i.e., life of the owner" should, in part, determine the style of a house. For the Bandini house, Greene & Greene fulfilled this requirement, and in the process found the genesis of the style that would define their careers. Interiors, Arturo Bandini house.

Some clients preference for building at the arroyo's edge is easily understood, however, not only for the sweeping views afforded by such a location but for the recreation it provided prior to development.

The Craftsman article notes that, "The tendency toward out-of-door life, the love of light and air and growing things is developing in the West." [62] It seems likely that such a tendency already existed in that part of the country and that many Easterners were only recently made aware of the West's unique natural gifts. In any case, Charles and Henry supported this trend, whether recent or long existing, via their designs — designs with integrated gardens, patios and porches, numerous routes of egress and a feeling of belonging to the landscape.

LIVING-ROOM IN THE HOME OF ARTURO BANDINI, ESQ.

Transplanted Easterners exerted significant influence on Greene & Greene at the earliest stage of their practice. The exponential growth in Southern California during the last decades of the 19th and first decade of the 20th centuries was due to migration — migration from the East and Midwest of those seeking opportunity, fortune, climate and good health. However, like the traveler seeking a hot dog in Paris, these newly minted Angelenos didn't always adapt to their new environment. A 1903 article by Grace Ellery Channing in Charles Lummis' *Out West* addressed this point. "We cannot blame our Eastern ancestors for modeling their homes and gardens, as they framed their lives and laws, after English, Dutch and German models; but when the Easterner moves West and plants his snow-shedding roofs beneath a shower of rose-petals, and builds him his Dutch or English lidless house upon a shadeless sidewalk and then immures himself — it is time to call him back to the decencies."[63]

Thus, Ms. Channing suggests, it was not uncommon for Southern California's new settlers to bring with them the styles they knew and with which they were comfortable. The Spanish missionaries had, of course, done much the same thing with the California missions which were constructed to recall, to the extent possible given the rudimentary tools available,

buildings from their native Spain. The mission fathers were well justified given the similar climates in Spain and Southern California. As Ms. Channing states, however, the Eastern and Midwestern arrivals, a group that included most architects practicing in the area, introduced a number of styles quite poorly suited to their adopted home.

An architect can do only so much to change a client's mind. Greene & Greene had for a time been fighting a quixotic battle, attempting to convince Pasadena's transplants to leave the traditional styles back East where they belonged.[64] They had had some success in incorporating climate-appropriate features, such as broader eaves to protect living spaces from the harsh sun but had not yet designed a truly Californian house. In 1903 they were engaged by Arturo and Helen Elliott Bandini, clients for whom no convincing was necessary. Arturo Bandini was the son of Juan Bandini, one of the old Spanish dons with substantial land holdings in the old Rancho system. He had grown up in a true California house — a casa de rancho, a style described quite well by Helen Elliott Bandini in her opus *History of California*. "The homes were generally built around a court into which all the rooms opened, and were constructed of adobe bricks such as were used at the missions. In the better class of homes

several feet of the space in the courtyard next to the wall were covered with tile roofing, forming a shaded veranda, where the family were accustomed to spend the leisure hours."[65]

The Bandinis requested a house that would recall the rancho homes of California's recent past. The Bandini house would not be large nor grandly appointed. It certainly would not be one of the more lucrative commissions for Greene & Greene.[66] Nonetheless, the Bandini house represented a significant opportunity for the brothers — it presented them with the occasion, for the first time, to design a house fully suited to its location. The result was a rustic, board and batten masterpiece with interior and exterior perfectly suited to the lifestyle of the clients.

With the Bandini house the Greenes had finally found a direction. Their well-known contributions to the development of the California Bungalow would soon follow. They were now on the evolutionary path toward their trademark style. Greene & Greene were certainly not alone in their recognition of the need for California houses. Fellow Pasadenan Elmer Grey spoke to this in a 1907 article in *The Craftsman*. Grey is quoted as saying of California architects: "If he

has a proper sense of the fitness of things he will not implant amid the semi-tropical foliage of California such architecture, for instance, as the Queen Anne or the Elizabethan."[67]

Around the San Francisco Bay, a number of architects created the California Bungalow suitable for the distinct climate of that area. This included eaves cut out above windows to allow in sunlight to dissipate the morning chill, quite unlike the requirement further south. Some of the best known architects in that area were in Berkeley, Bernard Maybeck and John Galen Howard, for example, where Charles Keeler articulated his version of the Arts & Crafts philosophy, California-style. "It has often been pointed out that all sound art is an expression springing from the nature which environs it. Its principles may have been imported from afar, but the application of those principles must be native. A home, for example, must be adapted to the climate, the landscape and the life in which it is to serve its part. In New England we must have New England homes; in Alabama, Alabama homes, and in California, California homes."[68]

The clients of Greene & Greene, particularly the wealthy, were helping to create the California country house.[69] They did not, of course, set out to do this, nor were they likely aware of it, but that is precisely what they did. Then as now, Pasadena's Orange Grove Avenue was known as "Millionaire's Row" for the string of elegant mansions along its length. Certainly the Gambles, Blackers and Fords, barons of industry, could have built there had they so desired. They, however, were not chasing acclaim or society. They sought the lifestyle afforded by locale. Marble mansions did not indulge that desire and were, at any rate, incongruous for that place and time.

One should not think of "country house" in the sense of country-style décor with stenciled furniture and punched-tin pie safes. The term, imported from England, denotes a house located outside the city. It is important to note that a country house is not necessarily a small or modest house. In the English idiom, in fact, these are typically impressive estates of the gentry. The United States also has its share of similarly impressive country houses. In *The American Country House*, the first example given by author Clive Aslet is Biltmore, the immense house built by George Washington Vanderbilt outside Asheville, North Carolina.[70] Clearly then, modest size is not a requirement.[71]

Nor is modesty of appointment a prerequisite. A 1914 *House Beautiful* article about bungalows in Southern California addresses this point. "Among all that Southern California has to boast, there is nothing of which she is more justly proud than the charm of her country homes; … Many of them are unrivaled in their completeness, thoroughly meeting not only the individual needs of the owner and of the climate, but the demands of really good building as well. The construction, the decorative lines, the arrangement of the rooms, even the least detail of interior finish, coloring and furnishing are planned in consistent relation to each other, so that every little part will aid, both in making the practical working of the house as convenient as possible and in the creation of an original artistic effect for the whole."[72]

With this definition in mind, it is quite clear that most Greene & Greene houses are in fact country houses. The Gamble house is included in a 1913 book entitled *American Country Houses of Today*.[73] The impressive Fleischhacker estate in Woodside is similarly represented in an article for *The Architectural Record*, by John Galen Howard, about country houses on the Pacific coast.[74] The Blacker, Ford, Robinson

and Pratt houses all fall into the category as well. One could argue that the Thorsen house is not a country house given its setting in Berkeley and its siting on a standard urban lot, but this only makes it the exception that proves the rule since it shares a great deal with its predecessors to the south.

The final word on the topic goes, quite appropriately, to John Ruskin, who spoke very eloquently on the subject of the English country house. His words are quite befitting the work of Charles and Henry Greene, two young men creating perfect houses an ocean and a continent away. "And in actual life let me assure you that the first 'wisdom of calm' is to plan and resolve to labour for the comfort and beauty of a home such as, if we could obtain it, we would quit no more. Not a compartment of a model lodging-house, not the number so-and-so of Paradise row, but a cottage all our own, with its little garden, its pleasant view, its surrounding fields, its neighbouring stream, its healthy air and clean kitchen, parlours and bedrooms. Less than this no man should be content with for his nest; more than this few should seek; …"[75]

The landscape of the Van Rossem/Neil house. A perfect illustration of Ruskin's "…cottage all our own, with its little garden…" View of north façade, Josephine Van Rossem house #1.

Poems of Wood and Light

"Every great architect is — necessarily — a great poet. He must be a great original interpreter of his time, his day, his age."
FRANK LLOYD WRIGHT

G od is in the details." These words are often attributed to modernist architect Ludwig Mies van der Rohe though it is unclear if he ever actually spoke them.[1] This fact hardly matters, however. The brilliantly brief phrase conveys to the listener an instantly understood, if previously unrealized, meaning: we get to the beauty of something by delving beyond the surface. That this concept is ascribed to a modernist, to the man who

said, "Less is more" is intriguing. Architecture of the Modernist Movement is typically austere, minimalist. One tends to think of such designs not in terms of details but rather form. Practitioners of modernism,

Afternoon sun through art glass windows throws a wonderful light and makes the silky mahogany glow. Detail, dining room server, 1908-09, David B. Gamble house, Pasadena, 1907-09.

however, are no different from designers before and since in this regard: details are critical.[2]

It might seem that modernism has little to do with the work of Greene & Greene. The Arts & Crafts movement was decidedly anti-modern. It was, in part, a rejection of the industrial age, whereas modernism was conceived as an architecture for the industrial age. Despite this apparent diametric opposition, there are sympathetic aspects to the movements. Recall that Arts & Crafts was also a repudiation of the overly ornate characteristics of the Victorian era, a move toward more honestly expressed construction with less adornment. A philosophy of less is more, if you will. One must be careful not to carry such analogy too far as clearly the reigning attitudes of the two schools were vastly dissimilar but it is an interesting line of inquiry.[3]

Of course, the modernist notion of architecture as transcending regional identity is completely anti-thetical to the work of Greene & Greene, whose houses were heavily influenced by their locale. It is also the case that the Greenes were highly aware of the people who would inhabit their buildings. No one-size-fits-all solution could have held any appeal for them. Despite the allure of Arts & Crafts for its emphasis on natural materials, honest construction and simple forms, modernism won, at least for a time. It made Arts & Crafts seem irrelevant and anachronistic, a throwback to the era of horses and buggies at a time when automobiles were screaming about the countryside.

Putting aside differences and similarities between these movements, "God is in the details" applies as well, perhaps, to the Greenes' designs as to any others. Details define Greene & Greene. As Morgan Yost noted, "The time spent by the brothers on each of their later jobs must have been enormous. Every detail was obviously supervised in execution after having been individually designed."[4] Thus, to understand the work of Charles and Henry Greene, one must gain an appreciation for the details that appear in their work and the extraordinary effort devoted to them.

To gain this appreciation, this understanding, a degree of deconstruction is required. However, deconstructing a masterpiece is likely to be less than completely satisfying. We can describe the component parts, but any such narrative is sure to be incomplete — a work of genius is always more than the sum of its parts. But because those parts are essential, even a partial understanding of them, of the design vocabulary, is valuable.

The Greene & Greene design vocabulary is rich and varied with a number of well-recognized elements. Among the best known are cloud lifts, ebony pegs and breadboard ends. Lifts and pegs, in particular, have been the subject of countless words — and rightly so.

Flawless in design and execution. Dining room armchair, 1909-10, William R. Thorsen house, Berkeley, 1908-10.

They are beautiful and essential to the look. There are other elements, however, that are equally important but less widely known. These include finger joints, *tsuba* shapes (a *tsuba* is a Japanese sword guard), carvings, shop-made handles and pulls, and intricate inlays. All contribute significantly to the signature style.

Greene & Greene were obsessive in their pursuit of detail nirvana. They would expend thought, effort and their clients' money on elements that few but the servants would ever see. The backs of cabinets are prepared and finished with the same care as the fronts.[5]

The most trivial features were designed by the architects rather than allocated from the parts bin. Doors and windows were designed anew for each commission. Furniture, interiors and structures were equal recipients of this attention.

There is, in effect, no distinction between furniture and woodwork. The woodwork and built-ins are so beautiful in design, execution and materials that they are elevated to the level of the best furniture. It's as if the rooms themselves are exquisite furnishings. That furniture and architectural details share common elements serves to enhance the effect. In fact, every piece of furniture was designed to occupy a particular place in a particular room, and each was a unique creation. There was no need for general designs that could fit into many settings. This fact allowed for a unity of design that has seldom been seen before or since. The same device, repetition of design elements, was also used to unify interiors and exteriors, a practice for which Greene & Greene were pioneers.

In the final analysis, it's impossible to express a formula for a well-designed Greene & Greene piece.

Adequate evidence for this claim exists in the form of very poor imitations. Even many "reproductions" are lacking. Though the style is hard to define, there are some adjectives that begin to capture the feel. Graceful is the first that comes to mind. This derives from the scale and proportion of the pieces but also from the easy interplay of components. Nothing seems forced or overdone. It is said that a good melody is inevitable. So it is with Greene & Greene furniture. What to add or remove to improve a piece? The answer is nothing. It's difficult to imagine it any other way.

Which brings us back to obsession; devotion to even the most trivial details. It's part of the Greene & Greene mystique. It's part of the Greene & Greene genius. It's part of the reason Greene & Greene continue to be relevant after more than 100 years.

This piece was designed for a small alcove where the back would never be seen, and yet the finish and detailing are perfect. Living room bookcase, 1908-09, Robert R. Blacker house, Pasadena, 1907-09.

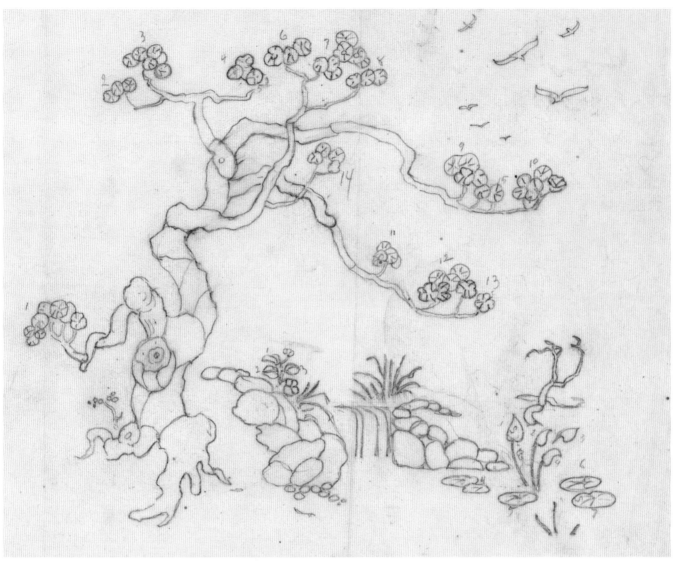

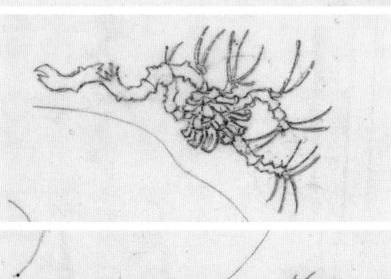

This inlay, closer to work for the Pratts than the Gambles, demonstrates how well and how quickly Charles Greene mastered this craft. Detail drawing, living room letter box, 1914, David B. Gamble house.

Unifying Themes

"The furnishings and gardens were their province in the later houses for the wealthier clients and they produced a unity that has never been surpassed."[6] This quote, by Morgan Yost in 1950, succinctly expresses one of the most important aspects of Greene & Greene design, the nearly total unification of every aspect of a project: exterior, interior, furniture, furnishings and landscape.

The Robert Blacker house is certainly one of the "later houses" to which Yost refers. In the dining room in that house, there are two small serving tables of the same design, a design that duplicates, in reduced scale, the dining table. The bottom stretchers of the tables include a pair of lift details symmetric about the center. Amazingly, the moldings on the wall behind the tables duplicate this lift element.

In a Greene & Greene home, it can be difficult to determine exactly where interior woodwork ends and furniture begins. Materials and execution are similarly beautiful, common themes serve to enhance the effect. The only practical difference is that the furniture can be moved. Or can it? Recall that each object was designed for a specific position, information that was sometimes included on original drawings. There were no generic forms designed to fit into many settings. This allowed for, even promoted, commonality of design, as dictating the position of a piece allowed the architects to fully integrate their creation.[7]

John Ruskin described "unity of feeling" as "the first principle of good taste ... the basis of all grace, the essence of all beauty."[8] He argued that a building must be true to itself and to its location and purpose. It is no great leap of logic to extend this reasoning to the furniture and other decorative objects in a house, to expect that the furnishings are true to the building, their location and purpose, to expect that the interior is in harmony with the exterior. Greene & Greene excelled at using common themes to unite interior with exterior, blurring the distinction between indoors and out. One example, a trademark feature common in many Greene & Greene exteriors, are wide eaves that overhang a house's walls. Many pieces of furniture mirror this trait with dramatic overhangs that are one of the defining features of the Greenes' style. Examples

TOP LEFT Attention to detail defined by example. One wonders if David and Mary Gamble ever saw these ebony pins. Detail, dining room table, 1908-09, David B. Gamble house, Pasadena, 1907-09.

LEFT Every piece of furniture was designed for a particular place in a particular room. The lifts on this table mirror the woodwork below. Dining room serving table, 1908-09, Robert R. Blacker house, Pasadena, 1907-09.

such as the Gamble entry hall table and the Freeman Ford server, both iconic pieces, beautifully illustrate the thesis. The Ford server is, in fact, defined by the wonderfully exaggerated overhang at each end.

Two less widespread examples, each from one of the Ultimate Bungalows, further illustrate this wonderful aspect of the work of Greene & Greene. Chinese cloud scroll patterns are a recurring theme in the entry hall of the Robert R. Blacker house. They appear on the legs of each of the many pieces of furniture. They appear on the top surface of at least one piece of furniture. And they appear on the ends of large, overhead beams that span much of this impressive space. These beams pass through the rear wall of the room, terminating on the patio at the back of the house, where each supports a copper and art glass lantern. Above each lantern, on the exterior end of the beam, is a scroll mirroring that found on the interior end. The effect, despite the simplicity of the device, is the feeling that each element works with every other. The scrolls do not accomplish this task alone, but they certainly amplify the effect.

The Blacker house was the second of the Ultimate Bungalows, the William R. Thorsen house, constructed in Berkeley in 1909-1910, was the last. One of the astounding facts about the Ultimate Bungalows is how little they have in common. To be sure, there are stylistic similarities — present are many of the most

TOP   Scrolls are a recurring theme in the entry hall, even carrying over to beam ends on the patio. Detail, hall stairs, Robert R. Blacker house.

ABOVE   A different scroll form is found on much of the furniture in the hall and less prominently on the stairs. Detail, hall plant stand, 1908-09, Robert R. Blacker house.

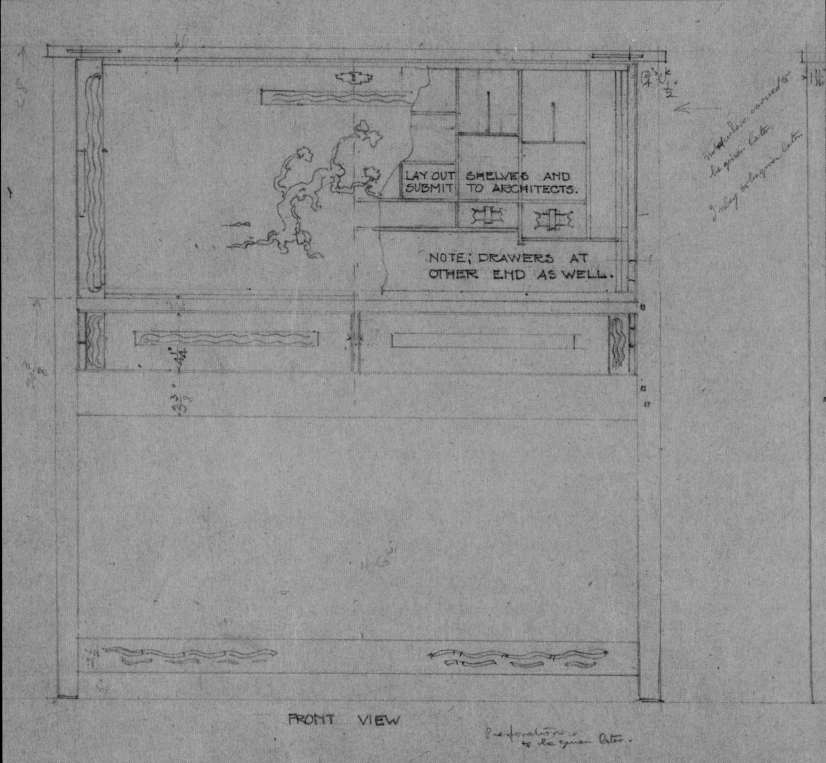

LAY OUT SHELVES AND
SUBMIT TO ARCHITECTS.

NOTE; DRAWERS AT
OTHER END AS WELL.

FRONT VIEW

DESK

1½ INCH SCALE DETAILS OF DESK & CHAIR.
CHA'S M. PRATT ESQ, IN THE OJAI VALLEY CAL
GREENE & GREENE ARCHITECTS 215-31

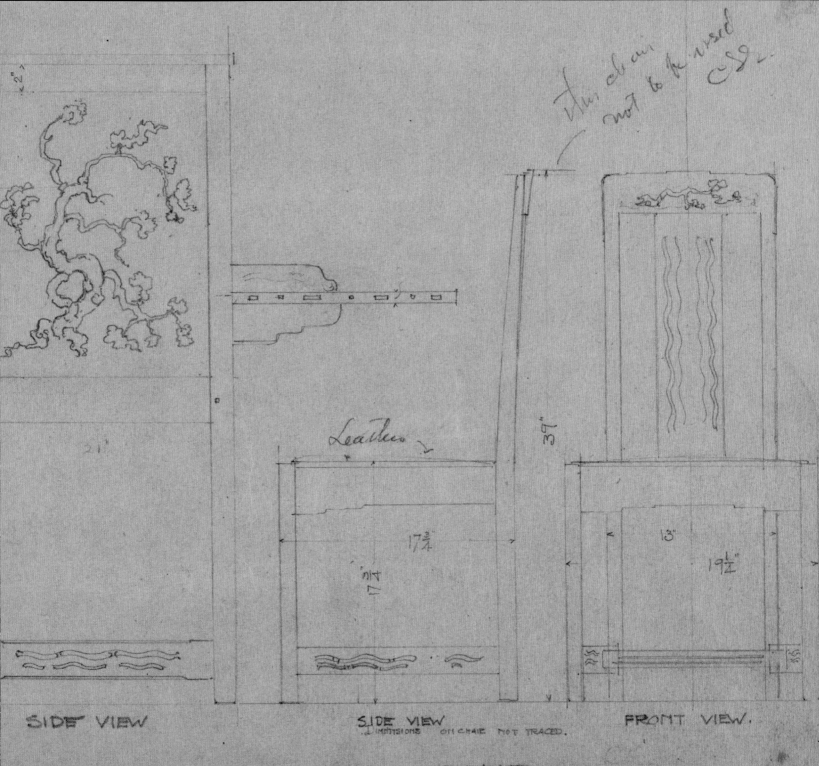

This chair
not to be used
CSG~

Leather

39"

17¾"

17¾"

13"

19½"

21"

SIDE VIEW

SIDE VIEW
DIMENSIONS ON CHAIR NOT TRACED.

FRONT VIEW.

CHAIR.

OR LIVING ROOM, FURNITURE FOR RESIDENCE OF
DRAWING Nº 4.

BOSTON BLD'G PASADENA CAL.

Notations on this drawing provide insight into the working
relationship between architects and craftsmen. Drawing, living-
room desk, c. 1912, Charles M. Pratt house, Ojai, 1908-10.

The nautical theme at the Thorsen house continues all the way to the sidewalk. Gate, 1908-10, William R. Thorsen house, Berkeley, 1908-10.

identifiable elements of the Greene & Greene style — but each is a new and distinct plan, a fresh design from the ground up. The Thorsen house, an urban mansion, contained fewer visible interior beams than some of its predecessors but included a large quantity of exquisite teak and mahogany trim and built-ins that are the rival of any designed by the brothers. The west-facing house, when built, had spectacular views of the San Francisco Bay, a nod to William Thorsen's maritime

interests. Continuing the nautical theme, the living room and two bedrooms each have a wall that forms an obtuse angle, giving the impression of a ship's prow. In the living room, "At the V-end can be seen the massive redwood beam which extends through to support the porch roof. This is another indoor-outdoor motif used to break down the barrier of the separating wall and one which they used many times."[9] Completing the theme, the redwood beam resembles the bowsprit extending from the bow of a sailing ship, as if to lead the house on a sail through the Golden Gate.

Some themes recur throughout an interior. The primary motif in the David B. Gamble house is the *mokko-gata tsuba form* (see the section on *tsuba*). This lobed shape is ubiquitous in the Gamble dining room, appearing in art glass, chair backs and, most significantly, the dining table top. The shape is carried throughout the house via the switch plates. It appears famously in inlays in the furniture in Mr. and Mrs. Gamble's bedroom. In the living room, there are *mokko-gata* ebony pegs on the library table drawer pulls, which themselves include the shape. In the first floor guest bedroom the profile is recalled in the metal frames of the custom-made beds.

The dining table and chairs for the Laurabelle Robinson house marked a turning point in Greene & Greene furniture designs, a move toward more elegant, less severe forms with more refined ornamental elements. The chairs, based on a Chinese Ming dynasty design, are particularly graceful, the reverse-arched crest rail and arms defining the piece. That concave rail/arm shape is an unusual element that is repeated in the arms of some living room furniture. The backs of the living room sofas also repeat the rectilinear shape of rails used, in various forms, in doors, both interior and exterior, throughout the house.

Even without the unifying features highlighted here, further evidence of the obsessive attention to detail that is a hallmark of their work, Greene & Greene houses would be considered, without question, at the highest level of American architecture and design. What the unifying themes provide is the additional touch, the *je ne sais quoi* that convinces one, perhaps subliminally, that they are in the presence of genius.

Ebony Pegs

Greene & Greene furniture is distinguished by a number of details: lift elements, breadboard ends, small reveals where components meet, broad overhangs, sinuous surfaces; the list is long. Perhaps the most iconic element of all, however, is the ebony peg. From the earliest pieces, Greene & Greene incorporated pegs in their work. Initially, they were round and made of oak,

ash or other woods similar to the primary woods of the furniture. The square ebony peg first appeared in furniture for the Dr. William T. Bolton house (1906).[10]

By the time the Greenes began using ebony pegs[11] in their furniture, the primary wood was typically, though not always, mahogany. The deep black luster of the highly polished ebony pegs is set off wonderfully by the satin finish of that reddish-brown wood. The use of ebony is by no means limited to square pegs. Ebony splines often decorate the joint between the breadboard ends and a tabletop and more whimsically shaped pieces were used in some furniture, such as concave diamonds in chairs for the Freeman Ford house. In most cases the peg surface is pillowed and protrudes slightly from the member that contains it.

Though in some cases pegs are purely decorative, in many instances they hide a screw that reinforces a joint or attaches a breadboard. Some might assert that a purely decorative peg runs counter to the Arts & Crafts philosophy that argues for largely functional forms. It is certainly true that many of the Greenes' furniture

designs are less austere, more ornamented than the designs of most of their contemporaries, but we should note that even Gustav Stickley pieces included inlays that served no purpose other than decoration.

Most woodworkers who have attempted to make a piece in the Greene & Greene style have struggled with the question of how to cut mortises for ebony pegs so that they are accurately sized and square to the piece. While no consensus exists — there are nearly as many solutions to this problem as there are woodworkers working in that style — Darrell Peart provides a very helpful discussion in his book on the topic of Greene & Greene details for woodworkers.[12] It is interesting for anyone who has confronted this dilemma to see the original pieces. Many of the pegs are not quite square, they are very slightly angled either side of vertical. We

will likely never know if this was born of the expediency necessary in a commercial workshop or if it was a conscious decision made to give the arrangements of pegs a more natural, less formal feel.

Greene & Greene continued to use ebony pegs in their furniture designs for only a brief time. Pegs are present throughout the period of the Ultimate Bungalows including a desk constructed for the Gamble house living room around 1914, much after other furniture for that house. At about the same time, the Greenes were designing furniture for the Cordelia Culbertson house. Furniture for that house is quite distinct from earlier forms and ebony pegs are largely, though not entirely, absent and ebony does appear around the perimeters of doors and drawers for some pieces.[13] Many would agree that the use of the ebony peg reached its zenith quite early on, in chairs for the living room of the Robert R. Blacker house.[14] Pegs at each end of the crest rails on those pieces seem to dance due to their varied sizes and wonderful arrangement.

LEFT A difficult material to work because it is brittle, ebony's use as accents are quite playful. Detail, dining-room chair, c. 1908, Charles S. Greene.

BELOW Designed after other Gamble pieces, this desk has a sleeker look. Detail, living room desk, 1914, David B. Gamble house, Pasadena, 1907-09.

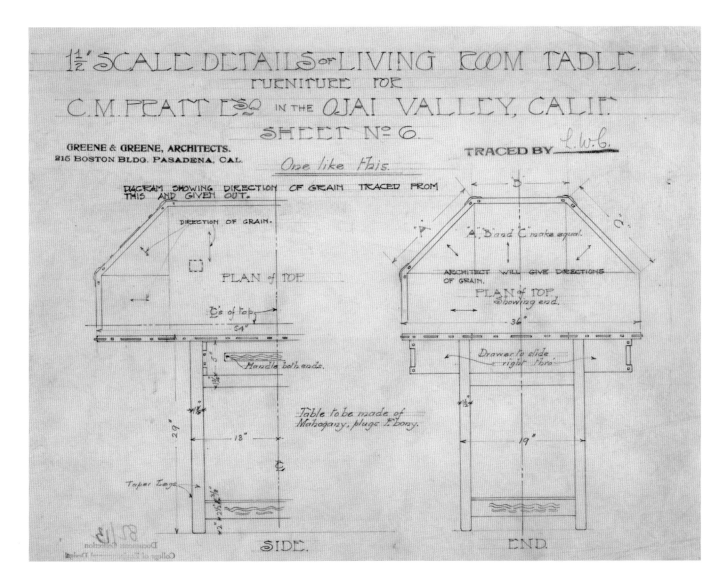

Greene & Green never failed to find interesting ways to incorporate construction methods as design features. Drawing, living room table, c. 1912, Charles M. Pratt house, Ojai, 1908-10.

Cloud Lifts

If ebony pegs are the most recognizable element of Greene & Greene furniture, then certainly cloud lifts are a close second. The cloud lift, a rise in a horizontal element such as a stretcher or apron, is a Chinese form, appearing for centuries in furniture from that country. It was first employed by Greene & Greene in furniture and decorative arts for the Adelaide Tichenor house (1904). One sure way to create a Greene-inspired piece of furniture is to design a rather generic form and then adorn it with pegs and lifts. Many lackluster (or worse) commercially available results attest to just this inclination. This fact reveals several truths. First, Greene & Greene were extremely sensitive in their use of the details in their design vocabulary. In their furniture, nothing seems superfluous or out of place. The details relate to one another, they are part of a cohesive whole rather than a collection of disparate elements. This, of course, is true at the meta-level as well: the elements in a house could be described in the same way.

Another fact revealed by the many poor imitations is that the seemingly simple features employed by the Greenes are actually quite difficult, and time-con-

suming, to implement well. This is likely not a revelation to anyone who has attempted to design and build something in the Greene & Greene style, though it might surprise a more casual observer. The cloud lift is a modest detail in terms of its complexity — even so, it can give fits to a designer. Countless posts on internet forums demonstrate that getting just the right form for a lift can be a challenge. Charles and Henry Greene may have thought so as well, given the broad variation of this element as used in their furniture.

How is it that such a simple detail could appear in so many varied forms? One answer is that, of course, it didn't have to be so. The Greenes could have created a single cloud lift boilerplate and used it injudiciously everywhere. That didn't happen because of the Greene & Greene propensity for extreme attention paid to the most minor design details. Thus, on the Gamble entry hall table we see on the upper aprons very small lifts

that rise perhaps ³/₁₆" with a very gentle radius while on the chairs in the same room we see lifts that are significantly more pronounced. In the examples above, the radii are smooth and gentle while in the Blacker dining room the transitions are much sharper.

On some pieces, the lift serves to lighten as when an apron is wider where it meets the legs — allowing for larger tenons — and narrower at the center after a series of lifts. The effect is quite similar to that achieved by arches on many Arts & Crafts pieces. On other pieces lifts serve to widen a member at its center, adding visual weight. In some cases, the detail appears on a vertical element. While technically not a lift, which is defined with respect to a horizontal element, the form is the same. Examples of this use appear on the base of the Gamble dining table and the legs of the Thorsen living room table (the latter complete with decorative scrolls at each lift). Perhaps the most inventive use of a lift detail exists on the beautiful Bolton gateleg table. To accommodate the gates when closed, the stretchers and aprons on the ends of the table are heavily sculpted with a cloud lift form, demonstrating

LEFT Lifts in this room are echoed by these marvelous, simple carving details. Detail, Living room sofa, 1908-09, David B. Gamble house, Pasadena, 1907-09.

BELOW Lower rails, which appear to be subtly curved, accent the lifts on this dining table. Detail, dining-room table, 1908-09, Robert R. Blacker house, Pasadena, 1907-09.

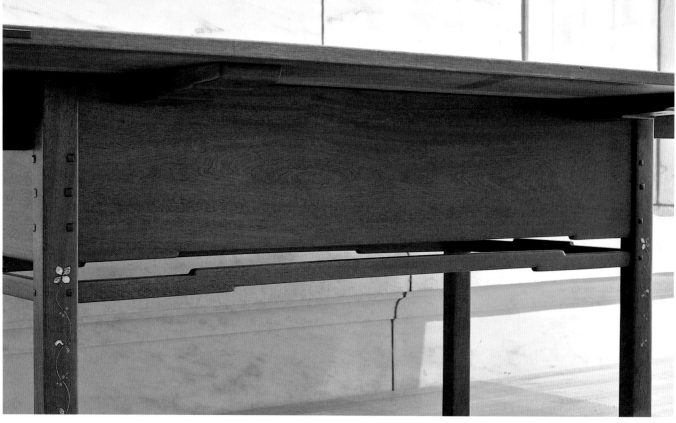

that, at least in this case, this detail can be both decorative and functional.

To drive home the point of variation, one last example, this from the Laurabelle Robinson house. On built-in cabinets in the dining room are lifts unique in the Greene & Greene world. Far more angular than typical lifts, they resemble nothing so much as a half dovetail and are a wonderfully inventive variation on the theme. These "dovetail lifts" are echoed, if only faintly, by elements in the main staircase, yet another example of using details to unify design.

TOP Is it or isn't it? This is certainly not a traditional lift though it serves the same purpose. "Dovetail lift" seems an apt description. Detail, dining room cabinet, 1905-06, Laurabelle A. Robinson house, Pasadena, 1905-06.

ABOVE A little known piece, this table provides another example of beautiful, inventive design. Living room gateleg table, 1907, William T. Bolton house, Pasadena, 1906.

Asymmetry

There was a time when symmetry was revered in Western architecture. Greek temples, Gothic cathedrals and American colonial houses each exhibit a high degree of symmetry on the exterior. In some cases, the concept is carried into the interior as well with central entries flanked by living and dining rooms. A search for new forms led eventually to a relaxed symmetry in which it was no longer necessary to have windows and doors in precise balance. The massing of the structure was still largely regular.

Quite distinct from the Western model, the Japanese have an affinity for asymmetry. Because symmetry is seldom found in nature, they believe, man-made structures should not be entirely symmetric. Tansu provide a beautiful example of this impulse.[15] These traditional cabinets are never symmetric. In the case of a step tansu (*kaidan-dansu*), shaped like a flight of stairs, the asymmetry is immediately obvious. However, even tansu with a regular overall shape always include some asymmetry, typically in the arrangement of drawers. This is an aspect of the aesthetic concept *wabi-sabi*, based on imperfection and impermanence.[16] Asymmetry is a form of imperfection, which is a sign of modesty, allowing for growth and improvement.

Asymmetry is not common in Greene & Greene furniture and furnishings. Certainly, many of their leaded glass motifs are asymmetric as are many, though by no means all, inlays. However, this derives largely from the natural inspirations for these designs. There are subtle asymmetries in some pieces, such as the leading in the Tichenor sconces (a geometric rather than natural design). In bedroom furniture for David and Mary Gamble the Greenes exhibit an unusual degree of asymmetry. The beautiful *mokko-gata tsuba* forms on the headboards and footboards of the beds are off center. In the matching chiffonier, there are two such shapes on one door and only one on the other. Most obviously, taking a cue from tansu design, drawers on that piece are not entirely symmetric. Perhaps it is not coincidence that this is one of their most successful furniture designs.

In Greene & Greene architecture asymmetry is much more common. It is sometimes subtle as in the firm's U-shaped houses, in which the legs of the U have different lengths. This detail is repeated in all of their houses of this form. Often however, the effect is more apparent as is the case with the porte cochere of the Blacker house. While the primary exterior form of the Blacker house is largely symmetric, the porte cochere is only partially balanced by the covered patio opposite — there is no mate to the massive clinker brick pier in the center of the circular driveway. The massing of the Gamble house is quite asymmetric with the sleeping porches and porch all to the right of the entrance. Similarly, the Robinson house has unbalanced massing and angles that are not matched opposite the main axis. And, of course, Charles Greene's own house is highly asymmetric and irregular. The octagonal living room is unbalanced by any other exterior feature.

The asymmetry in these designs creates visual interest. To a greater extent, however, it allows for a more natural interior plan as the architects were not constrained by the artificial requirement of a symmetric footprint. That is, the architects were free to fit the interior to serve the needs of the family, their interests and the environment in which they lived, rather than answering the dictates of traditional architectural rules. In this sense, asymmetry is a liberating influence not only for the architect but also for the homeowner.

LEFT Asymmetric drawer arrangement and tsuba placement help make this piece one of the best by Greene & Greene. Bedroom chiffonier, 1908-09, David B. Gamble house, Pasadena, 1907-09.

OPPOSITE Charles Greene's home was a test bed. This elevation is unusual, perhaps even quirky. Detail, north façade, Charles S. Greene house, Pasadena, 1902-15.

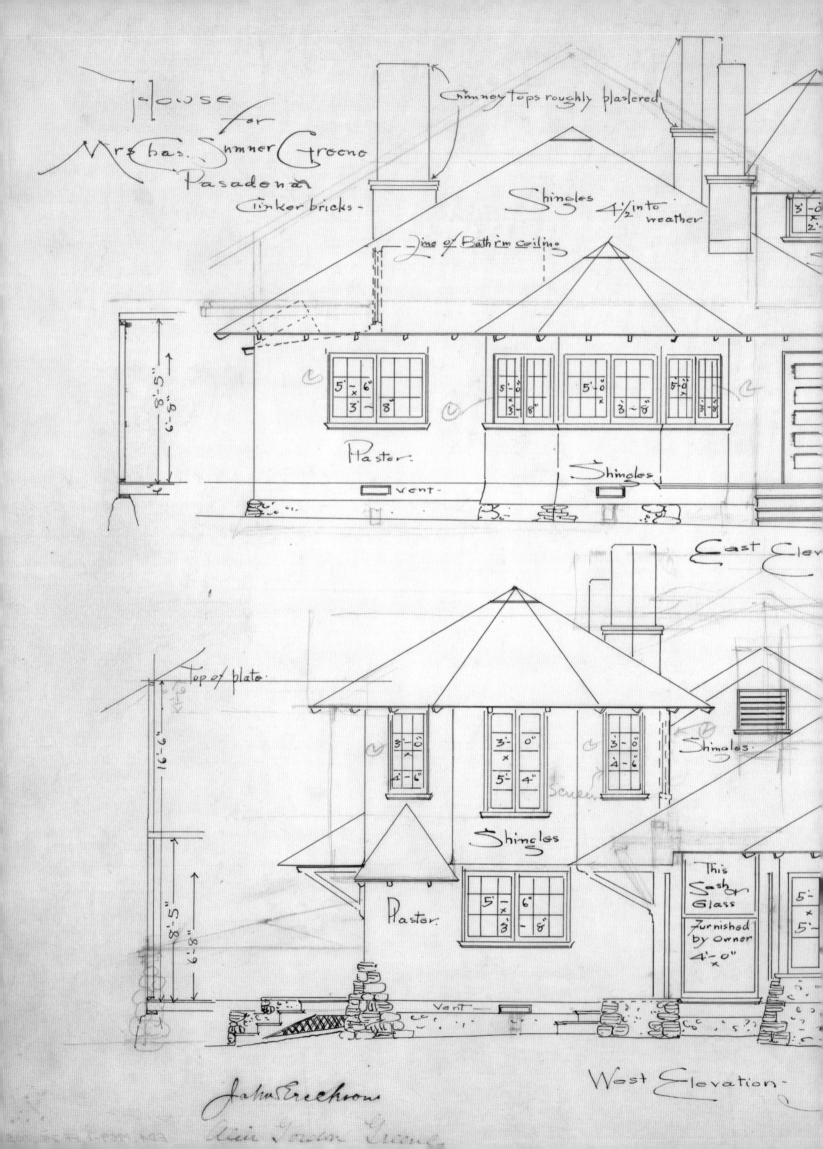

House for
Mr & Mrs. Chas. Sumner Greene
Pasadena
Clinker bricks.

Chimney tops roughly plastered

Shingles 4½ into weather

Line of Bath r'm ceiling

8'-5"
9'-8"

5'-6" × 3'-8"

5'-0" × 3'-8"   5'-0" ×   5'-0" × 3'-8"

3'-0" × 2'-

Plaster.

Shingles

Vent

East Elevation

Top of plate.

9'-1"

3'-0" × 4'-6"

3'-0" × 5'-4"

3'-0" × 4'-6"

Screen

Shingles.

Shingles

8'-5"
9'-8"

Plaster.

5'-6" × 3'-8"

This Sash & Glass Furnished by Owner 4'-0" × 0"

5'- × 5'-

Vent

John Erickson

West Elevation.

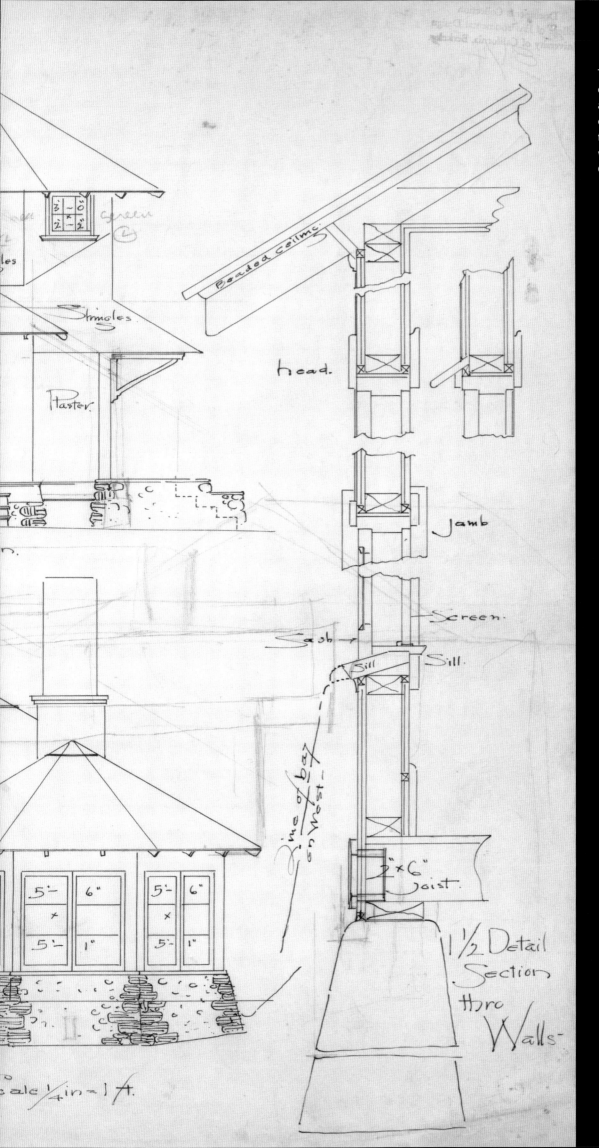

Scale 1/4 in = 1 ft.

head.

Jamb

Screen.

Sash

Sill   Sill.

Shingles.

Plaster.

Beaded ceiling.

Line of bay on West.

2"x6" Joist.

5'- 6"
x
5'- 1"

5'- 6"
x
5'- 1"

3'-0"
x
2'-2"

1½ Detail
Section
thro
Walls

The house Charles Greene designed for his family is unique and fascinating. These elevations depict an early use of unusual forms and massing. East and west elevations, Charles S. Greene house.

Broad Eaves

One of the most recognizable features of Greene & Greene architecture, perhaps the most recognizable and most imitated,[17] is broad eaves supported by exposed rafter tails. These are, in fact, two distinct attributes of the firm's vocabulary. Broad eaves, dictated by the often harsh sun present in Southern California, appeared first. Exposed rafter tails, in point of fact, projecting rafter tails, made their first appearance several years later. Earlier houses, such as the chalet-style house for Mrs. Lucretia Garfield (1904), included broad eaves but without exposed rafters (though roof-supporting beams, perpendicular to the rafters, project from the gables). Absent protruding rafters, the effect is less satisfying.

A wonderful feature of broad eaves in a climate such as that in Pasadena, is that they are most functional exactly when they are most needed. In the summer months, when the weather is hottest, the sun is highest in the northern sky. It is then that the eaves are

Perhaps the broadest overhang on any Greene & Greene house, this gable with brackets and beams is stunning. View of southwest corner, Robert Pitcairn, Jr. house, Pasadena, 1906.

maximally effective at reducing the quantity of direct sunlight entering through windows. In winter, when temperatures are lower and the sun is lower in the sky, the overhanging eaves are less preventive.

Farther north, where the sun is less intense, broad eaves are less welcome. In particular, in the San Francisco Bay region, where temperatures are lower and fog performs the task of reducing sunshine, eaves are typically far less wide. Adapting to this climate for the William Thorsen house, Greene & Greene employed narrower eaves for the first time in more than six years. They did not adopt that region's practice of indenting the eaves above windows. The iconic rafter tails still make their appearance and still cast "beautiful shadows" as Charles Greene explained to Mrs. Garfield years earlier (see page 86).

The eaves employed by Greene & Greene were not, of course, purely functional. If protection from the sun was the only goal, awnings could be bolted on above the windows, particularly on the western and southern elevations. No, the eaves serve a decorative purpose also. Their width adds a horizontal aspect to some designs, such as the chalet houses, and enhances that dimension on others, such as the Gamble and Blacker houses. The former with a strong horizontal presence due to the sleeping porches that dominate the north side of the house, the latter due also to the porte cochere that is a signature feature of that house.

While Greene & Greene surely incorporated broad eaves into their houses in response to the climate, it is interesting to note that two of the styles that influenced them also included this feature but for different reasons. Swiss chalets typically have widely overhanging eaves so that snow falling from the roof does not accumulate too close to the house where it could block doors and windows. Broad eaves are present in much Japanese architecture as well, where one purpose is to protect delicate paper walls from rain and snow.

Sidney Gamble, the second son of David and Mary Gamble, was a teenager when his parents built the Gamble house. While the house was under construction, Mr. and Mrs. Gamble took Sidney and younger brother Clarence on a trip to the Orient. Sidney was smitten with what he saw. After graduating from Princeton, he undertook graduate study in sociology and economics and entered the relatively new field of social economics. His interest in Asia, China in particular, led him to make several professional visits to that part of the world. An avid photographer, he studiously chronicled his travels. His photos, which appeared in *National Geographic* as well as a number of books, were largely forgotten until rediscovered by his daughters after his death.[18] In a truly wonderful quirk of fate, among the photographs[19] are several from Japan including at least one that perfectly illustrates the Japanese precursor to the Greene & Greene use of broad eaves, such as those found on the house that still bears his family's name.

The Gamble children were not members of the idle rich. Sidney Gamble became a prominent scholar, expert in China, where he traveled extensively. He traveled less widely in Japan, seen here.

Shadows

Shadows are ubiquitous. Even as children we see them, and notice them everyday. We gain an understanding of them from a very early age. We learn to make shadow puppets, and we learn that shadows change as the sun's position in the sky changes. Given that even young children have a reasonable understanding of this phenomenon, it may be unexpected that shadows are a design feature for architects, one that can significantly alter the character of a building.

Charles Greene certainly understood the decorative quality of shadows. In 1903-04 the firm was involved in designing a house for Mrs. Lucretia Garfield, widow of assassinated President James Garfield. Mrs. Garfield was quite active in the design process. In a letter of June 5, 1903, Charles Greene addresses his client's question regarding the beams that project from the house's gables. He writes, "The reason why the beams project from the gables is because they cast such beautiful shadows on the sides of the house in this bright atmosphere."[20]

The element in Greene & Greene architecture most responsible for casting beautiful shadows are exposed rafter tails. At the time the Garfield house was being designed, this feature had not yet appeared in their work. The first house to include exposed rafter tails was for Dr. Arthur Libby in 1905 though several smaller structures included them before that.[21] Watching the sides of a Greene & Greene house as the sun moves through the sky, there can be no doubt that Charles Greene was entirely correct. The projecting beams and rafters do indeed cast wonderful shadows that serve as simple but elegant ornament.

Charles Greene was not alone in his assessment of shadows. Clay Lancaster wrote of the Charles M.

Pratt house in Ojai, California, "Shifting shadows cast by these diversified shapes transfigure the house into a sentient being that changes moods with the hours of the day or night."[22] Contemporaneous with the Greenes, Charles Keeler wrote, "The decorative value of shadows cannot be well overestimated…"[23]

The decorative value of shadows is not limited to the exterior. Charles Keeler was, in fact, writing of the shadows created by exposed joists/beams in a house's interior. At the dawn of the 20th century, interior shadows were far more prominent than today. While electric lighting was universal in Greene & Greene houses, it was much dimmer than what is currently common. Docents at The Gamble House like to highlight the moth-shaped, stained glass shade on the living room table lamp. They point out that the purpose was to shield Mrs. Gamble's eyes from the powerful 15-watt bulb. While said somewhat in jest, this illustrates the far different character that rooms had in the evening at the turn of the last century.

In *Greene & Greene Masterworks*, Bruce Smith wrote about this element. He described the Gamble house living room quite eloquently and poetically, "At night these hanging lamps in the living room cast their strongest light, a gentle warmth that moves upward to reflect on the ceiling and then in all directions. Shadows remain in corners, under tables, and on the upper walls of the bay and inglenook, where the light cannot reach around the trussed beams."[24]

Greene & Greene furniture exhibits the same trait in miniature. Many small reveals create shadow lines

An early masterpiece that included features, interior and exterior, that became iconic elements for Greene & Greene. Southeast corner, Arthur A. Libby house, Pasadena, 1905.

that are almost as vital to the Greenes' style as any other element. Broad overhangs on tabletops throw their bases into shadow and draw the surroundings in as well. In some cases, as in the Gamble and Robinson dining rooms, table bases are themselves the sources of interesting shadowy detail. Intricate art glass lighting serves to enhance these effects.

TOP Beautiful shadows indeed, and not solely from exposed rafters and beams. The gardens and massing of the house play with sunlight as well. View of southwest corner, Robert R. Blacker house, Pasadena, 1907-09.

ABOVE One can imagine the subdued lighting of 100 years ago created a wonderful ambience in the evening. Living room inglenook, David B. Gamble house, Pasadena, 1907-09.

Chalets

The need to categorize seems deeply ingrained in the human psyche. When confronted with something new, the natural tendency is to try to fit it neatly into some pigeonhole with which we are already familiar. So it was that the Arroyo Terrace neighborhood, home to a significant number of Greene & Greene homes, came to be known as "Little Switzerland." It isn't difficult to see a Swiss chalet character in some of the firm's houses.[25] The broad eaves, projecting beams or brackets, cantilevered second stories and wooden construction are obvious common traits. Charles denied the influence some years later: "People of Pasadena called my first group of successful houses little Switzerland — from my own understanding there was nothing Swiss about it — It all started from my interest in Japanese early temple design."[26]

It is undoubtedly true that the way in which Charles used exposed, extended rafters to support broad eaves was influenced by Japanese forms. One cannot, however, ignore the evidence — a number of Greene & Greene houses, such as the Arthur Libby, John Phillips and Lucretia Garfield, bear more than a passing resemblance to the iconic Swiss houses.[27] One might reasonably conclude that this is mere coincidence except that Charles and Henry Greene were both exposed to the chalet style. At the Columbian Expo-

sition in Chicago, the brothers surely saw the Idaho building, a rustic log cabin with a definite chalet-like appearance.[28] Chalet forms also commonly appeared in architectural literature of the day, where the Greenes would certainly have encountered them.[29]

The number of Greene & Greene houses with a strong similarity to the commonly held view of a Swiss chalet is rather small. The chalet style, however, is not as narrowly defined as is commonly believed. While we may view the chalet as fundamentally four-square with a single main gable, there is wide variation in the details, and even basic form, of houses viewed as chalets in Switzerland.[30] William Dana describes chalets quite poetically in *The Swiss Chalet Book*. "The chalet motive is not Swiss; it is not Tyrolean, nor Himalayan. It is universal. And by reason of its inherent beauty it is adaptable to any site and any condition where land is plentiful, and where picturesqueness and harmony with the natural surroundings are the first consideration. The chalet is especially adaptable as a country house."[31]

This house represents an important step for Greene & Greene — it is one of their earliest complete designs, including furniture and fixtures. Southwest corner, Jennie A. Reeve house, Long Beach, 1903-04.

MRS. JENNIE A. REEVE'S HOUSE.

Pasadena, Cal.

Greene & Greene, Architects.

Before the Ultimate Bungalows, Greene & Greene designed
several chalet-style houses. View of south façade, John B.
Phillips house, Pasadena, 1906.

LEFT There is no one chalet form; there is great variation. This example from Bülach, Switzerland, contains most of the canonical elements.

BELOW Though not Swiss, the Idaho building at the 1893 Columbian Exposition certainly looks like a chalet. Charles and Henry Greene likely encountered the building while headed to California.

Thus, we may see a Swiss influence in a wider variety of Greene & Greene houses. Even the Gamble house has been described as "a chalet in the Japanese style."[32] Dana goes on to note the similarity in materials between the chalets common in California and their Swiss antecedents (red pine in Switzerland vs. redwood in California). It may be then that the similarity has as much to do with the approach to building and the general philosophy of what a home should be as it does with the outward appearance of the structure. In the end, it appears that those who coined, and perpetuated, the "Little Switzerland" label got it right after all, even if they didn't quite understand why.

Stairs

Greene & Greene interiors, particularly those for the Ultimate Bungalows such as the houses for David B. Gamble and Robert R. Blacker, are wonderlands for anyone with an affinity for a surplus of beautiful elements, complementarily arranged to provide the viewer with a sense of marvel and calm. Even in environments such as these, replete with the most astonishing wooden works of art, there is one facet of the interior that often stands apart: the staircase.

Stairs are, of course, primarily utilitarian, allowing one to move easily among the various levels in a building. Aesthetics and convenience aside, we could simply arrange ladders around the house to facilitate access to upper stories. One can, in fact, easily imagine many frontier homes with just such an arrangement. However, our homes are not strictly utilitarian. This leads us away from a strict interpretation of functionalism toward a philosophy in which we indulge our need for beautiful things. At its best, this philosophy allows for aesthetics without sacrificing function — a marriage with co-equal partners.

Greene & Greene stairs serve as perfect examples of this marriage, of the synthesis of the functional and the aesthetic. Those fortunate enough to have viewed the interiors of the Gamble and Blacker houses must certainly attest that the stairs in each are focal points; works of art that happen to serve a useful purpose beyond mere ornament. While it is obvious that these

Beautiful simplicity describes this stair and entry. Entry hall, William T. Bolton house, Pasadena, 1906.

stairs are advanced expressions of the stair-maker's art, it is also true, if less obvious, that they are exemplary in their function as well. Stairs in a Greene & Greene home almost always include a landing, breaking the run of treads, and typically a window to provide natural light (both features serve an aesthetic purpose as well).

Interestingly, landings and windows were not reserved exclusively for wealthy clients. Even relatively modest commissions included these features. One often reads that Greene & Greene eventually priced themselves out of the market because of the materials and detail in their designs. While there is some truth in this, we must recognize that many details were implemented in earlier, much less costly houses. One of the first rediscoverers of the Greenes, Jean Murray Bangs addressed this point, commenting on the democratic aspect of the firm's output. "While many, especially the later, Greene & Greene houses were large and expensive it could not be said that the architects designed only for the well-to-do. Rather they created the type form from which sprang the most delightful little houses we have ever had."[33]

In the grand commissions, the stairs take on a magical quality with banisters, balusters and newel posts combining to play the part of functional sculpture. As on the exteriors, individual elements are

identifiable but the key effect is that of a cohesive whole rather than a collection of parts. In more modest homes, there is always some piece that is interesting and unexpected. Quite often this manifests itself via the balusters which are frequently implemented quite creatively.[34]

It is worth noting that Peter Hall was an accomplished stair builder, which may have provided Greene & Greene with the confidence to attempt such intricate compositions. As the designs increased in complexity, Peter and John Hall, and the team working with them, rose to the occasion, answering the challenges set forth by Charles and Henry Greene and in the process providing us with some of the most exquisite interiors ever constructed.

OPPOSITE Lovely wood, art glass and wonderful detailing help make this stairway a masterpiece. Hall stairs, Robert R. Blacker house, Pasadena, 1907-09.

TOP Even relatively early Greene & Greene houses have stairs that are interesting, even if modest. Stairs, Josephine Van Rossem house #1, Pasadena, 1903.

RIGHT This inlay, very much an Arts & Crafts form, is highly unusual for Greene & Greene. Detail, stairs, Arthur A. Libby house, Pasadena, 1905.

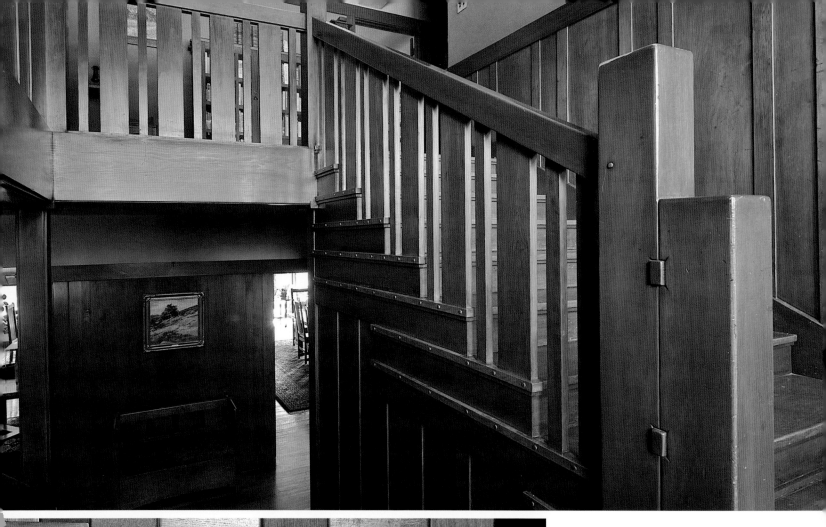

ABOVE   Straightforward details, such as rectangular pegs in the newel posts and round pegs in the treads, create interest. Detail, stairs, William T. Bolton house.

LEFT   Like pointillist painters, Greene & Greene created masterpieces by combining many elements, each quite simple in itself. Detail, hall stair, David B. Gamble house, Pasadena, 1907-09.

Chairs

From the time of the William Bolton house in 1906 to that of the Cordelia Culbertson house in 1913, Charles and Henry Greene designed hundreds of pieces of furniture.[35] That would stand as an impressive feat if it was their only accomplishment during that time. Of course, they also designed numerous decorative objects and about 30 houses during the period and shepherded most from conception to completion.[36] This fact only makes more remarkable the incredible variation found in the furniture designs during that span.

Some variation was inevitable if only as a result of evolution. Charles Greene was an artist, one who was not content to take the expedient course, to churn out designs that were largely unchanged from one commission to the next. He played in a world of the new and unexplored, his goal to create rather than recreate. This, however, provides only a partial accounting, for we see significant intra-house differences in addition to the more expected inter-house distinctions. This point is perhaps most obvious in an examination of chairs created by Greene & Greene.

The Greenes had ample opportunity to practice chair design. Historic photos show the living room of the Blacker house with at least five chairs and as many again in the entry hall. The Gamble house living room currently contains 10 chairs. Furniture drawings for the Ford house show three distinct chair designs for the living room alone. With the addition of chairs for bedrooms and dining rooms, the total can become quite large. Thus, we may find four or more chair forms within a single home even ignoring armchair/side chair/rocker variants. At some level, of course, a chair is just a chair, an arrangement of legs, a seat and a back. This constraint of functionality helps make the variation more wonderful, and in the hands of Greene & Greene, wonderful is exactly what it was.

As with many traditional chair styles, crest rails and back splats are the most obvious features of the majority of Greene & Greene designs. Chairs by the firm typically include a broad, heavily curved crest rail that is often ornamented. Backs usually incorporate a wide central splat sometimes flanked by narrower splats. Arms are quite sculptural, counter to the Arts & Crafts norm. Crest rail joints with rear legs are almost always adorned with ebony splines. There are exceptions to these rules of thumb. The Bolton hall chairs

Perhaps somewhat more traditional than typical for the Greenes, this chair includes a crest rail that sits between the rear legs rather than atop them. Living room armchair, 1907-08, Freeman A. Ford house, Pasadena, 1906-08.

have a broad top rail, but, like all elements in that design, it is straight. Chairs for the Robinson dining room include curved but very narrow crest rails. The design for the Bolton dining room does not contain splats but rather pierced horizontal slats.

Decoration for splats and crest rails derives in part from the unusual forms they often take with additional embellishment provided via inlay and ebony. Thorsen dining room chairs provide one of the best examples. The pierced splat grouping is brilliant, the

LEFT This form brings to mind chairs by Frank Lloyd Wright more than Greene & Greene. This furniture was the beginning of their best work. Hall chair, 1907, William T. Bolton house, Pasadena, 1906.

BELOW The lack of inlay on the back allows one to focus on the form of this chair. The arms flow wonderfully, and the splats are a work of art. Dining room armchair, 1909-10, William R. Thorsen house, Berkeley, 1908-10.

OPPOSITE A deceptive, beautiful piece that appears simple at first reveals wonderful details on closer inspection. Note the carving that mirrors the lifts. Living room rocking chair, 1908-09, David B. Gamble house, Pasadena, 1907-09.

LEFT The parallelogram shape of these legs is dramatic. Note also the round pin in the through mortise and tenon joint on the stretchers. Detail, dining-room chair, 1908-09, Robert R. Blacker house, Pasadena, 1907-09.

OPPOSITE This piece is a compact laboratory for Greene & Greene details. The ebony is more playfully used here than on most of the firm's work. Chair, c. 1908, Charles S. Greene (same design as dining room chairs for Freeman A. Ford).

ing a purely decorative offset effect. In both designs, the cross stretcher attaches via pinned, through mortise-and-tenon joints, as in the Thorsen chair. This stretcher arrangement was commonly employed by the Greenes. Often referred to as an H-stretcher for the obvious reason, the Greene & Greene version is closer to an "A" with a truncated top due to the extreme change in seat width from front to back. To help facilitate this, chair legs are parallelogram in cross section with edges parallel to the seat rails (the seat rails form an isosceles trapezoid).

One of the most interesting chair designs from Greene & Greene is not well known relative to pieces for the Blacker, Gamble and Thorsen houses. Dining-room chairs for the Freeman Ford house are superb, demonstrating the Greenes' ability to combine multiple elements into a seamless whole. Charles Greene must have thought so as well for he kept a chair of the same design, with different finish, in his studio. The basic form of the chair is quite straightforward; however, a number of details make it remarkable. The most obvious extraordinary feature is the ebony detailing on the splats. The pegs are playfully placed while dramatically long ebony accents run nearly full length. Viewed from the front, the rear legs are stepped above the seat rail, gaining width with height. The crest rail is pierced to create a handle, a device the Greenes used elsewhere. The front of each rear leg displays a geometric inlay in mahogany, also the primary wood for the chair. Front and rear seat rails are lifted, wider at the center than the ends. Side rails are lifted only at the back and surprisingly close to the rear leg, creating an unexpectedly beautiful effect. A narrow stile mirrors each front leg running from seat rail to stretcher. The overall impression created is one of harmony despite the numerous details.

shape accentuated by the narrow elements to either side of the main splat. Ebony and brass are subtly incorporated as the only applied decoration. The crest rail displays an inlay design that is continued in the top of the dining table. Arms are sinuous and transform from tall and narrow to wide and thin. In this design, the elements below the seat are quite plain with only delicate, pinned, through mortise-and-tenon joints on the H-stretcher for ornament.

In some cases, seat rails and stretchers are quite interesting. For the Blacker dining room chairs, stretchers between the front and back legs are tiered on their outer surface, a subtle effect that is lovely. The same components on the Ford living room arm chairs have lifts on both top and bottom edges creat-

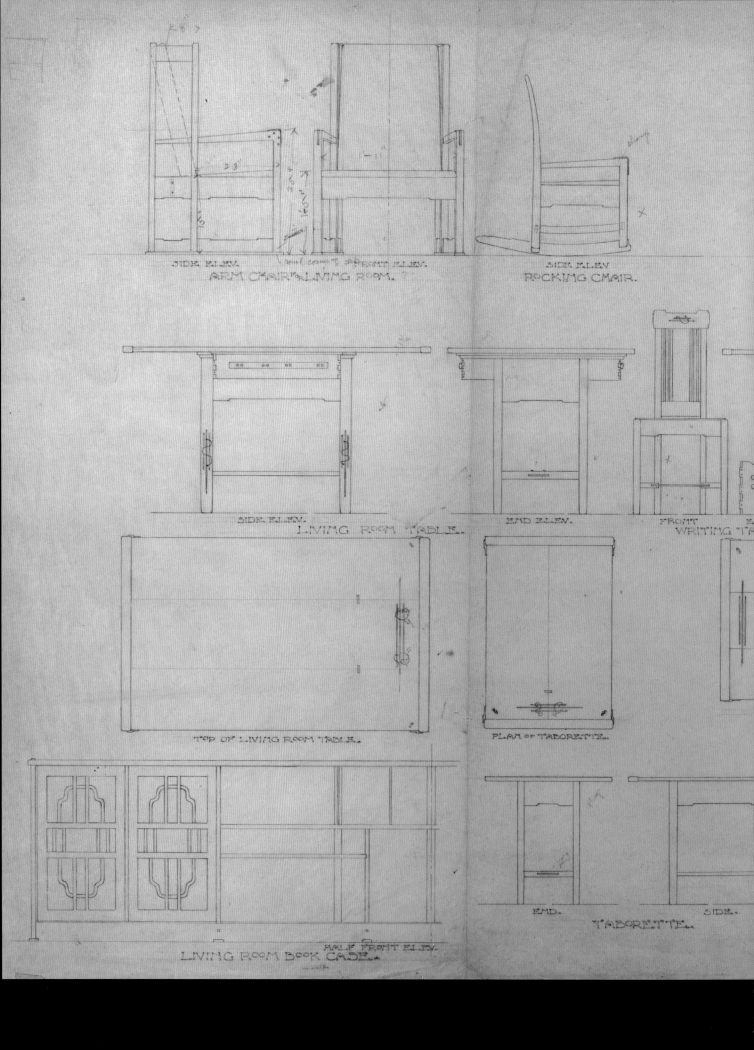

SIDE ELEV. FRONT ELEV.
ARM CHAIR LIVING ROOM.

SIDE ELEV
ROCKING CHAIR.

SIDE ELEV.
LIVING ROOM TABLE.

END ELEV.

FRONT
WRITING TA

TOP OF LIVING ROOM TABLE.

PLAN OF TABORETTE.

LIVING ROOM BOOK CASE.
HALF FRONT ELEV.

END.
TABORETTE.
SIDE.

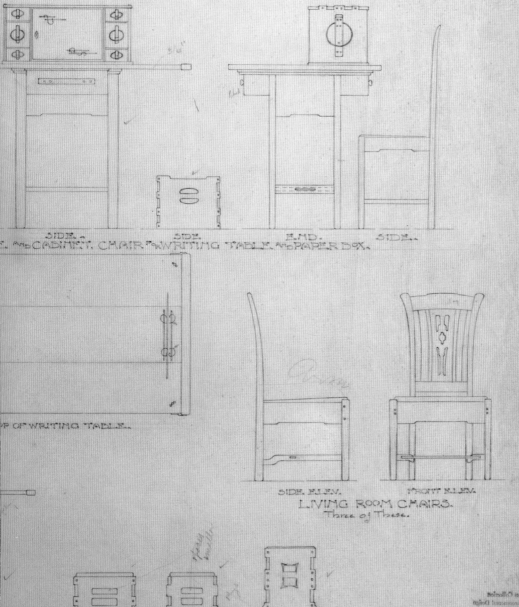

DESIGNS *for* FURNITURE.
FOR BUNGALOW FOR
FREEMAN A. FORD ESQ *at* PASA-
DENA CALIFORNIA.
GREENE *and* GREENE ARCHTS 215 *to* 231
BOSTON BLD'G PASADENA CAL..
SHEET N°   FEB 25 '08.

SIDE.
..CABINET. CHAIR *for* WRITING TABLE *and* PAPER BOX.

SIDE.   END.   SIDE.

TOP OF WRITING TABLE.

SIDE. ELEV.   FRONT ELEV.
LIVING ROOM CHAIRS.
Three of These.

SIDE.   END.   SQUARE.
FOOT STOOL.   PEDESTAL.

Three distinct chair designs for the living room, each a minor masterpiece. Very little of this furniture is available for public view. Drawing, living room furniture, 1908, Freeman A. Ford house.

Hijiki

The Greene & Greene design vocabulary is quite rich and complex. Even so, a number of elements are reused often, sometimes in slightly different versions or new combinations. This provides an effect that is both familiar and fresh. The living room of the William R. Thorsen house in Berkeley contains a stunning Arts & Crafts frieze that incorporates a marvelous Asian element that is unique in the Greene & Greene canon. It serves as testament to the lengths to which the brothers would go to meet the needs of their clients and achieve a pleasing, coherent environment.

In an architectural interior, a frieze is the section of wall above the picture rail. In the Arts & Crafts idiom, it is often distinguished by a wall covering or paint color distinct from that on the wall below. Charles and Henry Greene often used the frieze to very good effect. In the living room of the Gamble house, the frieze contains relief-carved panels. In the Blacker house living room, gold leaf covers lotus forms molded into the plaster. Even in less grand houses a frieze is almost always present though it may contain less decoration. In the Thorsen house, hand-painted dogwood branches grace the subtly colored plaster framed by exquisite wood trim.

This frieze is representative of the Arts & Crafts form, if somewhat more sophisticated. The hijiki are rather stylized, not unlike some Japanese examples. Detail, living room frieze, William R. Thorsen house, Berkeley, 1908-10.

Use of wooden elements in the frieze is certainly not unique to the Thorsen house. What differentiates the composition in that house is that the form of one feature is likely based on a traditional Japanese structural device. The device, known as *hijiki*, or bracket arm, is repeated throughout the frieze. *Hijiki*, literally translated as "elbow wood," were originally used as structural elements to support eaves in Buddhist architecture.[37] They evolved to become more elaborate, and in some cases purely decorative. Such is the case in the Thorsen house.

Hijiki are actually just a component of a larger, more complex system known as a *tokyou* (bracket system). Between the *hijiki* and the rafters were small bearing blocks known as *makito*. The *hijiki* itself rests on a large bearing block called a *daito* which is set upon the top of a pillar. *Hijiki* come in many forms. Closest to that used in the Thorsen frieze is *hakarihijiki*.[38] *Hakari* means balanced and, thus, *hakarihijiki* are balanced elbow brackets.

BUDDHIST ARCHITECTURE— STRUCTURE AND DETAIL

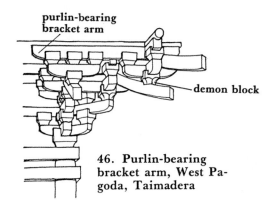

purlin-bearing bracket arm

demon block

45. Demon block, West Pagoda, Taimadera

46. Purlin-bearing bracket arm, West Pagoda, Taimadera

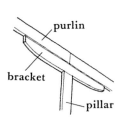

purlin

bracket

pillar

47. Boat-shaped bracket arm, Main Hall, Daisen'in, Daitokuji

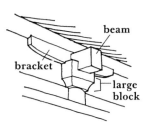

beam

bracket

large block

48. Large block and bracket arm, Dempōdō, Hōryūji

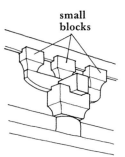

small blocks

49. Flat three block, Great Lecture Hall, Hōryūji

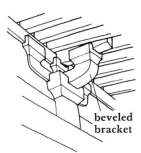

beveled bracket

50. Projecting three block, Main Hall, Chōkyūji

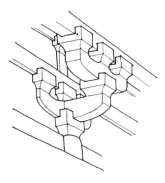

51. Projecting complex, Hokkedō, Tōdaiji

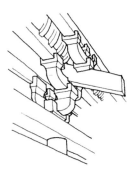

52. Two-step complex, Five-story Pagoda, Kaijūsenji

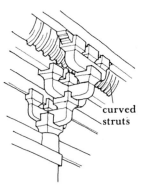

curved struts

53. Two-step complex, Main Hall, Daizenji

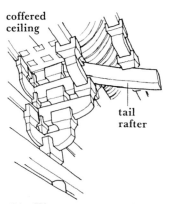

coffered ceiling

tail rafter

54. Three-step complex, West Pagoda, Taimadera

Not surprisingly, the Greenes didn't use an exact replica of the traditional form. The variant they included is somewhat simplified and includes a small central vertical element. There are similar Japanese forms that are sometimes described as resembling a pitchfork. One could also see in this form a stylized version of Neptune's trident, the central vertical element extending below the bracket as if forming a handle.

William Thorsen was a lover of ships. The Greenes incorporated their client's interest into the design for his house. The iron front gate includes a ship in relief. The south end of the living room is con-

Functional antecedents of the element appropriated by Greene & Greene. Even in Japan this component evolved significantly.

structed to recall a ship's prow, complete with beams that extend through the wall to the exterior. Thus, Neptune's trident is a fitting symbol for that room. It may at first seem dubious to consider such an interpretation. However, recalling the Greenes' penchant for obsessive attention to detail, gives one cause to consider the possibility.

Tsuba

Influences can manifest themselves in various ways. In some cases, the result is a very direct and literal application of source material. This could take the form of creating a near reproduction, or perhaps simply borrowing substantially from a piece. In other instances, the effect is more subtle. One may pay homage to a source, or make allusion to it, without explicitly making use of the original. Another category exhibits influence in a still less direct way. This might involve significant abstraction or use of some element in a context very different from the original. This latter case applies to the incorporation of the *tsuba* form into the Greene & Greene vocabulary.

A *tsuba* is the hand guard on a Japanese sword. Primary, among the several tasks they perform, is preventing the swordsman's hand from sliding onto the blade during a thrust. Additionally, they aid in the balance of the sword and allow the owner to convey status.[39] Most functional *tsuba* are constructed of forged iron (rather than cast iron which is more brittle)[40] though other metals are sometimes employed. Japanese swords consist of a number of separate components.[41] Thus, *tsuba* can be separated from the

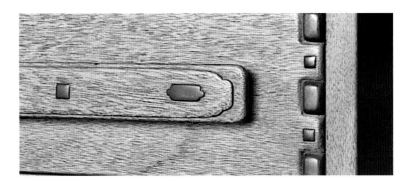

LEFT One of the *tsuba* from Charles Greene's collection. The *mokko-gata* form appears repeatedly in the work of Greene & Greene.

BELOW The shape of this ebony peg is amazing. Note that the form is repeated in relief on the drawer pull. Detail, living room table, 1908-09, David B. Gamble house, Pasadena, 1907-09.

sword, which they often are, and collected. It is through Charles Greene's interest in, and collection of *tsuba,* that they are relevant to the work of Greene & Greene.

One often reads that a piece of furniture is "*tsuba*-shaped" or that the form of an element is derived from *tsuba*. Such statements are not entirely accurate since there is no single shape for *tsuba*. The most common shape is round, though it would be senseless to describe round elements as referencing *tsuba*. No, the *tsuba* favored by Charles Greene are characterized as *mokko-gata*, or lobed shape.[42]

The first use of this form by Greene & Greene is in lighting for Adelaide Tichenor. The shape is not a dominant element in that house. In fact, the furniture is largely rectilinear and a little severe, similar in fundamental form to the Arts & Crafts archetype. Though furniture for the Bolton house demonstrates a leap forward in sophistication, it is still more rectilinear than organic. One point of departure is a gateleg library table with a *mokko-gata* top. The base is also quite sophisticated and original. Designed slightly before the Bolton furniture, however, the dining room table for the Laurabelle Robinson house provides the first appearance of the *mokko-gata* form as a substantial element in Greene & Greene furniture. The Robinson table is a point of departure for the Greenes — it is the first piece of furniture designed by the firm to exhibit an organic, sensual form due not only to the *mokko-gata* top, but also the elements in the pedestal base.[43]

With Robinson furniture constructed in 1907,[44] the possibilities for Charles Greene's designs going forward were nearly limitless. Over the next two years, he created an astounding number of pieces for his masterpiece, the Robert R. Blacker house, where the *tsuba* is used very sparingly, and his best known commission, the David B. Gamble house. In the Gamble house, the *tsuba* makes a return, this time as a sig-

nificant design theme. For the Gamble dining table, Greene & Greene revisit the form of the Robinson table, but with the addition of ebony highlighting the hand-rubbed mahogany. The *mokko-gata* form appears throughout the dining room, turning up in leaded glass, chair back splats and switchplates (which carry the shape through the house).

It would be difficult to chronicle every appearance of *tsuba* influence in the Gamble house, but it is quite easy to identify the most elegant, indeed one of the most beautiful decorative elements in the Greene & Greene canon. In furniture for Mr. and Mrs. Gamble's bedroom, there are *mokko-gata* ebony inlays and ebony-ringed *mokko-gata* cutouts, in each case fitted with brass pins. One marvels at the genius that conceived of such a detail and the craftsman that so expertly executed it. And with that, having perfected the form, Greene & Greene abandoned it — the *mokko-gata* *tsuba* all but disappeared from their designs.

Perhaps the most elegant and challenging use of the *mokko-gata* form appears in the Gamble bedroom. Detail, bed footboard, 1908-09, David B. Gamble house.

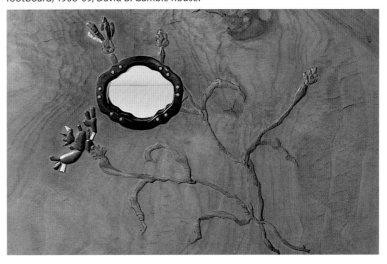

As a unified suite of furniture, this set
may be the supreme expression of the
Greene & Greene aesthetic. Drawing,
bedroom furniture, 1908-09, David B.
Gamble house.

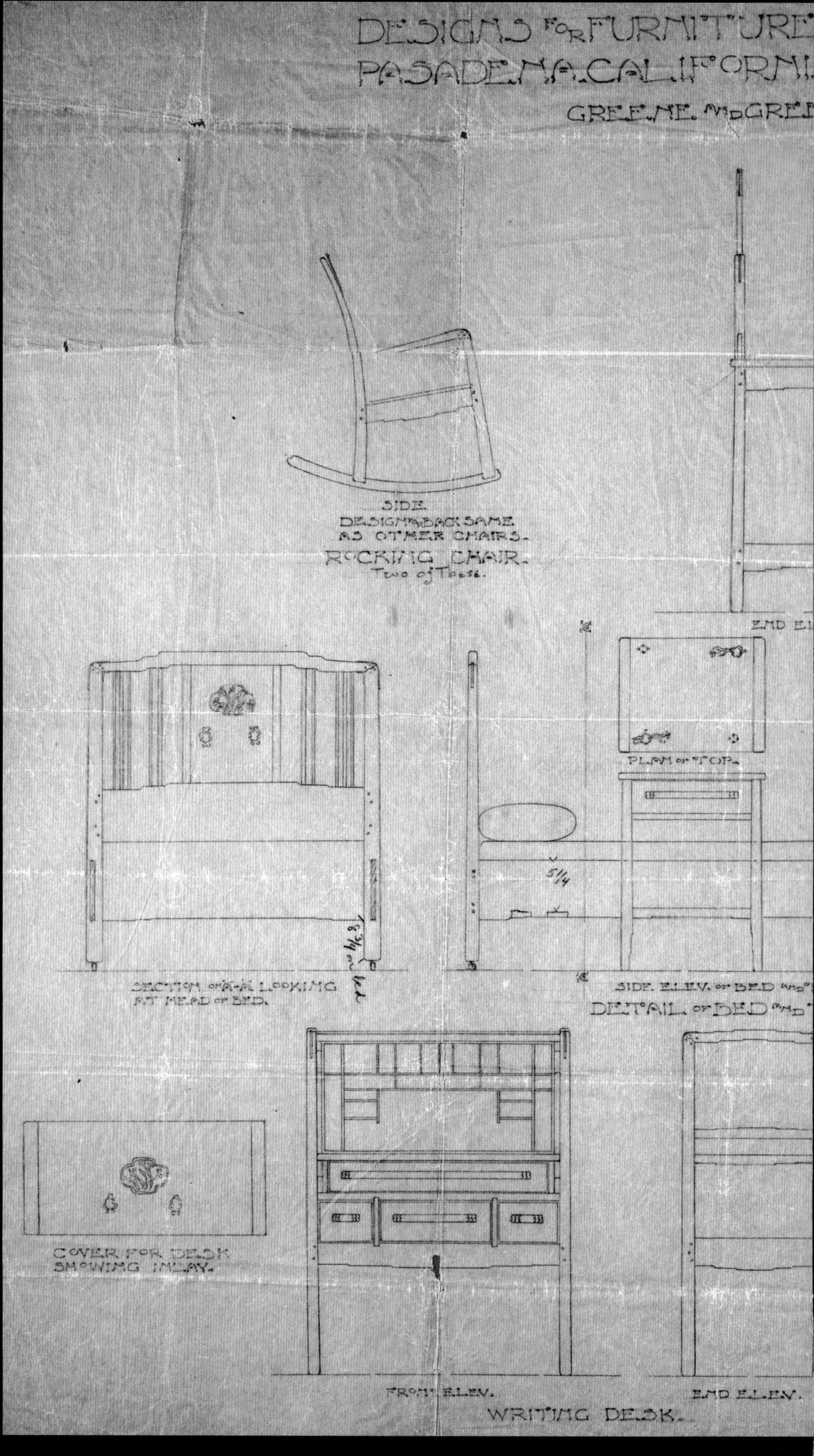

DESIGNS FoR FURNITURE
PASADENA CALIFORNI
GREENE MᴄGREE

SIDE.
DESIGN⋅BACK⋅SAME
AS OTHER CHAIRS.
ROCKING CHAIR.
Two of These.

END EL

PLAN of TOP.

SECTION on A-A LOOKING
AT HEAD of BED.

SIDE. ELEV. of BED and
DETAIL of BED and

COVER FOR DESK
SHOWING INLAY.

FRONT ELEV.

END ELEV.

WRITING DESK.

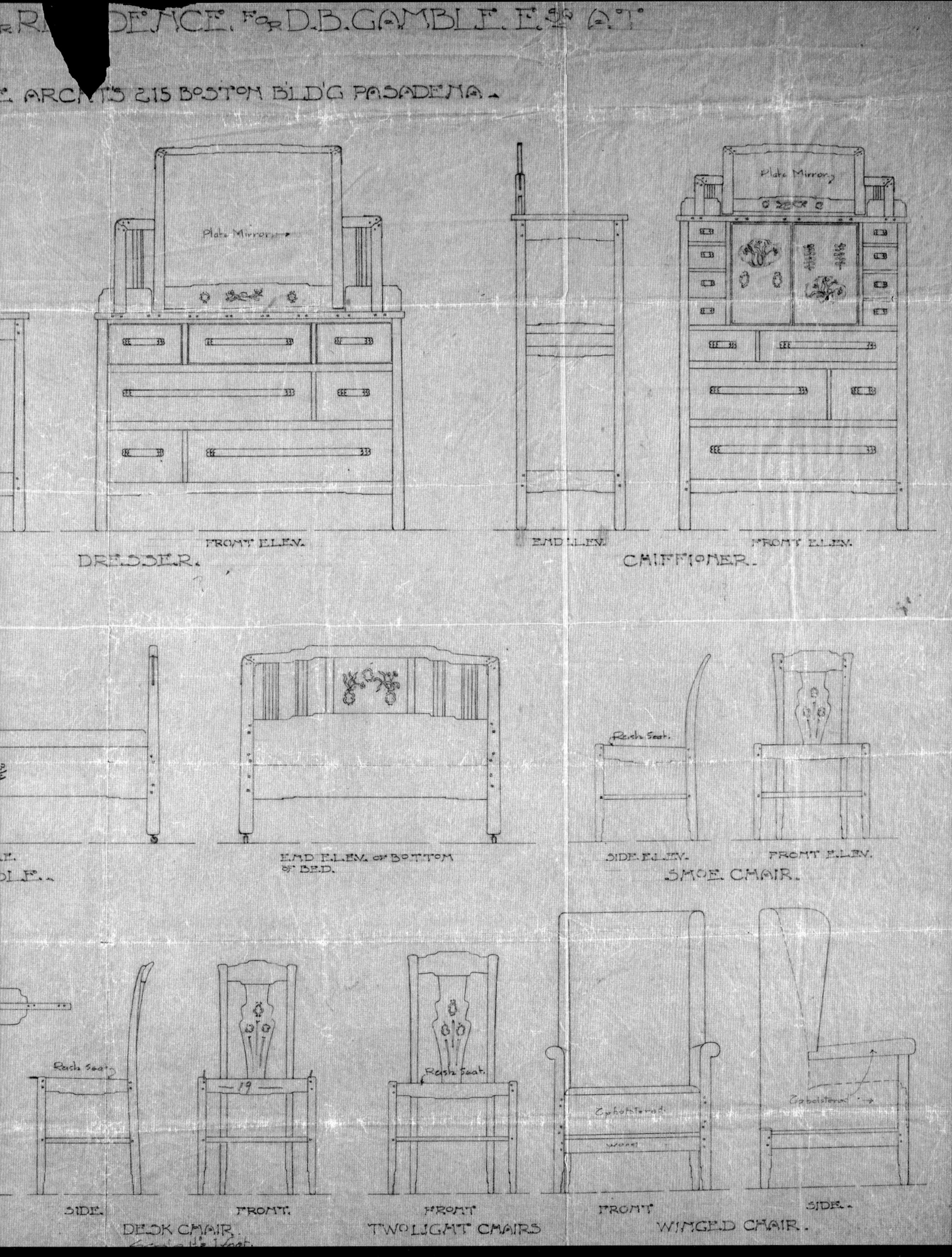
DENCE. FOR D.B. GAMBLE. ESQ. AT
ARCHTS 215 BOSTON BLD'G PASADENA.
Plate Mirror
FRONT ELEV.
DRESSER.
Plate Mirror
END ELEV.
FRONT ELEV.
CHIFFONIER.
END ELEV. OF BOTTOM OF BED.
Rush Seat.
SIDE ELEV.
FRONT ELEV.
SHOE CHAIR.
Rush Seat
19
Rush Seat.
Upholstered
Wood
Upholstered
SIDE.
FRONT.
DESK CHAIR.
FRONT
TWO LIGHT CHAIRS
FRONT
SIDE.
WINGED CHAIR.

Hidden Construction Details

Knowledge changes the way we perceive things. A deep understanding of music, for example, certainly alters the listening experience. Thus, a musician surely hears music differently than does one to whom it is a mystery. Similarly, woodworkers see furniture differently than do others. They are deconstructionists. They may admire the aesthetic qualities and craftsmanship of a chair or a table, but the admiration is certainly accompanied by thoughts of what the eye cannot see, of the hidden details that help make the piece what it is.

British author Douglas Adams had an interesting view of the world and a very entertaining way of putting ideas into words. He said, "If you try and take a cat apart to see how it works, the first thing you have on your hands is a non-working cat."[45] That is a valid point, and undoubtedly true. There is an obvious corollary for furniture. While it would be fascinating to disassemble a piece of furniture by Greene & Greene

This rare view reveals the working of table extensions. The two scuffed members extend through the apron to support leaves. Other details of construction are apparent as well. Detail, dining room table, 1908-09, Robert R. Blacker house, Pasadena, 1907-09.

to determine how it was constructed, the end result would be a pile of wood, a non-working piece of furniture. Of course, the cat analogy breaks down at this point because we are likely to have much greater success reassembling the furniture than the cat. That is also a valid point, and I'll be the first to wish you good luck in arguing that position to the owner of a Greene & Greene original.

All this is to say that we are somewhat restricted in the methods by which we can determine the construction of historic furniture. We can, if we are fortunate, crawl around, peer under and behind. If we are very fortunate, we may even be able to open and look

inside. Experts can employ technology such as X-rays to reveal hidden secrets.[46] And we can rely on those with experience building furniture to explain the techniques, if only somewhat speculatively.

Drawers provide a reasonably easy entry point to the interior of a case piece. A drawer rather quickly reveals its details of construction. It is well known that Greene & Greene drawers are not dovetailed but rather are built with a type of lock joint. (Finger joints, also used on many drawers, are discussed elsewhere in this chapter.) This joint, in which a tongue on each end of the drawer front fits into dadoes on the drawer sides, is strong and not labor-intensive. Drawer backs fit into dadoes in the sides and are secured with screws. Bottoms are typically solid wood and mate with grooves in the drawer front and sides but extend below and beyond the drawer back. Excluding those with more creative systems for movement, drawers typically have one or two oak runners attached to the bottom with screws. One interesting detail is that drawer sides are usually stepped at front and back to provide smaller bearing surfaces. This allows for easy movement while also preventing the drawer from tipping as it is pulled out. In some cases, the steps appear on the top and bottom edges of the sides. The back is sometimes stepped as well.

Furniture for the William Thorsen house in Berkeley was not constructed in Peter Hall's Pasadena shop. Instead it was made on-site in a makeshift shop in the house's basement. For this reason, construction of Thorsen furniture is slightly different from its Pasa-

dena cousins. Drawers there, in both freestanding furniture and built-ins, are constructed with half-blind dovetails at the front. Drawer backs are secured with wooden dowels — as many as ten dowels are employed on each side of a drawer.

It is worth noting that all of the methods discussed here appear on furniture designed and built during the Greenes' collaboration with the Halls. Some techniques, such as the lock joint used on drawers, certainly came from the craftsmen rather than the architects. If detailed shop drawings ever existed, none

The varied colors and textures of mahogany, ebony and brass are combined to great effect in this beautiful table. Detail, hall table, 1908-09, David B. Gamble house.

survive today. Thus, we cannot be certain about the origins of some of these details. About one thing we can be certain: the collaboration was synergistic and benefited everyone involved.

One of the most intriguing details in any Greene & Greene furniture are the brass "pins" that secure ebony runners to the drawers for the entry hall table in the Gamble house.[47] These pins are, in fact, brass screws that have been filed to remove enough of the head to give them the appearance of pins. This provides the holding power of a screw but with a more elegant, less utilitarian, appearance than would be afforded by a screw. A close examination shows just the hint of a slot on several of the screws, just enough to alleviate one's disbelief that such a labor-intensive method was used to construct an element so seldom seen. The result, of course, is striking, with the brass beautifully accenting the dark ebony. The Greenes continued to use this detail. It appears repeatedly in furniture for the Cordelia Culbertson house, for example. Interestingly, this detail does not appear on the ebony-wrapped doors of the sideboard from the William R. Thorsen house.[48] This despite the fact that furniture for the Thorsen house was designed and built in the period between the Gamble and Culbertson houses. This argues that use of this technique

was an aesthetic choice rather than purely a method of construction.

The title of this section applies particularly well to one construction detail employed by the Greenes and the Halls. Quality furniture has been constructed using mortise-and-tenon joints for a very long time. This form of joinery provides for significant long-grain surface area for glue, and it can be easily augmented, via drawboring, for example, for additional mechanical strength. One minor problem with traditional mortise-and-tenon joints is that visible gaps can develop over time due to wood shrinkage. A construct that combats this is the housed mortise. A housed mortise is really a mortise within a mortise. More specifically, the primary mortise resides within a much shallower secondary mortise. The secondary mortise does not fit a tenon but rather the entire end of the tenoned member. While this reduces the probability of visible gaps arising in the future, it increases significantly the work required. It is a visible joint — no shoulder hides it — and, therefore, it is difficult and time consuming to implement well.

ABOVE A modern housed mortise on a recreation of a Blacker dining room chair. It creates significant additional labor in the name of aesthetics. Detail, mock-up of dining room chair, Jim Ipekjian.

RIGHT A study of construction secrets: glass installation, shelf breadboards and supports, hinges, and brackets on the interior of the piece. Detail, living room bookcase, Robert R. Blacker house.

As we have seen, Greene & Greene used art glass often. While it appears most frequently in lighting and grand entries, clear leaded glass is also found in furniture and built-ins. It may seem like a minor point, but something has to hold the glass panels in place. For the very small panels typical in lighting, the solution is often as simple as small nails into the frames bent slightly to contact the glass. Clearly this method is not suitable for much larger panels. A common technique is to use thin wood strips to hold the glass into rabbets in their frames. The strips are typically screwed or nailed in place to allow for removal should repair of the glass become necessary. This technique becomes somewhat more complicated when, as is the case in the Blacker house living room bookcase, the glass is divided in the frame and some components are quite small and have curved shapes.

Exposed Construction Details

Arts & Crafts furniture is distinct from preceding styles in a number of significant ways. Incorporation of less applied decoration while simultaneously creating ornament by highlighting joinery and construction details is, perhaps, most interesting. In many pieces, in fact, joinery is the dominant feature. Think of the wonderful through-tenons on many pieces. Recall the more dramatic keyed tenons on some bookcases and tables. Or pegged joints in which the peg is left dramatically proud of the surface. In each case, the joinery attracts attention and honestly announces its purpose.

Exposed joinery is certainly quite common in Greene & Greene furniture (and architecture) though the forms may differ somewhat from those used by other designers of the era. Pegged joints are standard and through-tenons appear on some pieces, but the Greenes took exposed joinery to a higher, more elegant level and expanded beyond typical joinery. In fact, when describing a Greene & Greene piece, it is insufficient to discuss exposed joinery. In order to fully capture this aspect of their work one must be more comprehensive; the discussion must include the broader topic of exposed construction details.

This, of course, begs the question, "What are exposed construction details?" In Greene & Greene furniture this term applies to traditional joinery in addition to features such as stacked hinges and drawer runners that are creatively incorporated into the design. Use of the word "feature" in the previous sentence is deliberate — as with exposed joinery, these

Through-tenons figure less prominently in Greene & Greene furniture than in that by some other Arts & Crafts designers, but, when used, are used well. Detail, dining room table, 1907-08, Laurabelle A. Robinson house, Pasadena, 1906-07.

exposed construction details are critical to the visual effect and are central elements in the final result. They may even be the primary focus, intended to draw the viewer into the piece and the process of its creation.

Shelves are often quite simple, not much more than a plank of wood. Greene & Greene shelves are somewhat more complex. They often incorporate breadboard ends, and, despite being concealed, the breadboards include ebony pegs. Incredible details once again. Long shelves, particularly those that will support heavy loads, present a design dilemma. If made sufficiently thick to prevent sagging, the shelf will appear heavy. If made sufficiently thin to give a pleasing appearance, the shelf will sag. One solution employed by the Greenes was to step the shelf along its length. Thus, at the front edge the shelf has a pleasing profile, but across most of its width it is thick enough to provide sufficient strength.

Shelf support mechanisms range from very simple to quite interesting. The simplest form is familiar to anyone old enough to walk — a series of holes with pegs inserted to support the shelves. Of course, the pegs are often made of ebony and sometimes engage shallow mortises on the shelves. An uncommon take on a common solution. In other versions, the holes are replaced with sawtooth standards that engage the

shelf. Shelves for some furniture in the Cordelia Culbertson house have "pegs" built in. These are actually very small legs that pivot on a pin and engage rectangular holes in the standards. One wonders whether this arrangement solved some recognized problem or was merely a flight of fancy.

Some details are quite humble. Such is the case with board-and-batten construction of doors and cabinets. Greene & Greene neither originated nor

Imagine the added complexity of constructing a shelf in this way. The detailing is flawless and awe-inspiring. Detail, livingroom built-in case, 1909-10, William R. Thorsen house, Berkeley, 1908-10.

significantly altered the board-and-batten archetype. What they did, as with many other construction details, was put their unmistakable stamp on it. In the case of board-and-batten construction, this consisted

LEFT An intact kitchen, now more than 100 years old, is rare. Even the wood counters are original. Kitchen, Caroline S. de Forest house, Pasadena, 1906.

BELOW Screw slots still aligned, these cabinets are much the same now as when built. Detail, kitchen cabinet, 1906, Caroline S. de Forest house.

Certainly not necessary to support this small door, stacked hinges, used often by Greene & Greene, were likely a design statement. Detail, secretary, c. 1911, Cordelia A. Culbertson house, Pasadena, 1911-13.

Not used exclusively on furniture, stacked hinges also appeared in architectural contexts. Detail, living room doors, William R. Thorsen house.

of ensuring that the slots of all of the pan head screws, used to attach the battens, were aligned. Typically, the slots run with the grain, vertically on stiles and horizontally on rails, though in some instances the slots are vertical regardless of the grain direction. It is surprising to see that in many cases these slots are still aligned more than 100 years later.

This level of attention to detail, while nearly unthinkable today, is common in the work of Charles and Henry Greene and Peter and John Hall. One must wonder whether this practice originated with the Greenes or with the Halls. There does not appear to be any documentary evidence to answer the question. We can, however, speculate based on available facts. In this case, the relevant data take the form of board-and-batten doors in houses that predate the Halls' association with Charles and Henry Greene. For example, doors in the Jennie Reeve house (1904) include screws with slots aligned. The same is true in the Charles Greene house (1902) and the house for Martha, Violet and Jane White (1903). That all were originally constructed prior to the Greene/Hall association, suggests that this particular compulsion belonged to Greene & Greene. However, we cannot ignore the fact that these houses have been modified. The screw heads could have been aligned years later by subsequent homeown-

ers aware that this detail exists in other houses, though this seems a far less likely explanation.

Nineteen. That's the number of hinges on each door of the curio cabinet designed by Greene & Greene for Belle Barlow Bush.[49] With no context, this single data point might lead one to believe that this is a large, imposing piece of furniture. It is not. It has an imposing presence due to the elegant design and flawless execution, but is a diminutive piece, measuring just over 2 feet tall. Stacking butt hinges, in resemblance of piano hinges, was a common practice for Greene & Greene (the only furniture on which they used an actual piano hinge was, appropriately enough, pianos). While certainly providing a great deal of strength for doors with heavy leaded glass panels, this arrangement was just as certainly overkill from an engineering perspective. Consider that the main entrance doors in many Greene & Greene houses weigh a great deal. Most, however, are hung in more conventional fashion, using only three, or perhaps four, hinges. For example, the massive entry doors to the Gamble and Blacker houses do not utilize stacked hinges. Certainly these doors contain enough mass to have warranted use of the technique. The only explanation is that this was a design element, and a most unexpected one at that.

It is worth noting that larger pieces didn't necessarily incorporate more hinges — hinge dimensions increased with furniture dimensions. Hinge lengths varied from roughly one inch to several inches. The French doors separating the living room from the entry hall in the Thorsen house provide an interesting case study. Each of the two bifolding doors is hung using five hinges: two at top, two at bottom and one in the center. The bifold joint, however, incorporates 26 hinges (each 3"-long) in a stacked arrangement running the length of the doors. Once again, we see evidence that use of large numbers of hinges is not purely functional. If it were, certainly it would have been used to hang the doors in their opening as well as to hinge the sections of each door.

Another interesting detail concerning hinges is also quite surprising. When touring the Gamble house, one can easily suffer sensory overload. There are simply too many gorgeous objects present for one's brain to fully process all of the visual stimuli. Some things simply must go unnoticed. So it is not unexpected that many visitors don't see this detail. It is not visually beautiful, though there is a conceptual beauty and elegance. On doors with only three hinges, the middle hinge is not centered between the top and bottom hinges. Imagine the middle hinge as a fulcrum. Gravity, and leaning house guests, try to move the door toward the floor. The hinges fight these forces with the upper hinge doing much of the heavy lifting. Moving the middle hinge up reduces the torque applied to the

TOP The golden ratio would certainly have been known to Charles and Henry Greene. Surely, it is no accident that it describes the distances between these hinges. Dining room patio doors, David B. Gamble house, Pasadena, 1907-09.

ABOVE Scarf joints as used by the Greenes in interior trim were almost entirely decorative. Detail, hall woodwork, William R. Thorsen house.

top hinge. Now for the surprising part: The distance between the middle and lower hinges is 1.618 times the distance between the upper and middle hinges. The figure 1.618 just happens to be a common approximation for the golden ratio, a factor that has for centuries been used to define pleasing proportions and sound design.[50] Of course, in that context it is typically used to determine the aspect ratio of a tabletop or cabinet door. Its use for spacing hinges inspires a certain degree of awe.

A scarf joint is used to join two elements, such as wood planks, end-to-end allowing for the creation of longer pieces than those available in the stock on hand. Often, though not exclusively, used in architectural trim, this joint, if oriented appropriately, offers the advantage of near invisibility even if the joined elements separate slightly. In keeping with the Arts & Crafts philosophy of honest, exposed joinery, Greene & Greene made no effort to conceal scarf joints. On the contrary, they incorporated them into the design and put them on display.[51]

For scarf joints commonly employed in trim work, angled cuts are made on the front of one element and the back of the other so that the joint is minimally visible as only a line running across the grain. In the variant employed by Greene & Greene, the top and bottom edges of the members are cut so that when joined, the entire joint is visible. Thus, Greene & Greene scarf joints are more like those used for joining structural timbers. Use of such joints was common and increased as the old-growth forests were depleted, and availability of the massive timbers they yielded declined.

The form of scarf joint most commonly used by the Greenes is similar to a halved and undersquinted scarf. This joint is quite similar to a half-lap. Undersquinting refers to angling the vertical cuts of the joint, a prac-

LEFT This scarf joint is enhanced by the addition of a lantern to light a stairway. Detail, stair woodwork, Freeman A. Ford house, Pasadena, 1906-08.

BELOW Greene & Greene also made use of structural scarf joints, used when timbers of sufficient length are not available. Detail, attic, Mary E. Cole house, Pasadena, 1906-07.

tice that helps resist twisting of the members. Greene & Greene also used, on occasion, a stop-splayed and undersquinted joint. In this version, the laps are cut at an angle rather than parallel to the lengths of the members.[52] In either case, the joints were keyed or pegged.[53] Additionally, Greene & Greene had the edges of the joined members eased, thus eliminating the possibility that the joint would disappear into the wood grain.

Scarf joints are another detail for which there may have been a Japanese influence. The keyed version employed by Greene & Greene bears a resemblance to the Japanese *kanawa-tsugi*.[54] Defined as a housed, rabbeted, half-blind, tenoned scarf joint, the *kanawa-tsugi* is actually a more complex joint than those Greene & Greene used. However, this joint appears similar to Greene & Greene examples due to the key (*komisen*) used to lock the members in place. Particularly in architectural trim, the Greenes used a joint more like the *okkake daisentsugi* except for the oblique, rather than parallel, nature of this joint.[55] *Okkake daisentsugi* lack the tenons, top and bottom, of the *kanawa-tsugi* permitting it to slide together from the side. Also missing is the key through the face of the joint. Rather *okkake daisentsugi* are pinned, less obviously, through the top and bottom surfaces.[56]

Perhaps no joinery element was more transformed at the hands of Greene & Greene than the simple finger joint. Usually a utilitarian method of joining boards at the corner of a box (such as a drawer or case), the finger joint provides great strength due to the large amount of gluing surface. However, it is not typically very decorative. Therefore, its use in fine furniture had always been limited. Perhaps the exposed end grain, on both front and side, also plays a role in the low esteem afforded the finger joint. Even in applications where hidden, as in drawer construction, its more respected cousin, the dovetail, was far more common and considered a hallmark of well-constructed furniture. This is the point in the narrative where one expects to read that Greene & Greene changed all that, raising this lowly joint to high status and common use. Constrained by fact rather than Hollywood license, our tale doesn't take that turn.

The truth is that Charles and Henry Greene did transform the finger joint into a featured element, perhaps even *the* featured element on several of their furniture designs. Also true, however, is that the transformation was neither long lasting nor widespread. The dovetail continues to this day to be the gold standard for drawer construction and, to a lesser degree, for carcass construction as well. But for those few wonderful years, the Greenes' joinery creation graced furniture and architectural trim. There are several distinguishing

TOP Each finger in this joint is a different width, creating additional interest in a beautiful feature. Detail, hall table, David B. Gamble house.

ABOVE The exaggerated reveals on this finger joint add appeal where typically there would be none. Detail, hall woodwork, William R. Thorsen house.

characteristics of the Greene & Greene finger joint. Not all are present in all examples. The fingers are wider than in the traditional, utilitarian version; fingers can have variable sizing within a joint; and the fingers typically stand proud of the surface of the mating board. In some trim the fingers extend significantly, while on most drawers the effect is far more subdued and on some drawers, as in the Blacker house, only the fingers on the drawer sides are proud, those on the front are flush with the sides. In some cases, as in the mantels in several houses, there are only several fingers — two on one board and one on the other. The single finger can be quite large, perhaps as much as several inches. Despite the many variations, the common heritage is obvious as is the wonderful effect this feature creates.

A relative of the finger joint, the bridle joint makes an appearance in several Greene & Greene designs. Bridle joints are a form of open mortise-and-tenon.[57] This means that a through mortise is cut at the end of a board resulting in a mortise that is open on three sides. The mating tenon is visible on two sides, one side being hidden by the closed end of the mortise. This joint is particularly attractive in frame construction as in the Gamble house fern table and living room bookcase. In both pieces, bridle joints are used in frame construction of the tops. In these instances, the joint is adorned with square ebony pegs.

Every aspect of the Gamble stairs is exquisite. Here, finger joints, scrolls, pegs and beautiful materials work together beautifully. Detail, hall stairs, David B. Gamble house.

In some cases, several of these details are combined in a single masterpiece. Such is the case with the entry hall table from the David B. Gamble house. Two drawers in this table combine perhaps the ultimate expression of finger joints found in the Greenes' work with a wonderful example of brass "pins" and yet another original detail: imaginative and beautiful drawer runners. Typical drawer runners are purely functional. They are often made of a secondary wood and are fully hidden from view until the drawer is removed. Greene & Greene brought drawer runners out of hiding and into full view. Two examples, in particular, merit discussion.

Not least among the wonderful details in the Gamble entry hall table are sensual, sculptural ebony drawer runners that are a highlight of the design. In this table, the drawers hang from their runners. Ebony strips, dovetailed at the corners, are attached to the top edges of the drawers (with the aforementioned brass pins). The strips are wider than the drawer sides, overhanging them to the outside of the drawer box. Two-tiered ebony runners attach to the table, adjacent to the legs on either side and in the center, between the two drawers.

These runners engage the drawers, supporting them just above the upper stretchers. Because of the deep black color of the ebony, the runners are not immediately obvious, and the drawers appear to float. On closer inspection, the true nature of this mechanism is apparent and becomes a key feature of the table.

A very different but equally creative drawer arrangement is found on the living room library table from the Charles M. Pratt house (design for the house began in 1908 but the living room furniture was not designed until 1912). In this design, the single drawer is supported directly by the legs. Drawer construction utilizes finger joints in which the drawer front has one centered finger and the sides have two fingers top and bottom. The drawer runner is integral to the side: the drawer side is stepped across its width, much thicker in the center than at the edges. This step corresponds exactly with the finger on the front so that in elevation view it is concealed. The step engages a mating, subtle cutout in the legs suspending the drawer and providing a beautiful, unexpected solution to this ubiquitous design dilemma.

RIGHT Even lowly drawer runners are elevated to high art, a sculpture in ebony. Detail, hall table, David B. Gamble house.

BELOW A study of detailing in a small piece, this clock must have had a commanding presence. Sadly, it is unknown if it still exists. Mantel clock, 1908, Belle Barlow Bush (William T. Bolton house), Pasadena, 1906.

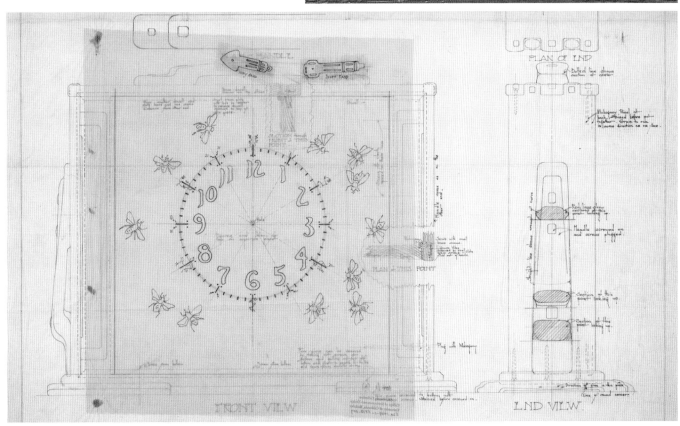

Blacker House Details

Charles and Henry Greene considered the Blacker house to be their masterpiece. Built beginning in 1907 for retired lumber baron Robert R. Blacker and his wife, Nellie Canfield Blacker, the Blacker house is commonly considered the first of what are now known as the Ultimate Bungalows.[58] Aesthetics are quite personal, but one can hardly argue with the Greenes' choice. The Blacker house is a masterpiece in every respect.

Thanks to the considerable efforts of the current owners, the magnificence of this house, never far below the surface, is once again fully evident. The past, however, was not always kind to the pride of the Oak Knoll neighborhood.[59] Nellie Blacker lived in the house until her death in 1946. Throughout her life the house remained in excellent condition. Henry Greene, who maintained a working relationship with Mrs. Blacker, visited as late as 1945 or 1946.[60] In a 1942 letter to brother Charles Greene, he reported happily on the fine condition of the house.[61]

After Mrs. Blacker's death, the house's fortunes changed dramatically. There was a yard sale in which

much of the furniture was sold. The magnificent 5-acre parcel was subdivided, leaving the house on a significantly smaller lot. The garage and keeper's house were sold off. Finally, in the well-known "rape of the Blacker house," the house was purchased by investors with the sole intention of stripping it of original lighting fixtures and art glass. To see the house in its current condition, one couldn't believe that it had suffered such indignities.

For the Blacker house, Greene & Greene inherited a footprint and floor plan from fellow Pasadena archi-

Interior and exterior are both fantastic. Note the beams projecting not only in the gables but below as well. View of South façade, Robert R. Blacker house, Pasadena, 1907-09.

tects Myron Hunt and Elmer Grey. While the Greenes made only minor changes to the physical dimensions of the structure, the elevations and materials they chose are dramatically different.[62] One significant exterior addition is the powerful porte cochere that juts at an angle from the front entrance to the circular terminus of the driveway, providing cover for arriving guests. Presaged by a more modest version on the Mary Cole house (1906), the porte cochere, supported at the outboard end by a massive clinker brick pier, is perhaps the signature element of the house. The roof for the terrace at the opposite side of the house provides balance for the porte cochere while allowing for a degree of asymmetry as well.

The 1905 commission for Henry and Laurabelle Robinson gave Greene & Greene the opportunity to create a large estate including furniture for several rooms. This move toward creating a complete environment was an important development but ultimately only a step along the path to even more complete designs to come. The Blacker house represents a quantum leap in this regard. Designs for this estate include the 12,000 square foot main house, a garage, the groundskeeper's house, gardens — with a substantial pond — and furniture and decorative arts for almost every room. In the interval between these two projects, Charles Greene developed and refined the firm's trademark style, particularly with regard to furniture design.

In the Blacker house we find a startlingly cohesive collection of objects each of surpassing beauty and quality. This does not mean that there is a sameness in these objects. Quite the contrary is the case — there are a number of different themes in various rooms of the house. Despite the variation, rooms flow one into another and are unified through use of materials and subtle recurring elements such as the rounded corner brackets in windows throughout the house.

In addition to a number of details that we now recognize as elements of the Greene & Greene vocabulary, the Blacker house contains several features seldom or never used in other works by the firm. Some, such as tree of life inlays in the bedroom and scrolls in the magnificent entry hall, are discussed in other sections. The double brackets used in the interior corners of living room furniture are among the most striking details in the Greene & Greene repertoire and one of the most recognizable today. Certainly, Charles and Henry Greene must have understood the success of this detail. Why then did it not appear in other houses when many other details were used more commonly? Perhaps even then they understood that in the Blacker house they had created a unique environment, one that would define their careers. Befitting that status, they may have chosen to retire details used there.

The double brackets mentioned above, sometimes referred to as "Blacker brackets," are nearly ubiquitous in the living room furniture. They appear on chairs, a sofa, tables and a magnificent bookcase with leaded glass doors. So frequently do these brackets appear in the living room that it is somewhat astonishing that they do not appear in any other room of the house. Typically used in the void at the right angle meeting of a leg and a rail, brackets were also used in the frame and panel sides and the leaded doors of the bookcase. The brackets on the bookcase may be the best illustration of the underlying nature of this form: The Blacker

The Blacker living room is home to several details not seen elsewhere. This piece includes them all. Living room bookcase, 1908-09, Robert R. Blacker house.

ABOVE Blacker brackets in mahogany and lead. This iconic detail didn't stay long in the Greene & Greene arsenal. Detail, living room bookcase, Robert R. Blacker house.

RIGHT High detail density — leg indents, brackets, breadboard ends, splines, pegs, all in a couple of square feet. And it all works together seamlessly. Detail, living-room bookcase, Robert R. Blacker house.

bracket is, in effect, a modified, exaggerated form of cloud lift — one that is applied rather than integral to the rail. While the open center of the bracket form is clearly distinct from cloud lifts, the result is the same — a rise in a horizontal line.

Another detail unique to the Blacker house living room is much more subtle but quite beautiful and clever. Near the bottoms of the legs on every piece of furniture in the room, there is a small indent, nearly as wide as the leg. Several inches in length, the indents increase in depth and stop short of the leg bottom. The surface of the indent is slightly pillowed at the edges, mirroring the eased edges of the legs. The indent detail adds visual interest to the legs by creating shadow lines and texture. In some cases, they also serve to lighten the leg, similar to a slight taper, but without the exceedingly traditional appearance that detail imparts.

Notations and marks on these drawings allow us to imagine Charles Greene and Peter Hall poring over them together. Drawing, dining room and hall furniture, 1908-09, Robert R. Blacker house.

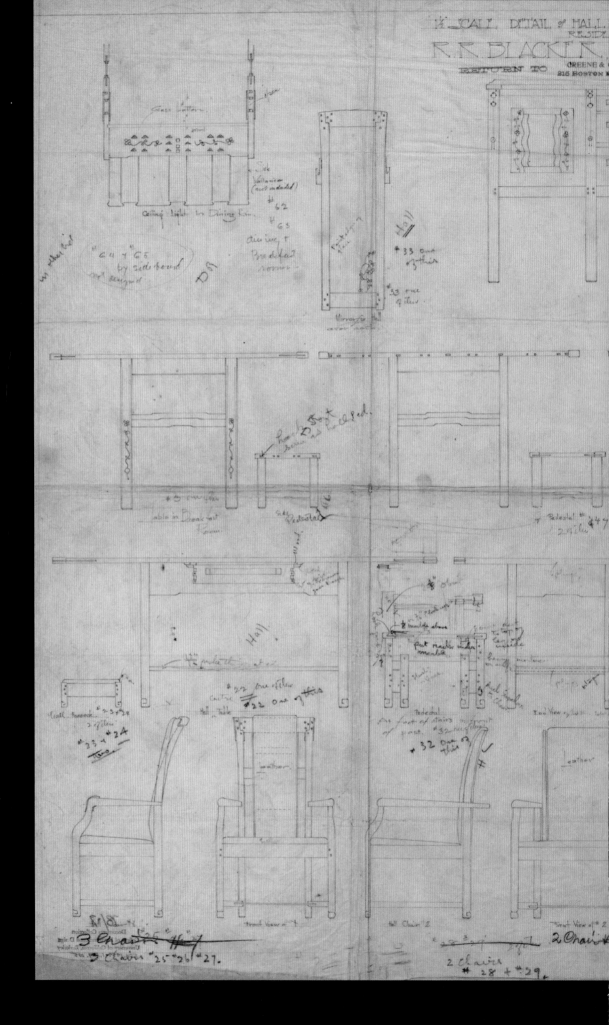

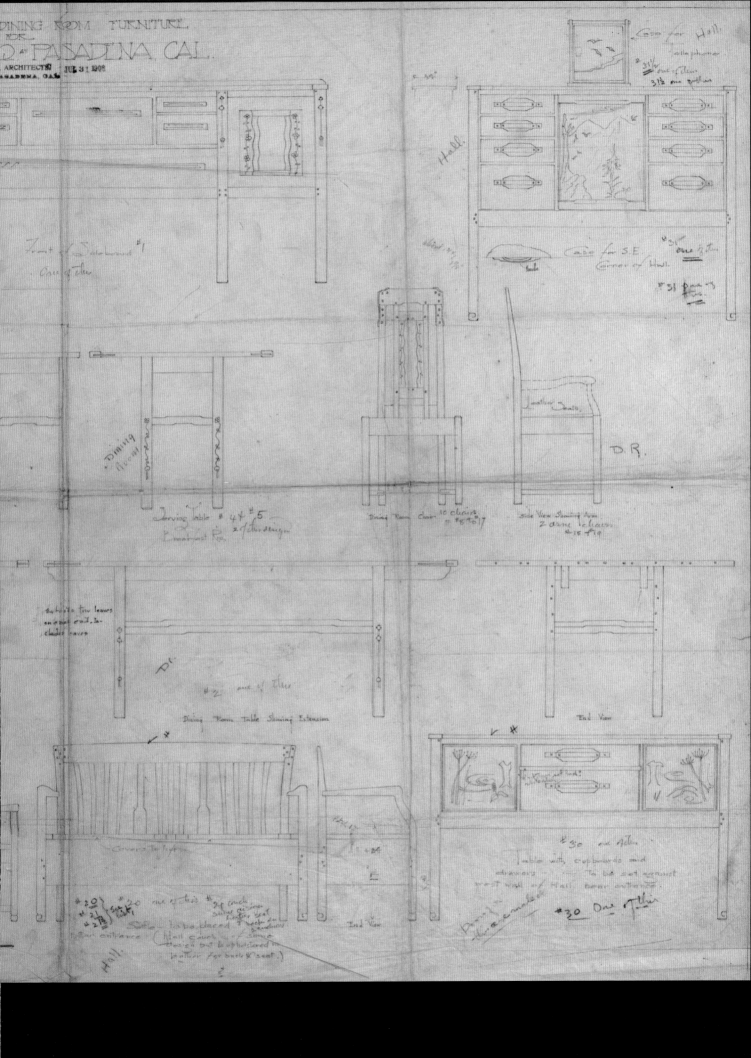

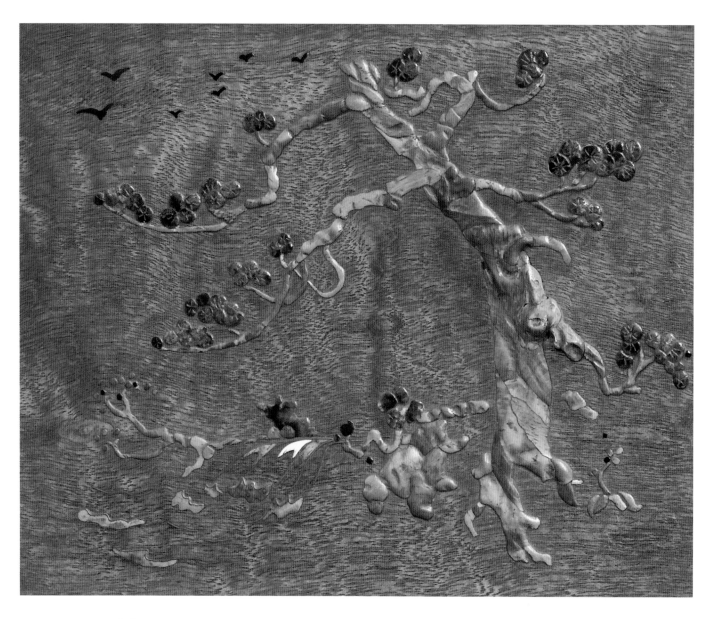

Inlay

As is surely plain by now, wonderful details are often the highlights of Greene & Greene furniture. Consider the crest rails on the Blacker living room chairs or the finger-jointed drawers on the Gamble chiffonier or the carved elements on the Thorsen living room desk. Each of these features greatly enhances the pieces on which they appear without dominating or overwhelming. Even in the context of such considerable beauty, one form of detail frequently stands out as simply incredible: the inlays that often grace tabletops, door panels, legs and chair backs.

While Greene & Greene inlays are unusual in some ways, they share at least one important attribute with other Arts & Crafts varieties: they are inspired by, and depict, natural forms. This is consistent with Japanese and Arts & Crafts influences as both emphasize nature, not only with respect to inlays but in general. This subject is distinct from the common historical Western forms which were predominately geometric. Despite the common theme, Greene &

Certainly among the best Greene/Hall inlay work, this piece shows an amazing sensitivity in design and implementation. Stock selection is inspired. Detail, living room letter box, 1914, David B. Gamble house, Pasadena, 1907-09.

Greene inlays are distinct even from others by Arts & Crafts designers. Consider the beautiful examples on pieces designed by Harvey Ellis for Gustav Stickley. Ellis' designs helped bring a new grace and delicateness to Stickley's offerings. Inlays certainly play a significant role in conveying this effect. These inlays typically depict flowers in highly stylized form. As with many Greene & Greene inlays, they often stand out as a defining element.

In contrast, inlays by Charles and Henry Greene are usually quite realistic with a three-dimensional appearance. There is little need for imagination to deduce what is being depicted. On the living room table (circa 1910) from the William Thorsen house, for example, the inlays, in the form of long-stem roses, are extraordinarily lifelike. The thorns appear ready to draw blood. Veins in the leaves are inlaid ebony, a remarkable achievement given their delicate dimensions and the brittle nature of the material. Shading on the leaves is achieved by singeing the wood in hot sand, adding to the three-dimensional quality. Flower petals are of vermillion — heart wood for darker petals and sap wood for lighter. The stems are primarily of koa. The overall effect is quite spectacular.

The conveyed three-dimensionality is the result of trompe l'oeil (as in the shading mentioned above) but more importantly to the fact that the inlay is, indeed, three-dimensional. Most Greene & Greene inlays are, in actuality, three-dimensional in that the inlaid elements stand proud of the field in which they are inlaid. These bolection inlays are able to convey a realism that would be otherwise impossible. Another benefit is a tactile quality that further summons fingers to surfaces that beg to be touched due to the silky finish.

Such extraordinary results can arise only from a synergistic relationship between designer and craftsman. Neither alone can achieve the goal. The craftsman needs the inspired design from which to begin, while the designer must rely on the skill and intuition of the craftsman. Clearly, both elements were present

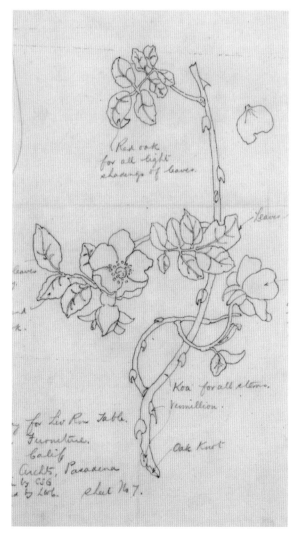

LEFT AND ABOVE   For this very literal inlay, every species is called out by the architect and is expertly handled at the bench. The result speaks for itself. Detail, living room table, c. 1910, William R. Thorsen house, Berkeley, 1908-10.

in the collaboration between the Greenes and those in the workshop of Peter and John Hall. Not only did Charles Greene sketch the inlay for the Thorsen table, he called out on the drawing the species of wood for each element. Even so, the success of the final result was largely dependent on decisions and execution at the bench by the craftsman. Inlays of this type are brought to life by appropriate stock selection and shaping. The best design cannot succeed except via these skills.

Another exceptional example of the designer/ craftsman relationship appears in the living room desk made for the Gamble House in 1914. A true work of art, it invokes one of Charles Greene's favorite motifs: trees and birds in flight. The inlays seemingly come to life due to extreme care in selecting stock that is sensitive to the intended effect. This is especially evident in the tree trunk that crashes through the two-dimensional barrier to draw the viewer into the scene. The swirling grain of the background is also an important element — straight grain would have provided a less natural appearance. It is worth noting that the desk and let-

ABOVE AND OPPOSITE TOP More abstract and stylized than most Greene & Greene inlays, this depiction of the tree of life (opposite top) is a recurring theme in the Blacker bedroom, including the desk above. Detail, bedroom desk, c. 1908, Robert R. Blacker house, Pasadena, 1907-09.

terbox for the Gamble living room were designed well after most other furniture for that house. In the intervening years, Charles had further developed, perhaps perfected, his inlay designs. This work bears a stronger resemblance to furniture for the Charles M. Pratt house than to any other for the Gambles.

Not all Greene & Greene inlays are so literal and lifelike. Many of their earlier inlays are more stylized, in keeping with the typical Arts & Crafts form. Some inlays in the Robert R. Blacker house fall into this category — abstract forms inspired by nature. In the owner's bedroom, the inlay motif is a depiction of the tree of life. This theme, symbolic of the interconnectedness of all life-forms, is consistent with Charles Greene's interest in Eastern philosophies, an interest

he indulged heavily later in life. The rather abstract form he designed (circa 1908), implemented in copper, silver, mother-of-pearl and fruitwood, appears on many pieces in the room — in some cases the tree trunk is several feet long, in others merely inches. Furniture for the bedroom is of mahogany with ebony accents.

As the Blacker inlays illustrate, Greene & Greene used many materials other than wood in their inlay designs. In addition to copper, silver and mother-of-pearl, all mentioned above, semi-precious stones, lapis lazuli, for example, and brass were used. Of course, the more expected broad assortment of woods also appear. The effect of the unexpected materials is both startling and immediately pleasing. Mother-of-pearl is used to particularly good effect in a number of pieces. The almost iridescent quality of the shell material unites very well with stained glass elements used liberally throughout many Greene & Greene houses.

Silver is brought to life in inlays for furniture in the Gamble house guest bedroom. The spidery metallic forms, accented with ebony and vermillion, appear surprisingly natural. To help achieve this effect, the width of the silver varies and the surface has a subtle texture. Smooth and uniform material would not be at all effective. In some cases, the lines are punctuated with silver dots, adding to the variability.

An illustration of the incredible variety in Greene & Greene inlays. Like some other details, this appears in only one room. Bedroom letter box, 1908-09, David B. Gamble house.

Carving

"Wood carving was a near religious experience for Charles Greene."[63] It was a lifelong avocation, one that yielded beautiful results for a number of clients. One can easily imagine that the bench work performed by a designer would best serve as a prototype rather than the finished product. This was certainly not the case with Charles Greene's carvings. He displayed a genuine talent for both design and execution of carved panels.

After moving to Carmel in 1916, Charles Greene devoted significant time to building and modifying the studio that became his refuge and his canvas. Few aspects of the small structure escaped Charles' touch. On approach, the whimsical brickwork and wonderfully carved front door announce their pedigree. Inside, the carved doors are the highlight, though the plaster above, stamped by the Greene children while perched on Charles' shoulders, are also very interesting. The mental image of the younger Greenes stamping the wet plaster with their father as their ladder casts Charles in an endearing, familial light.

The carving on the doors varies between lighthearted and impressive. There are several scenes, including one depicting Susannah and the Elders, that well illustrates Charles' skill. Perhaps most remarkable

Gamble and Blacker furniture gets more attention, but this piece is one of the firm's best. The carved feature at the rail/leg joint is simply wonderful. Detail, living-room table, c. 1910, William R. Thorsen house, Berkeley, 1908-10.

are the doors between the small entrance hall and the spacious main room. Here we see symbols carved on the rails and stiles alongside pencil and chalk sketches of planned but never executed additions. This glimpse inside the creative process is fascinating. Being in that place, one has a palpable sense of Charles Greene's presence, as evidence of the mind, and hand, of the master are everywhere.

Carving took hold of Charles Greene at the Manual Training School of Washington University in St. Louis. There, as part of the woodworking course, both brothers had hands-on training. While it would be some time before Charles would make professional use of this preparation, clearly it served him well. As with furniture design, knowledge of the process likely aided him in the design of carved panels and details, allowing him a high degree of empathy for the craftsmen who would implement his ideas.

In the James Culbertson house (1902) we see the first significant use of carved panels. Given that James

ABOVE The story of Susannah and the Elders as carved by Charles Greene. Charles may not have been a master carver, but he was certainly talented. Detail, bathroom door, 1923-57, Charles Greene studio, Carmel, 1923-24.

RIGHT Relief-carved panels were often employed by Greene & Greene. This example is particularly lifelike. Entry hall panel, c. 1907, James A. Culbertson house, Pasadena, 1902-14.

Culbertson and the Greenes collaborated to create the firm's initial Arts & Crafts house, the maxims that appear on a number of the panels come as no surprise. Natural themes also appear frequently, carved in deep relief. It is unfortunate that many of the panels were removed from the house during a renovation, making it impossible to experience the full impact of seeing them en masse and in situ as the architects intended.

Carved details found in Greene & Greene houses vary greatly in form. From the very literal and detailed panels in the Culbertson house to much less detailed low-relief carvings found in the Gamble house living room to the abstract, almost art deco frieze in the Robinson house sunroom, each project offers something unique. In yet another example of using details to unify various aspects of a design, we see in the Robinson house, carving details carried from the frieze into the wonderful square table also found in the sunroom. Similarly, in the Gamble house we find exceptionally simple carved details on the rails of living room furniture. They echo not only the cloud lifts on the same rails but also the amazing beams that are a primary feature of that room.

Reportedly carved by Charles Greene himself, these wall panels combine natural subjects, such as the rising sun, with a motif that could be described as art deco. Detail, sunroom, Laurabelle A. Robinson house, Pasadena, 1905-06.

For this piece, and others in this house, nearly every aspect of design was a departure from the signature style, with the exception of quality and attention to detail. Drawing, living room screen, c. 1911-15, Cordelia Culbertson house, Pasadena, 1911-13.

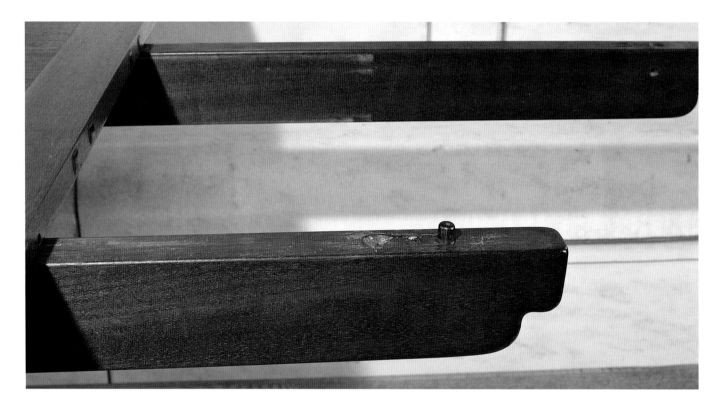

Table Extensions

It has been well documented that one hallmark of Greene & Greene commissions is extreme attention to detail. No aspect of a design was considered too trivial to receive the designer's touch. Even so, one could easily imagine that in some cases overwork and inertia might have led to repeated use of an established design element, particularly if that element was not central to the overall effect of the piece. Consider the extension mechanism for a dining room table. While it is certainly important to plan for this detail early in the design process due to the impact it could have on structural elements, it is not, in most cases, an aesthetic feature. Why not simply perfect one form of slide and use it whenever possible, saving considerable effort in the process? One might have asked that question of Charles Greene as he developed a number of interesting extension mechanisms and found creative ways to integrate them as design features, in some cases to stunning effect.

The dining room table for the Robert Blacker house serves as a good example, not simply of an imaginative extension mechanism but also of the Greenes' attention to detail. The top of the table is solid mahogany. Viewed from above, it does not appear to allow for expansion. Running beneath the tabletop, flush with the underside of the top, is a set of four beams or arms, each of which slides to extend from one end of the table. Thus, a pair of beams pierce the wide apron at each end to support leaves. In a delightful surprise, the outermost leaf at each end is held in place by an ebony and brass pin concealed

The Blacker extension mechanism is simple and efficient. Note the ebony used for the alignment pin. Detail, dining room table, 1908-09, Robert R. Blacker house, Pasadena, 1907-09.

in each arm. The pins could have been made of any common wood. That the Greenes chose ebony further demonstrates their obsessive nature. The pins are rotated into position after the arms are extended.[64] Each end could accommodate multiple leaves, which were fitted together with indexing pins.

The dining room table designed by Henry Greene for the Richardson house is a study in simplicity, befitting that house's rural setting on a working citrus ranch. Similar to the Blacker dining room table, the top is not divided — extension occurs at the ends rather than in the center. In this case, however, the leaves are integrated into the table, one hinged at each end. Ingenious brackets, two at each end, serve to hold the leaves in place when folded under and support them when raised. It is the brackets that distinguish this mechanism from others of similar form.[65]

While not technically an extension mechanism, the gateleg table designed for the living room of the William Bolton house and built for Belle Barlow Bush, the house's first occupant, merits discussion. Like the other mechanisms under consideration here, gatelegs did not originate with Greene & Greene. As with many other design elements, however, they found a way to take a known form and improve on it, making it more graceful and beautiful. A classic problem with gateleg tables is how to accommodate the gate when closed.

ABOVE Possibly the most exquisite table extension mechanism ever devised. It glides effortlessly even today. Detail, dining room table, 1908-09, David B. Gamble house, Pasadena, 1907-09.

RIGHT Though in continuous use for more than 80 years, this table is in impeccable condition. A simple design, it contains several trademark elements. Dining room, Walter L. Richardson house, Porterville, 1929.

Greene & Greene solved the problem by introducing offset stretchers and rails, allowing the swinging leg to easily nestle in place.[66]

Certainly the most elegant implementation of an extension mechanism graces the dining room table in the David B. Gamble house.[67] For this table, Charles Greene took a typical sliding almost effortlessly extension mechanism and sculpted it into a truly spectacular, sculptural design element that serves as one of the dominant features. The slides consist of a series of nested runners, implemented in mahogany, each allowing the table to extend farther. The parts are expertly fitted in a wonderful marriage of engineering and craftsmanship. After 100 years the movement is still silky smooth and reassuringly precise, the elements sliding almost effortlessly to the fully extended length of 123 inches. At the center of the table, polished ebony indexing pins serve to align the table halves as they glide together. It is difficult to imagine that a more beautiful solution to this problem exists anywhere.

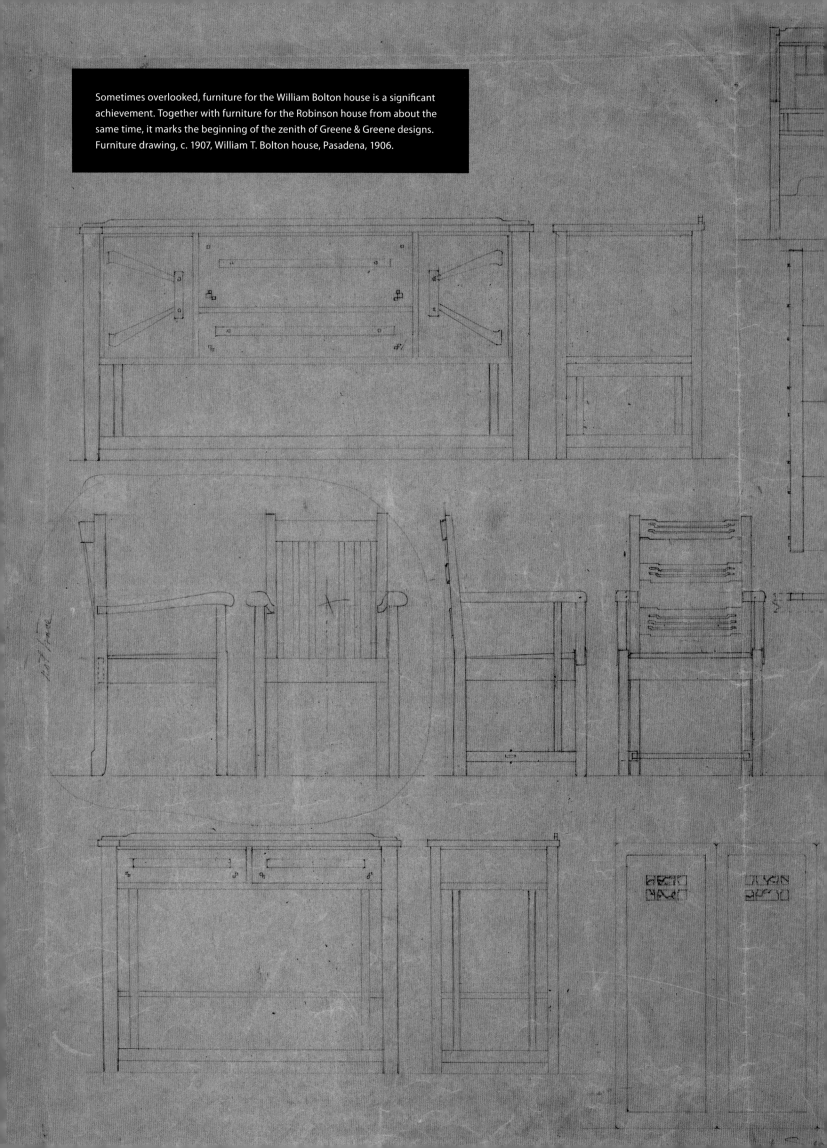

Sometimes overlooked, furniture for the William Bolton house is a significant achievement. Together with furniture for the Robinson house from about the same time, it marks the beginning of the zenith of Greene & Greene designs. Furniture drawing, c. 1907, William T. Bolton house, Pasadena, 1906.

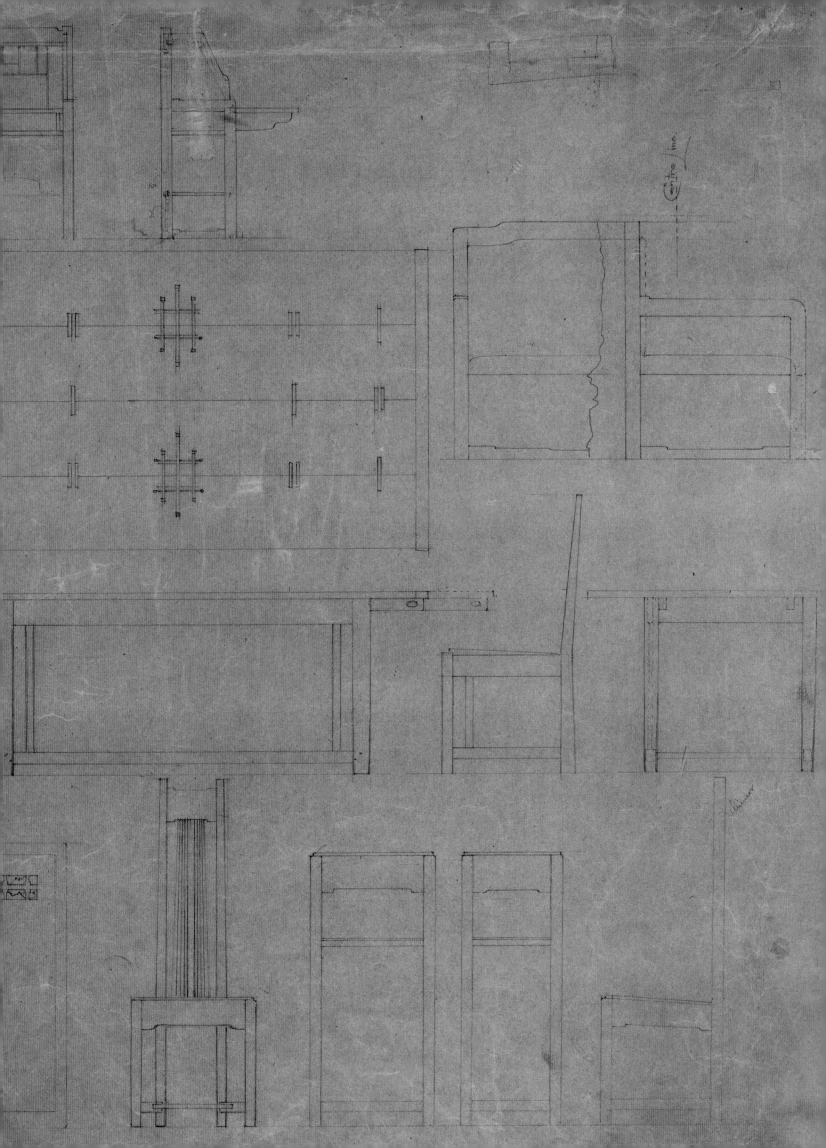

Lighting

Lighting was an important and integral aspect of Greene & Greene houses with designs adding significantly to the aura of both interiors and exteriors. This is quite distinct from the modern practice of lighting design in which professionals seek to optimize lighting patterns and locations for dramatic effect. It seems unlikely that anyone considered such installations a century ago, perhaps due to the limited selection of lighting options — 15-watt incandescent bulbs don't afford many choices.

No, for the Greenes', lighting design meant creating beautiful fixtures that were at once complementary with the overall design of the house and, in some cases, expressive works of art. Lighting designed by the

RIGHT Subtle asymmetry and the first use of a *tsuba* shape by the Greenes are just two of the features that make this sconce interesting. Living room sconce, 1904-05, Adelaide M. Tichenor house, Long Beach, 1904-05.

BELOW For this magnificent re-implementation, Kokomo Opalescent Glass reformulated the green glass — the original formulation is no longer available as it requires hazardous chemicals. Living room lantern, 1908-09, Robert R. Blacker house, Pasadena, 1907-09.

firm appeared in many more houses than did furniture. In wonderful homes such as those for Mary Reeve Darling, Edgar Camp, Jenny Reeve, Adelaide Tichenor and F.W. Hawks, we see interesting, if sometimes simple, designs that presage the more elaborate fixtures to come. Sconces in the Hawks house include round pegs that protrude significantly, perhaps as much as any others in a Greene & Greene design, a dramatic touch on a straightforward fixture. In the Ultimate Bungalows, we see lighting fixtures that are truly definitive statements of the Greene & Greene aesthetic.

Greene & Greene lighting falls into several categories not at all unique to the firm: sconces, lanterns (hanging and mounted), chandeliers, ceiling fixtures and table lamps. While none of these types originated with the Greenes, they adapted each type to their own purposes and in the process created forms that are unmistakably theirs. There is incredible variation in Greene & Greene lighting, much of which is not attributable to evolution. Consider dining room chandeliers in the Blacker and Robinson houses. While there is a hint of familial resemblance between the two fixtures, they are quite distinct. The chandelier from the Dun-

ABOVE LEFT By 1909, Greene & Greene had designed many sconces. Yet they found ways to make each unique and worthy of note. Living room sconce, 1909-10, William R. Thorsen house, Berkeley, 1908-10.

ABOVE RIGHT The inglenook is flanked by a pair of wonderful lanterns suspended from impressive beams. The upturned ends of the top set an Asian tone. Living room lantern, 1908-09, David B. Gamble house, Pasadena, 1907-09.

can/Irwin house, with individually suspended, fluted glass shades on black chains, is almost completely dissimilar. Perhaps the only clue to common heritage is the wooden ceiling treatment.

Among the most distinctive lighting elements from Greene & Greene are the sconces and hanging lanterns in the Ultimate Bungalows. Even within a house there is considerable variety in lighting fixtures. In the Thorsen house living room, sconces are rectangular forms with heavily sculpted tops and art glass sides. Though it may be overactive imagination, the glass appears to depict a marine plant, playing to the nautical theme. Also in the living room is a form of lighting very unusual for its day — flush-mounted

ceiling fixtures. A hanging lantern at the upstairs landing includes cutouts similar to those on the flower stand designed for that house.[68]

The Gamble house includes a large number of wonderful lighting fixtures. Perhaps best known are the hanging lanterns that flank the living room inglenook. These are an iconic Greene & Greene design. The basic form is standard but the thin top with upturned ends distinguishes the piece and lends an Asian feel. The cleats from which the piece is suspended, via leather straps, are quite sculptural.[69] Another well known fixture, one that is a real departure from most interior lighting designed by the Greenes, is the pair of hanging lanterns in the entry hall. Constructed primarily of brass, the top is arched in the manner of the roof over the entrances of many Japanese temples, appropriate given the location of these lanterns.[70] A crane and red rose motif is used above the panels to include elements from the Gamble family crest.

The Blacker house contains fixtures that nearly span the spectrum of complexity. In several rooms are sconces with fabric skirts as shades and wooden forms that are relatively simple. The dining room is among these. The dining room chandelier was designed to include a skirt as well, though it appears that this aspect of the design was not implemented.

Teak, ebony, silver, leather and art glass melded into a beautiful, functional work of art. Hall lantern, 1908-09, Robert R. Blacker house.

The entry hall hanging lanterns are one of the most pleasing decorative arts elements designed by Greene & Greene. The sinuous top provides a rare use of the lift form. The art glass panels on two opposing sides depict birds in flight while the other pair show flowers and have an unusual peaked shape, perhaps evocative of mountains. Subtle silver inlay on the bottom rails echo the themes. In the living room we find what may be the most stunning lighting element in any Greene & Greene home: six mahogany and intricate art glass basket lanterns. In old black-and-white photographs of the living room, these lanterns appeared, in my opinion, bulky and uninspiring. Viewing them in person quickly changes that view. They are quite remarkable and a highlight of an amazing room. They are also unique. With less immediate presence than the basket lanterns, the living room table lamp is quietly spectacular. The shade, in particular is a testament to the woodworking skills of the Halls' craftsmen. A flared octagon, each side consists of a mahogany panel beautifully carved to depict flowers and whimsical geometry. The shade is topped with an amazingly carved octagonal ebony cap.[71]

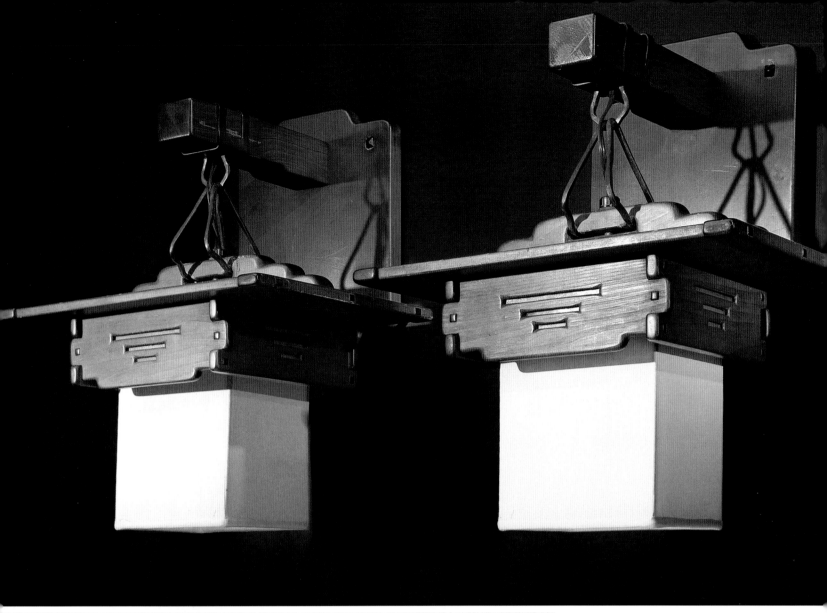

ABOVE An informality, attributable to silk skirts, alters the effect of the otherwise standard Greene & Greene elements. Bedroom sconces, 1908-09, Robert R. Blacker house.

LEFT Greene & Greene lighting is not exclusive to interiors. Since at least the Jennie Reeve house, the brothers designed wonderful exterior fixtures as well. Exterior lantern, 1906-08, Freeman A. Ford house, Pasadena, 1906-08.

LANTERN DETAILS. ~ ~ ~

RESIDENCE FOR MRS L. G. PORTER, AT
LOS ANGELES, CAL. SHEET Nº 41.

GREENE & GREENE, ARCHITECTS.
215 BOSTON BLDG. PASADENA, CAL.

TRACED BY L.W.C. from original tracing.

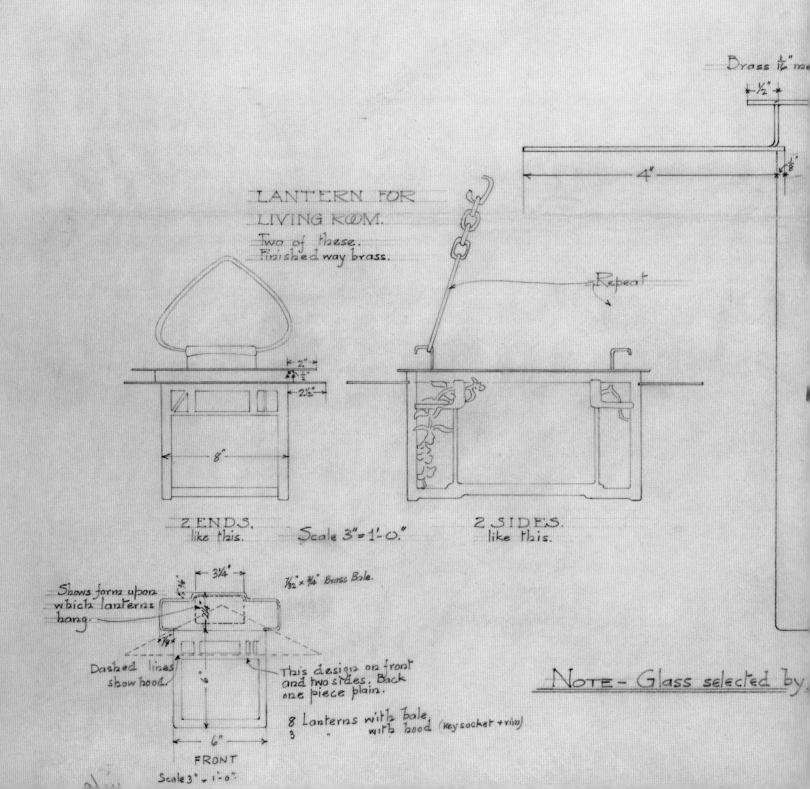

LANTERN FOR
LIVING ROOM.
Two of these.
Finished way brass.

Brass 1/16" me

4"

Repeat

2 ENDS, like this. Scale 3" = 1'-0." 2 SIDES. like this.

3 1/4"

1/32" × 3/4" Brass Bale.

Shows form upon which lanterns hang.

Dashed lines show hood.

This design on front and two sides. Back one piece plain.

8 Lanterns with bale,
3 " with hood (key socket + rim)

FRONT

Scale 3" = 1'-0".

NOTE - Glass selected by

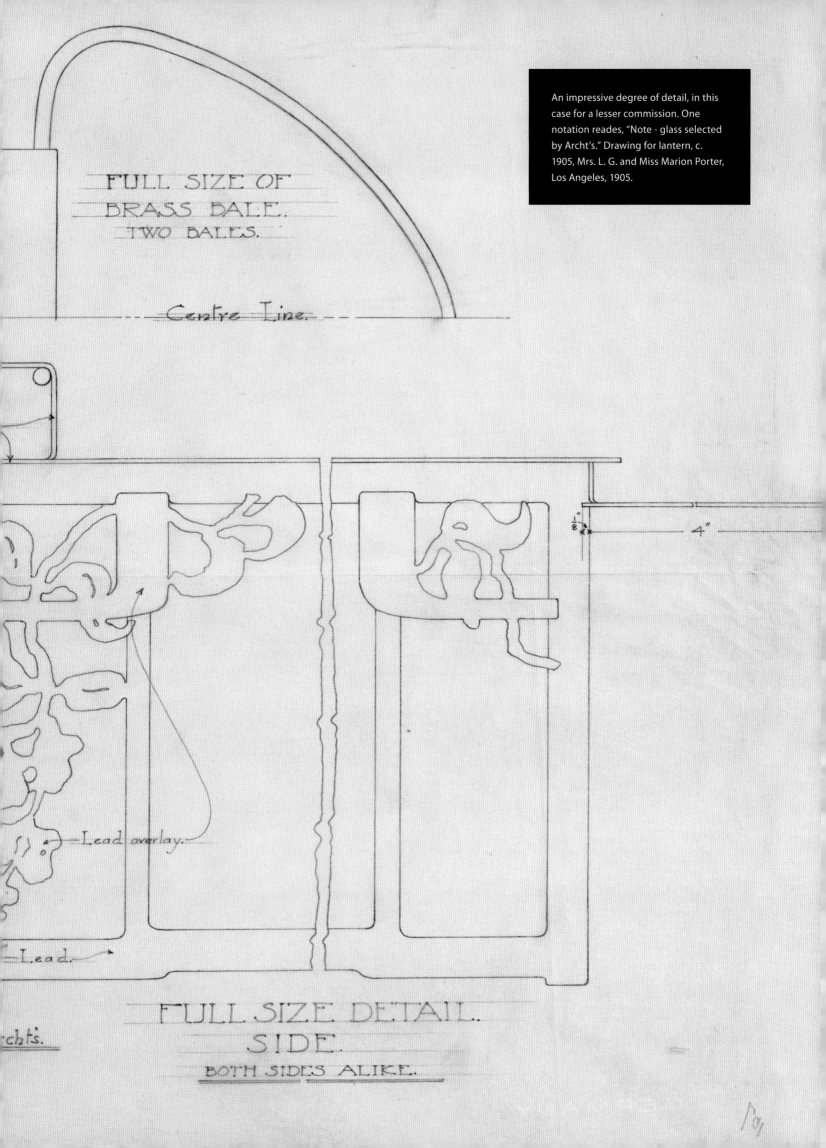

FULL SIZE OF
BRASS BALE.
TWO BALES.

Centre Line.

Lead overlay.

Lead.

rchts.

FULL SIZE DETAIL.
SIDE.
BOTH SIDES ALIKE.

$\frac{1}{8}$"

4"

An impressive degree of detail, in this case for a lesser commission. One notation reades, "Note - glass selected by Archt's." Drawing for lantern, c. 1905, Mrs. L. G. and Miss Marion Porter, Los Angeles, 1905.

Art Glass

Museums are home to many unusual objects. At the Rock & Roll Hall of Fame and Museum, one can see the clothes worn by Bruce Springsteen for the cover shot of the "Born in the USA" album. In the National Museum of American History, one finds the kitchen from Julia Child's Massachusetts home. On display at the American Museum of Natural History is a 1,000 pound hunk of stibnite adorned with hundreds of naturally formed, sword-like crystals. And in a Dallas museum, one can see the front door of a house. In a history museum this might not be a particularly unusual exhibit. In this case, however, the door is in the Dallas Museum of Art. Yes, a front door as art. Strange. That is until one sees the door in question: the front entry to the Robert R. Blacker house.

Clearly, this is no ordinary door. In fact, it is not a single door but rather three doors grouped into a single entry. The main door, much broader than is typical, is flanked by two smaller doors, each play-

This recreation of the main entry is an important part of the restoration of the Blacker house. No photo can do justice to the wonderful light coming through the glass. Set of doors (reproduction), c. 1985-87, Robert R. Blacker house, Pasadena, 1907-09.

ing the role of an oversized and entirely functional sidelight. The design is seamlessly integrated into the overall scheme of the house and the detailing, fit and finish are equal to that of fine furniture. Even with these impressive qualities, the doors are defined by a different element: the art glass.

Art glass is a frequent sight in Greene & Greene houses. In addition to appearing in entry doors, it turns up in windows, cabinets, furniture and lighting fixtures as well.[72] Its use in doors is not limited to entries as some interior doors include glass panels. The door from the dining room to the butler's pantry in the Gamble house includes a glass panel that continues the primary theme in that room — the *mokko*

Roughly 30,000 visitors each year pass through this door. More than a century after construction, it is still exquisite. Set of doors, c. 1908, David B. Gamble house, Pasadena, 1907-09.

gata tsuba. The same is true of windows — in several cases, there are art glass windows between two interior spaces, for the purpose of promoting airflow, something to which the Greenes paid special attention. For example, the owners' bedrooms in the Pratt and Gamble houses include this feature.

Lighting certainly provides the most frequent use of art glass with some truly spectacular examples: the Robinson dining room chandelier is a marvel not only for the intricate leaded glass but also for the remarkably inventive counterweighted fixture; the marvelous form of the Blacker entry lanterns, executed in teak and accented with iridescent and opaque glass, is one of the most compelling designs by Greene & Greene. However, doors provide the most spectacular use of glass, perhaps due to the scale, perhaps due to the exceptional beauty in an unexpected place.

As with every device employed by Greene & Greene, their art glass is unusual but not outlandish, innovative but not alien. Large panels, in particular,

resemble paintings. There are large expanses comprised of a single piece of glass punctuated by fine details executed with many small pieces. The glass work exhibits an organic quality that derives, in part, from the natural subject. The Blacker house entry depicts flowering vines climbing a trellis, the foliage and flowers providing glimpses of blue, red and green against the golden brown background. The trellis, represented in the lead lines of the panels, angles upward from the bases of the three doors and is echoed by stiles in the doors' wooden construction. A small trellis above the main entry continues the theme, drawing the eye up toward the magnificent tiered ceiling and flush light fixture.

The Ford house entry is a departure for Greene & Greene. The subject is inspired by nature and by man.

The frame of the single door portrays a rather abstract human figure with broad, sculpted mullions for legs and torso and a wide rail providing the outstretched arms. This form is not immediately apparent but once discerned is entirely obvious.[73] The art glass portrays a Native American ceremonial dress comprised of peacock feathers. The feathers continue into the transom above the door and above the panels that flank it. Two broad doors on either side of the entry hall, one to the living room, the other to the dining room, contain small glass panels that carry the feather motif of the entry into the house's interior. Outside the entrance hang two metal lanterns with wonderful iridescent glass panes.

The entry to the Gamble house is certainly the best known in the Greene & Greene canon. One might imagine that this results from that house being open to the public and the subject of countless photographs. Certainly that is the case, at least in part. However, the eminence of the Gamble doors just as certainly derives from the doors themselves for they are the most beautiful in any Greene & Greene house. Thought for years to illustrate a California live oak tree, the art glass is now believed to depict a black Japanese pine, its broad canopy spanning the main door and two smaller doors on either side.[74]

A different, less natural theme is found in this glass. Native American forms were common in arroyo culture. Door, 1907-08, Freeman A. Ford house, Pasadena, 1906-08.

The branches also continue into the transom which is large and interesting. Those above the smaller side doors are nearly triangular with a beautifully-formed hypotenuse breaking the largely rectangular form. This element was likely suggested by the hall stairs which project from the entry hall ceiling meeting the door wall at the north transom and providing one more example of a wonderful, decorative solution to a design dilemma.

With their extremely high level of craftsmanship, Peter and John Hall allowed Charles and Henry Greene to mature and evolve as designers, to create increasingly intricate and complex pieces, comfortable in the knowledge that their contractor could implement them with sensitivity and expertise. Some believe that the Greenes and Halls pushed each other in a good-natured game of chicken, each pair trying to make the other blink first. There is no evidence that anyone blinked — the houses, furniture and decorative objects attest to the skills and creative growth of designer and craftsmen. The Hall shop could provide

most of what Greene & Greene required but not every-thing. For art glass they turned to Emil Lange, from whom they were able to assume excellence on a par with woodwork from the Halls.

Lange, a former employee of Tiffany Studios, was a supremely talented artist. The organic char-acter of Greene & Greene art glass, attributed above to subjects drawn from nature, is also due to Lange's methods. That is perhaps the primary reason for the exceptional feel conveyed by his pieces. Several tech-niques serve to distinguish the works he created for Greene & Greene. Layering of glass to achieve variation in light transmission and color is one such technique. In some cases, one can see the layered elements in a rare opportunity to peer behind the curtain. Another technique, perhaps the most notable, is the high degree of variability in the width of the lead work. Rather than serving only to connect glass elements, the lead itself is integral to the aesthetics. It serves purposes both functional and decorative, a recurring trait in the work of Greene & Greene. The effect, achieved by manipulating lead solder with a variety of soldering iron tips,[75] increases the textural quality of the work in what is typically a highly textural medium. The result is an informality and brilliant organic character that

During winter months, when the sun is low in the sky, the afternoon light in the dining room glows with the color of this amazing window. Dining room window, c. 1908, David B. Gamble house.

fits perfectly with the country houses that were the Greenes' domain.

Evidence of this approach appears in the form of a drawing for a lantern for a commission that is not very well known. In 1905, Greene & Greene designed a resi-dence in Los Angeles for Mrs. L.G. and Miss Marion Porter. The lantern in question includes panels with a foliage motif and corner brackets similar to those on the Robinson dining room chairs and Blacker windows. The drawing calls out this detailing as "Lead over-lay." The overlay ignores the boundaries of the panel, making the scene appear spontaneously alive. This lovely piece serves to reinforce the democratic aspect, described by Jean Murray Bangs, in the work of Greene & Greene: even relatively modest houses received many of the same touches that make the Ultimate Bungalows, as well as many other houses designed by the firm, masterpieces of American architecture.

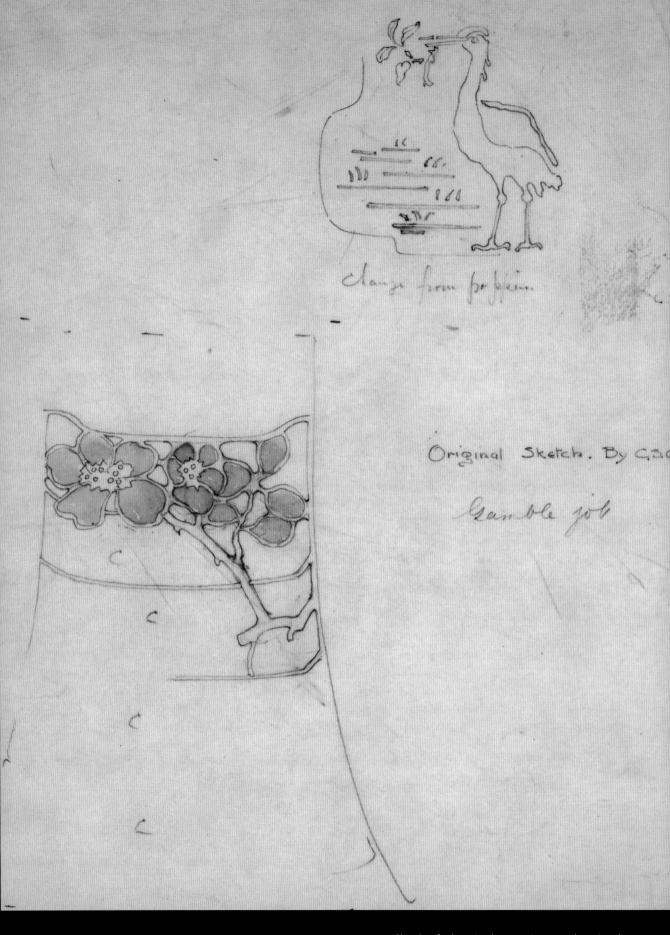

Change from pp ...

Original Sketch. By G.S.G

Gamble job

Sketches for hanging lanterns (crane and rose) and guest-
room sconces provide a glimpse of the creative process.

Pulls & Escutcheons

It is not particularly surprising that in high-end custom furniture even small details are designed and made by the craftsman. This is one of the perqs for clients willing and able to spend large sums of money for functional art. Drawer pulls, door handles and even escutcheons[76] are fully integrated into the design since they are part of the design rather than an off-the-shelf addition selected from a catalog and glommed on. Thus, Greene & Greene are not unique in their use of custom elements such as these. It is surprising, however, that they were able to continue this practice even during their busiest period, that several year span during which they designed the Ultimate Bungalows and several hundred pieces of furniture.

Shop-made pulls and escutcheons appeared in Greene & Greene furniture and built-ins beginning with the earliest pieces. These are rather simple in keeping with the furniture, but even at the outset the

Two of these imposing bookcases flank a window that once had a view of the bay. Shelves are stepped to provide strength and a lighter appearance. Living room bookcase, 1908-10, William R. Thorsen house, Berkeley, 1908-10.

Greenes attended to the small details. In the living room of the Jennie Reeve house, there is a wonderful built-in curio cabinet that backs to the bench of the well-known inglenook. On each leaded glass door is a simple pull that complements the piece and echoes the through tenons on the upper and lower rails. Pulls for furniture in the Adelaide Tichenor house are more complex, incorporating a lift motif, though still crude when compared to the firm's later work. Simple, oversized, rectilinear wooden escutcheons appear on pieces in both houses as well.

Custom escutcheons are absent from many projects, not reappearing regularly until the Ultimate Bungalow period. At that time, the escutcheons included

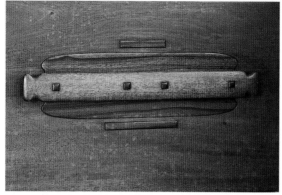

This drawer demonstrates the wonderful variety achieved with relatively simple building blocks. A similar flange, behind the pull, was used in the Blacker house entry hall. Detail, living-room bookcase, William R. Thorsen house.

Significant effort expended for a very small detail. This shop-made escutcheon is a wonderful accent. Detail, living-room bookcase, William R. Thorsen house.

Are those *tsubas*? In the Blacker house? The pull on the central door grows out of the carved scene. Entry hall chest, 1908-09, Robert R. Blacker house, Pasadena, 1907-09.

Pulls must be interesting to be noticed amidst so much beauty. These are particularly sculptural. Detail, bedroom chiffonier, 1908-09, David B. Gamble house, Pasadena, 1907-09.

in most of the Greenes' pieces were quite small, barely proud of the door or drawer surface and of a stepped geometric shape. It is tempting to see in that shape a form of *mokko-gata*, though one stylized and comprised entirely of straight line segments. However, another likely inspiration can be found in the arroyo culture that existed along the dominant geographic feature of Pasadena's western edge. The rusticity that was a key element of this culture was wonderfully complemented by Native American styles, which were common then as now. One can easily recognize in Greene & Greene escutcheons throughout this period, Native American geometric forms.

Development of drawer pulls follows that of the firm's furniture. Designs became increasingly sophisticated and sculptural. In some cases the pulls are a significant design element. Even within a single house there is often significant variation. Using the Gamble house as a case in point, we see very sparse pulls on the first floor with those in the entry hall exhibiting a particularly

modern appearance. By way of contrast, in David and Mary Gamble's bedroom the three-tiered pulls are rather whimsical and a noteworthy feature of that furniture.

One should almost expect that the Blacker living room would contain a drawer pull form not found elsewhere, in keeping with the unique details present in that room. The ebony and mahogany pulls on every drawer in the room do not disappoint. Each pull consists of three horizontal ebony bars, increasing in length top to bottom, and a mushroom-profiled mahogany grip set atop them. It is difficult to imagine these pulls on other Greene & Greene furniture, but it is difficult to imagine this furniture without this distinctive feature. Two case pieces in the Blacker entry hall each contain two different pull forms. Those on the drawers consist of a horizontal bar-style pull over a lobed backplate. A similar form was used later in the Thorsen house. The doors on these pieces are carved with a mountain scene. The pull takes the form of a gnarled tree, a vestigial branch providing purchase for fingers.

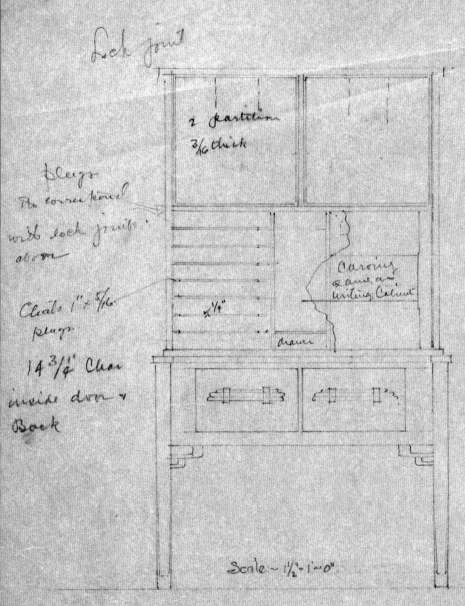

Lock joint

2 partition
3/16 thick

plugs
to correspond
with lock joints
above

Cleats 1" x 5/16"
plugs

14 3/4" Clear
inside door &
Back

2 1/4"

drawer

Carving
same as
writing Cabinet

Scale - 1 1/2" = 1'-0"

MAHOGANY MUSIC CASE for LIVING R'M.
HOUSE for R. R. BLACKER, Esq. AT OAK KNOLL.
SHEET No 74   DEC. 22nd 09.

GREENE & GREENE, ARCHITECTS.
215 BOSTON BLDG. PASADENA, CAL.
TRACED BY _____
DATE 12/22/09

A drawing that depicts many of the details for which Greene
& Greene are famous. Drawing, living room music case, 1909,

Culbertson Sisters' House Details

Charles and Henry Greene are best-known for a number of very beautiful houses designed and built during a very brief period. The houses, furniture and decorative items created during that time, and the style they defined, are now considered the quintessential Greene & Greene typeforms, and for good reason. Even so, the Greenes designed a number of important houses before and after that very productive period: the James Culbertson house, the D.L. James house, the Fleishhacker estate and the Culbertson Sisters' house are examples.

James Culbertson was a notable early client for Greene & Greene Architects. In 1911, his three maiden sisters, Cordelia, Kate and Margaret, commissioned the Greenes to design a substantial house in the fashionable Oak Knoll neighborhood.[77] The project included designs for gardens as well as a large number of pieces of furniture. It was their largest commis-

ABOVE Monumental size doesn't preclude elegance. Beautiful stock and typically attentive detailing instill grace in this 12-foot wide behemoth. Hall bookcase, 1911-13, Cordelia A. Culbertson house, Pasadena, 1911-13.

LEFT Looking beyond the surface reveals the pedigree of this piece. Shelf with breadboards and ebony pegs. Detail, bookcase, Cordelia A. Culbertson house.

sion to that time. In 1917, the Culbertson sisters sold the house to wealthy widow, Mrs. Elisabeth Allen. Mrs. Allen, who would later marry Francis F. Prentiss, would continue to engage the Greenes for 20 years.

The Cordelia Culbertson house represents both a departure and a return for Greene & Greene. For the basic form of the house, they returned to the U-shaped courtyard style used to great effect for several previous clients including Arturo Bandini and Freeman Ford. Similarities end there. The Culbertson house bears little resemblance to the "wooden style built woodenly"[78] of most of their earlier masterpieces. An increased formality is perhaps the best way to describe the different character found here.

Furniture for the Culbertson house is similarly distinct from the trademark style associated with the Greenes. Both more formal and more traditional, the pieces are striking and, like all Greene & Greene furniture, perfectly fit their environment. But these pieces do not immediately announce their heritage. One piece, an immense, wonderful bookcase comprised of six separate units and measuring roughly 12-feet wide and 7½-feet tall, is, interestingly, in the possession of the Property Department at Warner Bros. Studios. No one knows exactly how or when it arrived there.[79] Some years ago, department managers undertook to inventory and appraise pieces in their warehouse. An appraiser suggested, quite impressively given the dissimilarity from their trademark forms, that the bookcase might be by Greene & Greene. She contacted Randell Makinson who, upon viewing the imposing piece in the company of Ted Bosley and Jim Ipekjian, quickly verified its pedigree.

From basic form to detailing to finish, these pieces are unusual in the Greene & Greene catalog. Yet there

ABOVE Ebony accents and cloud lifts on the gate rails tie this piece to the better known Greene & Greene style. Garden room gateleg table, c. 1912, Cordelia A. Culbertson house.

BELOW This escutcheon may be the firm's best. An absolutely brilliant form, beautifully executed. Detail, living room secretary, Cordelia A. Culbertson house.

are clues to their lineage. Shelves are constructed with breadboard ends complete with ebony pegs. Doors and drawer fronts are wrapped in ebony secured with brass screws, heads filed to remove the slot.

Bookmatched veneers are a dominant feature of the Culbertson house furniture. Greene & Greene occasionally used this device but rarely put it so prominently on display. The perfectly prepared surfaces shimmer showing off the figure of the mahogany. Inlays on these pieces are a departure from the highly expressive, naturally inspired examples common over the previous several years. Restraint, abstraction and symmetry are the watchwords here. Some aspects of these designs exhibit an art deco feel. Escutcheons on the secretary may show this most strongly. Rectangular with a slightly rounded surface, they have a top edge that is stepped at each end and subtly engraved with horizontal lines. As is so often the case with Greene & Greene details, this is delicate and beautiful. Interestingly, the escutcheons are not uniform throughout the case pieces. Those on the bookcase described above differ from those on the secretary in form and material. Both are unique for Greene & Greene and are quite wonderful.

Restrained lines serve as the backdrop for Greene & Greene ornament: rather reserved inlay, wonderfully shaped pulls and ebony banding with beheaded brass screws. Living room secretary, c. 1911, Cordelia A. Culbertson house.

PLAN OF DRAWER "A".

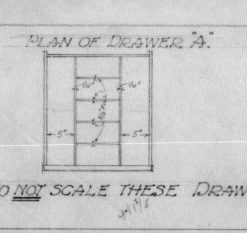

PLAN

NOTE - DO NOT SCALE THESE DRAWINGS, USE FIGURES AND FULL SIZE DE

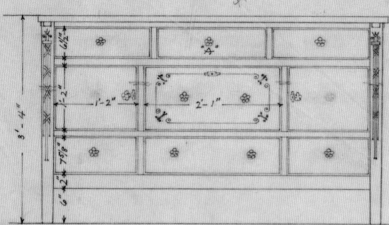

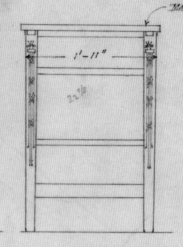

MARBLE TOP

FRONT.

SIDE.

Inch scale.   SERVING TABLE.

PIECE No 8

MISS C.A.CULBERTSON DIN

THIS DRAWING TO BE AFFIXED

cutting for
blueprint

These pieces are about proportion
and inlay. Note the rough sketches
in the margins. Drawing, dining
room furniture, 1911-13, Cordelia
Culbertson house.

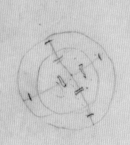

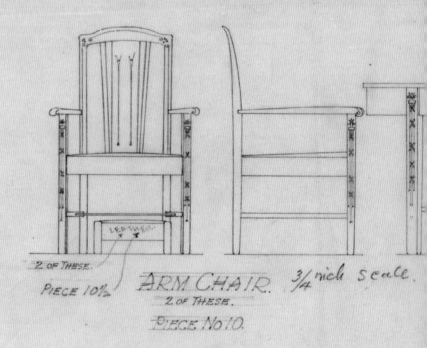

2 OF THESE.

PIECE 10½   ARM CHAIR. ¾ inch scale.

2 OF THESE.

PIECE No 10.

DETA

RESIDENCE

JOB No 27

G.

SCALE 1"= 1'-0"

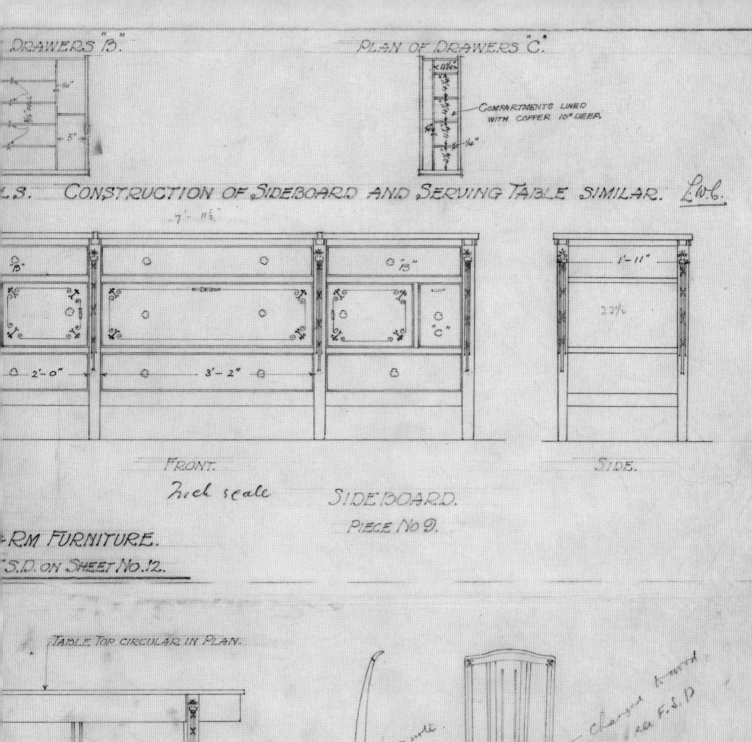

DRAWERS "B." PLAN OF DRAWERS "C."

1¼"
COMPARTMENTS LINED
WITH COPPER 10" DEEP.
¼"

5"

LS. CONSTRUCTION OF SIDEBOARD AND SERVING TABLE SIMILAR. *L.w.C.*

7'-11½"

"B"

1'-11"

2-½

2'-0" 3'-2" "C"

FRONT. SIDE.

½ inch scale SIDEBOARD.

PIECE No 9.

-RM FURNITURE.

S.D. ON SHEET No. 12.

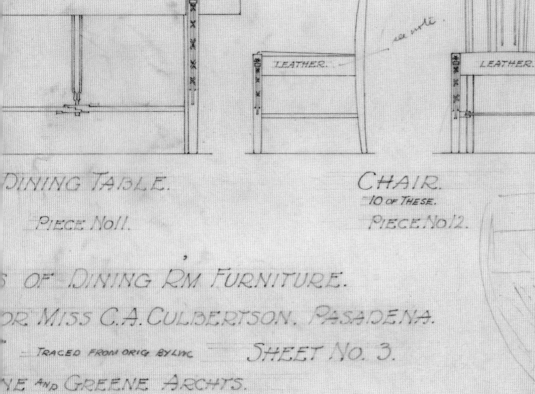

TABLE TOP CIRCULAR IN PLAN.

LEATHER. LEATHER.

see note. changed to wood — see F.S.D

DINING TABLE. CHAIR.

10 OF THESE.

PIECE No II. PIECE No 12.

S OF DINING RM FURNITURE.

OR MISS C.A. CULBERTSON. PASADENA.

TRACED FROM ORIG BY LWC SHEET No. 3.

NE AND GREENE ARCHTS.

PASADENA.

A Century Later

"A man may die, nations may rise and fall, but an idea lives on."
JOHN F. KENNEDY

In the early years of the 20th century, Charles and Henry Greene designed, and Peter and John Hall and their workmen built an impressive body of work, including some of the most highly regarded pieces to arise from the Arts & Crafts movement. A century later, an ever broader audience appreciates the Greene & Greene legacy thanks to the efforts of many individuals. These include the enlightened owners of Greene & Greene houses, museum curators, the staff of The Gamble House and a number of craftsmen who continue the craft of the Greenes and Halls by creating new works in their style. This latter group includes many talented woodworkers, glass artists and architects — far too many to discuss here. Instead we highlight three individuals responsible for inspired, and inspiring, reproductions and new creations, and one destination that introduces visitors to the Greene & Greene style in a magical setting.

Clearly inspired by Greene & Greene, this hanging lantern pays homage but is also original. Note the variation in width of the lead work. Woodwork by Thomas Stangeland. Dining room lantern, 2006, John Hamm.

John Hamm

Each fall, on the third weekend in October, Pasadena plays host to a highly anticipated event — Craftsman Weekend. A venture of Pasadena Heritage, Craftsman Weekend gives visitors the opportunity to tour historic homes, including bungalows in Pasadena's Bungalow Heaven neighborhood and, quite often, a house by Greene & Greene. Houses on the schedule in recent years have included the Cordelia Culbertson house, the Edgar Camp house, the Caroline de Forest house, the Laurabelle Robinson house and the Freeman Ford house. In addition, each year the weekend includes a marketplace where antique dealers and craftspeople exhibit and sell their wares. Included in the market-place is a silent auction.

During Craftsman Weekend 2007, I bid on a beautiful, small art glass panel made by one of the exhibitors. Looking as though it was straight out of a Greene & Greene house, this piece already had a place in my home, if only in my mind. That's as close as it came to my home — I was outbid. I learned later that the successful bidder was 12 years old, I had lost to a

While this window frame is obviously Greene & Greene, the glass is not. The birds are hand-cut from lead sheet. Window, 2008, John Hamm.

child. Apparently, a well-funded child. More than two years later, I can still see that beautiful stained glass, by Southern California artist John Hamm, so similar in style to the wonderful work of Emil Lange.

John Hamm knows the work of Greene & Greene. He is a long-time docent at the Gamble house and has done conservation work there. His work — reproduction, conservation or original — also appears in the Freeman Ford house, the William Thorsen house, the Laurabelle Robinson house and the Robert Blacker house. The glass in the Blacker front doors and tran-som, three layers thick, is by John, done in the late 1980s after the original doors were removed from the house and sold.

John does not work exclusively in the style of Greene & Greene. His portfolio is varied and includes traditional work, modern designs and at least one Tif-fany lamp reproduction. The methods used are varied as well to suit the project. For the organic feel required for some Greene & Greene pieces, he uses copper foil construction to facilitate the broad variation in the width of the leading, while many other jobs call for more conventional lead came assembly. Regardless of the technique, the results are beautiful and worthy of a place alongside the original work so stunningly executed by Emil Lange a century ago.

Darrell Peart

Seattle-based woodworker Darrell Peart designs and builds high-quality furniture in the spirit of Greene & Greene. While Darrell does make some reproductions, he is best known for his original pieces. In particular, his line of Aurora case pieces are a wonderful modern interpretation of the Greene & Greene aesthetic. Modern in this context means well-suited to a 21st century home, with pieces such as a media cabinet (100 years ago, a media cabinet had another name: magazine

ABOVE Combining the Greene & Greene vocabulary with his own touches (drawer pulls, curved, lifted rails) makes this piece both familiar and new. Media cabinet, 2007, Darrell Peart.

RIGHT A tsuba-inspired top with a more traditional rectangular base makes for a light, modern interpretation in this piece. Tsuba table, 2009, Darrell Peart.

stand). As one would expect of studio furniture, fit and finish are perfect. This may help explain a backlog of work that often approaches a year.

In addition to making furniture, Darrell writes frequently about topics related to the work of Greene & Greene. His book, *Greene & Greene: Design Elements for the Workshop* is a must have for any woodworker with an interest in the Greenes. Each year Darrell teaches a handful of woodworking classes at the William Ng School of Fine Woodworking in Southern California and the Port Townsend School of Woodworking in Washington.

Jim Ipekjian

Jim Ipekjian has the distinct pleasure of working in Pasadena, California, home to most of the houses designed by Greene & Greene. His shop is a short drive from the Gamble house (one might be tempted to say "short walk" except in Southern California). At any given time, it is quite likely that the shop contains a Greene & Greene reproduction in some state of semi-completion. Jim's reputation has been built, and maintained, on such pieces — exquisite reproductions of Greene & Greene designs. His relationships with clients are often ongoing and long lasting. He has been involved with the restoration of the Blacker house for roughly 15 years.

Jim's pieces are all but indistinguishable from originals. In fact, he marks each piece to ensure that there is never a question as to its origin. Impressively, Jim creates each piece from start to finish, including inlays and glass. It is likely that no living person knows more about Greene & Greene furniture. Because of that knowledge, Jim leads the monthly Details & Joinery tours at

TOP AND ABOVE Many hobbyist woodworkers create furniture in the Greene & Greene style. This piece includes pegs, lifts, finger joints, breadboard ends and "sunburst stiles" that draw from elements in windows at the Gamble house. Chest, 2007, David Mathias.

ABOVE   Accurately recreating an inlay such as this may be more difficult than making it the first time. Detail, Blacker living room desk, c. 2006, Jim Ipekjian.

LEFT   Is it real or is it Ipekjian? Faithful re-implementations of original Greene & Greene designs . Detail, Blacker living room armchair, c. 2007, Jim Ipekjian.

the Gamble house, giving participants a rare opportunity to examine original pieces and ask questions of one of the few people who might know the answer.

Lodge at Torrey Pines

As mentioned in the Preface, the Lodge at Torrey Pines is located on a magnificent site overlooking the Pacific Ocean in La Jolla, California. The current incarnation of the lodge, one befitting the setting, is a recent invention. Once more like a roadside motel than a high end hotel, the Lodge at Torrey Pines is now a monument to the best work of Charles and Henry Greene. The public spaces of the lodge contain elements from the Gamble, Blacker, Thorsen and Pratt houses, somehow incorporated into a structure that must meet the rigorous building codes of a modern hotel.

On approaching the lodge, one rounds a bend and encounters a porte cochere inspired by that at

the Blacker house, signaling even the uninitiated that this is a unique inn. Walking through the art glass entrance, one enters the lobby, which is the most satisfying of the lodge's Greene & Greene vignettes. It is a very inviting spot with architectural details and furniture working in concert to achieve a warmth seldom found in a hotel. The dining room of the signature restaurant is also quite compelling, complete with Blacker basket lanterns in the center of the room and Gamble hanging lanterns at booths around the perimeter. Enhancing the experience are truly outstanding food and service. The energy that owner Bill Evans brought to creating the lodge has continued in the way that it is run. As with Greene & Greene, attention to detail — in this case, for customer care — is paramount.

That statement applies as well to the work of John Hamm, Darrell Peart and Jim Ipekjian. Whether consciously or subconsciously, each pays tribute to Greene & Greene not only with the work that they produce but also with the way in which they work. Paying attention to the details, and getting them right, was one of the keys to the success enjoyed by Charles and Henry Greene. So it is in the present day. Some, it would seem, still recognize the extraordinary and are willing to engage talented craftsmen in order to obtain it.

TOP With the Pacific Ocean and sunset through the window and a multitude of Greene & Greene-inspired furniture and decorative arts, this is a very inviting spot. Lobby, The Lodge at Torrey Pines, La Jolla, 2002.

ABOVE It is unlikely that any other hotel in the world has an entrance similar to this one. As was true 100 years ago, there are cheaper ways to build but arguably none more beautiful. Detail of east façade, The Lodge at Torrey Pines.

Afterword

"A man will turn over half a library to make one book."
Samuel Johnson

During two days in September, 2009, I drove roundtrip from Columbus, Ohio to Boston, Massachusetts. Roughly 25 hours of driving in a 36-hour period. The reason? The Museum of Fine Arts, Boston, had granted me permission to photograph the Freeman Ford serving table while it was there as part of the Gamble house centennial exhibition. Thirteen months earlier, I had made a similar whirlwind trip to the High Museum of Art in Atlanta. There were other, less grueling trips to Detroit, Pittsburgh, Cleveland and St. Louis. And, three trips to California, including one circuit from Pasadena to Berkeley to Carmel and back.

I have no idea how many hours I spent driving, photographing, researching and writing. It's probably best that way. If I could divide any income to be derived from this venture by the number of hours invested, I would certainly be in violation of minimum wage laws. But no one with any sense undertakes a project such as this for money. Nor do they do it for fame. Neither is a likely outcome. So what causes someone to do this? For me, and I suspect for others, the reason is quite simple: a love for the work of Charles and Henry Greene, a profound respect for their many accomplishments and a desire to share the beauty and inspiration with others. I can't imagine any other professional circumstance for which I would drive 1,550 miles in a day and a half. The fact is, despite the long hours and bleary eyes, I loved every minute of it.

There are many ways to label the last two years, during which I've worked on this book. They have been a tremendous learning experience. To be sure, they have been a lot of hard work. But, the way I think about these years is that they have been a genuine privilege. It's been a privilege to meet so many wonderful people. Without exception, every homeowner, curator, registrar, librarian and staff member has been gracious and generous. It has been a privilege to work with my editor, David Thiel. His enthusiasm and his willingness to compromise in pursuit of an uncompromised result, has made this process a pleasure. It has been a privilege to share this experience with those brave enough to undertake to read this, the end result of these years. Foremost, however, is the privilege of witnessing firsthand the incredible houses and furniture designed by Charles and Henry Greene.

Anyone who has read this far must understand that this is not a critical work. It was never my purpose to turn an impartial eye toward Greene & Greene, to evaluate their output objectively. I am a convert, an unabashed zealot. Though not generally given to proselytizing, I embarked on a crusade, albeit one with a modest goal. If a few readers gain an appreciation for the work of the Greenes through this book, then the effort will have been entirely rewarding.

This process has given me a greatly increased respect for writers. Writing is work. Writing well is arduous. Beginning is almost impossible. It is humbling to recognize that all of the agony over how to organize the information, all of the internal debates about word choice, all of the hours spent reading and rewriting are of little consequence. The photographs, and by extension the houses and furniture, are far more important. To say that a photograph is worth a thousand words is to sell the photograph short. To put it another way, it is not difficult to imagine this book with photos but no text, but it is impossible to imagine it with text but no photos. This has, of course, been a great gift. In the end, no one will remember what's been written here. All they will remember is the beauty and grace created by a small number of men a century ago. And that is exactly as it should be.

Photo Credits

COVER: Courtesy of The Gamble House, USC. Photo by David Mathias.

PAGE 1: Courtesy of The Gamble House, USC. Photo by David Mathias.

PAGE 2-3: Courtesy of The Gamble House, USC. Photo by David Mathias.

PAGE 5: upper: Photo by David Mathias. Author photo Courtesy of The Los Angeles County Museum of Art. Photo by Tom Moore.

PAGE 6: The Nelson-Atkins Museum of Art, Kansas City, Missouri. Purchase: acquired through the generosity of Mr. and Mrs. R. Hugh Uhlmann, F91-23. Photo by John Lamberton.

PAGE 7: Photo by David Mathias.

PAGE 8: Photo by David Mathias.

PAGE 9: Courtesy of Sigma Phi. Photo by David Mathias.

PAGE 11: Courtesy of The Gamble House, USC. Photo by David Mathias.

PAGE 12: inset: Courtesy of The Gamble House, USC. Photos by David Mathias.

PAGE 13: Courtesy of The Gamble House, USC. Photo by David Mathias.

PAGE 14: Courtesy of The Gamble House, USC. Photos by David Mathias.

PAGE 15: Courtesy of Sigma Phi. Photo by David Mathias.

PAGE 16: lower: Courtesy of The Gamble House, USC. Photos by David Mathias.

PAGE 17: Courtesy of The Gamble House, USC. Photos by David Mathias.

PAGE 18: Designed by Charles Sumner Greene (American, 1868-1957), executed by Peter Hall Manufacturing. Secretary, 1911. Mahogany with inlays of various woods, 208.3 x 137.8 x 61.0 cm. The Cleveland Museum of Art. Gift of Mrs. John A. Hadden 1981.76.

PAGE 19: Courtesy of The Gamble House, USC. Photo by David Mathias

PAGE 20: Photo by David Mathias.

PAGE 21: Photo by David Mathias.

PAGE 22: Photos by David Mathias.

PAGE 23: upper: Courtesy of The Hungtington Library, Art Collections and Botanical Gardens. Photo by David Mathias. lower: Courtesy of Guardian Stewardship.

PAGE 24: inset: Photo by David Mathias. lower: Courtesy of Bruce Smith.

PAGE 25: Manual Training School Collection, University Archives, Department of Special Collections, Washington University Libraries.

PAGE 26: From the collection of David Mathias.

PAGE 27: left: Courtesy of Christie's. right: High Museum of Art, Atlanta; Virginia Carroll Crawford Collection, 1985.320. Photo by David Mathias.

PAGE 28: Courtesy of Guardian Stewardship.

PAGE 29: upper: Courtesy of Guardian Stewardship. lower: Private collection. Photos by David Mathias.

PAGE 30-31: Photo by David Mathias.

PAGE 32: Photo by David Mathias.

PAGE 33: upper: *Western Architect*, Vol. 13-14, April 1909. lower: Courtesy of Guardian Stewardship.

PAGE 34: Courtesy of Westridge School. Photo by David Mathias.

PAGE 35: Courtesy of The Gamble House, USC. Photo by David Mathias.

PAGE 36-37: Photo by David Mathias.

PAGE 38: Photo by David Mathias.

PAGE 39: Courtesy of Hirschl & Adler Galleries.

PAGE 40: upper: Courtesy of The Gamble House, USC. lower: Courtesy of Guardian Stewardship. Photos by David Mathias.

PAGE 41: Courtesy of The Gamble House, USC. Photo by David Mathias.

PAGE 42: lower: Courtesy of The Gamble House, USC. Photos by David Mathias.

PAGE 43: Photo by David Mathias.

PAGE 44: Sketch by Clay Lancaster. Courtesy of the Warwick Foundation.

PAGE 45: Courtesy of Gary Hall.

PAGE 46: Courtesy of Guardian Stewardship.

PAGE 47: Photo by David Mathias.

PAGE 48: *The Craftsman*, Vol. 1 No. 1, October 1901.

PAGE 49: upper: Sketch by Clay Lancaster. Courtesy of the Warwick Foundation. lower: Photo by Tom Moore.

PAGE 50: *House Beautiful*, Vol. 102, No. 8, August 1960. Photo by Ezra Stoller.

PAGE 51: *House Beautiful*, Vol. 102, No. 8, August 1960.

PAGE 52: Courtesy R. H. Porter Family. Photographs © 2009 Museum of Fine Arts, Boston. Reproduced with permission. Photos by David Mathias.

PAGE 53: Photo by David Mathias.

PAGE 54: Courtesy of the Western Historical Manuscript Collection – University of Missouri-St. Louis.

PAGE 55: Photo by David Mathias.

PAGE 56: upper: Edward S. Morse, *Japanese Homes and Their Surroundings*. Courtesy of Dover Publications. lower: International Studio, Vol. XXX, January 1907.

PAGE 57: lower: Courtesy of the Huntington Library, Art Collections and Botanical Gardens. Photos by David Mathias.

PAGE 58: Photo by David Mathias (with respect to Julius Shulman).

PAGE 59: upper: Photo by David Mathias. lower: From the collection of Geoffrey Goldberg.

PAGE 60-61: Photo by David Mathias.

PAGE 61: Sketch by Clay Lancaster. Courtesy of the Warwick Foundation.

PAGE 62: *House Beautiful*, Vol. 36, No. 1, June 1914.

PAGE 63: *House Beautiful*, Vol. 36, No. 1, June 1914.

PAGE 64: Photo by David Mathias.

PAGE 65: *House and Garden*, Vol. 12, No. 2, August 1907.

PAGE 66: lower: Courtesy of The Gamble House, USC. Photos by David Mathias.

PAGE 67: Courtesy of The Gamble House, USC. Photo by David Mathias.

PAGE 68: The Nelson-Atkins Museum of Art, Kansas City,

Missouri. Purchase: acquired through the generosity of Mr. and Mrs. R. Hugh Uhlmann, F91-23. Photo by John Lamberton.

PAGE 69: David B. Gamble house, Charles Sumner Greene Collection, Environmental Design Archives, University of California-Berkeley.

PAGE 70: upper: Courtesy of The Gamble House, USC. Photos by David Mathias.

PAGE 71: Photos by David Mathias.

PAGE 72-73: Charles M. Pratt house, Charles Sumner Greene Collection, Environmental Design Archives, University of California-Berkeley.

PAGE 74: Courtesy of Sigma Phi. Photo by Tom Moore.

PAGE 75: Minneapolis Institute of Arts, The Putnam Dana McMillan Fund.

PAGE 76: upper: Charles Sumner Greene (American, 1868-1957) & Henry Mather Greene (American, 1870-1954); Side Chair c. 1908; mahogany, ebony and leather; 37⅞" x 20" x 18½"; Carnegie Museum of Art, Pittsburgh. Photograph © 2008 Carnegie Museum of Art, Pittsburgh. lower: Courtesy of The Gamble House, USC. Photo by David Mathias.

PAGE 77: Charles M. Pratt house, Charles Sumner Greene Collection, Environmental Design Archives, University of California-Berkeley.

PAGE 78: upper: Courtesy of The Gamble House, USC. lower: Courtesy of the Detroit Institute of Arts. Photos by David Mathias.

PAGE 79: upper: Courtesy of the Huntington Library, Art Collections and Botanical Gardens. Photo by David Mathias. lower: Greene & Greene Archives, The Gamble House, USC.

PAGE 80: Courtesy of The Gamble House, USC. Photo by David Mathias.

PAGE 81: Photo by David Mathias.

PAGE 82-83: Charles S. Greene house, Charles Sumner Greene Collection, Environmental Design Archives, University of California-Berkeley.

PAGE 84: Courtesy of Westridge School. Photo by David Mathias.

PAGE 85: Sidney D. Gamble photographs, Duke University Rare Book, Manuscript, and Special Collections Library.

PAGE 86: Arthur A. Libby house, Charles Sumner Greene Collection, Environmental Design Archives, University of California-Berkeley.

PAGE 87: lower: Courtesy of The Gamble House, USC. Photos by David Mathias.

PAGE 88: *Architectural Record*, Vol. 20, October 1906.

PAGE 89: Photo by David Mathias.

PAGE 90: upper: As reproduced in William S. B. Dana, The Swiss Chalet Book, William T. Comstock, Co., New York, 1913. lower: Courtesy of Archives and Special Collections, Dickinson College, Carlisle, PA.

PAGE 91: Photo by David Mathias.

PAGE 92: Photo by David Mathias..

PAGE 93: lower: Courtesy of the Huntington Library, Art Collections and Botanical Gardens; Gift of D.J. Puffert in honor

of his daughter, Tiffany K. Puffert, and the Virginia Steele Scott Foundation. Photos by David Mathias.

PAGE 94: lower: Courtesy of The Gamble House, USC. Photos by David Mathias.

PAGE 95: Courtesy R. H. Porter Family and the Huntington Library, Art Collections and Botanical Gardens. Photo by David Mathias.

PAGE 96: Courtesy of The Gamble House, USC. Photo by David Mathias.

PAGE 97: left: Courtesy of Guardian Stewardship. Photo courtesy of Sotheby's. right: Courtesy of The Gamble House, USC. Photo by David Mathias.

PAGE 98: Minneapolis Institute of Arts, The Putnam Dana McMillan Fund.

PAGE 99: Charles Sumner Greene (American, 1868-1957) & Henry Mather Greene (American, 1870-1954); Side Chair c. 1908; mahogany, ebony and leather; 37⅞" x 20" x 18½"; Carnegie Museum of Art, Pittsburgh. Photograph © 2008 Carnegie Museum of Art, Pittsburgh.

PAGE 100-101: Freeman A. Ford house, Charles Sumner Greene Collection, Environmental Design Archives, University of California-Berkeley.

PAGE 102: Courtesy of Sigma Phi. Photo by David Mathias.

PAGE 103: Sketch from Kazuo Nishi and Kazuo Hozumi, *What is Japanese Architecture Architecture?: A Survey of Traditional Japanese Architecture*, Kodansha International, Tokyo, 1996. Courtesy of Kazuo Hozumi and Kodansha International.

PAGE 104: upper: Greene & Greene Archives, The Gamble House, USC. Lower: Courtesy of the Huntington Library, Art Collections and Botanical Gardens. Photo by David Mathias.

PAGE 105: left: From the collection of Randell Makinson. right and lower: Courtesy of The Gamble House, USC. Photos by David Mathias.

PAGE 106-107: Greene & Greene Archives, The Gamble House, USC.

PAGE 108: Courtesy of the Detroit Institute of Arts. Photo by David Mathias.

PAGE 109: upper: Saint Louis Art Museum, Friends Endowment and funds given by the Marjorie Wyman Endowment Fund, the Joseph H. and Elizabeth Bascom Trust, the Richard Brumbaugh Trust in memory of Richard Irving Brumbaugh and Grace Lischer Brumbaugh, an anonymous donor, and the Allen P. and Josephine B. Green Foundation. lower: Courtesy of The Gamble House, USC. Photos by David Mathias.

PAGE 110: Courtesy of The Gamble House, USC. Photo by David Mathias.

PAGE 111: upper: Courtesy of Jim Ipekjian. Photo by David Mathias. lower: The Nelson-Atkins Museum of Art, Kansas City, Missouri. Purchase: acquired through the generosity of Mr. and Mrs. R. Hugh Uhlmann, F91-23. Photo by John Lamberton.

PAGE 112: Courtesy of the Huntington Library, Art Collections and Botanical Gardens. Photo by David Mathias.

PAGE 113: upper: Courtesy of Sigma Phi. Photo by Darrell Peart. lower: Photos by David Mathias.

PAGE 114: left: Designed by Charles Sumner Greene (American, 1868-1957), executed by Peter Hall Manufacturing. Secretary, 1911. Mahogany with inlays of various woods, 208.3 x 137.8 x 61.0 cm. The Cleveland Museum of Art. Gift of Mrs. John A. Hadden 1981.76. right: Courtesy of Sigma Phi. Photo by David Mathias.

PAGE 115: upper: Courtesy of The Gamble House, USC. lower: Courtesy of Sigma Phi. Photos by David Mathias.

PAGE 116: upper: Photo by David Mathias. lower: Photo by Tom Moore.

PAGE 117: upper: Courtesy of The Gamble House, USC. lower: Courtesy of Sigma Phi. Photos by David Mathias.

PAGE 118: Courtesy of The Gamble House, USC. Photo by David Mathias.

PAGE 119: upper: Courtesy of The Gamble House, USC. Photo by David Mathias. lower: Belle Barlow Bush Furniture, Charles Sumner Greene Collection, Environmental Design Archives, University of California-Berkeley.

PAGE 120-121: Photo by David Mathias.

PAGE 122: The Nelson-Atkins Museum of Art, Kansas City, Missouri. Purchase: acquired through the generosity of Mr. and Mrs. R. Hugh Uhlmann, F91-23. Photo by John Lamberton.

PAGE 123: The Nelson-Atkins Museum of Art, Kansas City, Missouri. Purchase: acquired through the generosity of Mr. and Mrs. R. Hugh Uhlmann, F91-23. Photos by John Lamberton.

PAGE 124-125 Robert R. Blacker house, Charles Sumner Greene Collection, Environmental Design Archives, University of California-Berkeley.

PAGE 126: Courtesy of The Gamble House, USC. Photo by David Mathias.

PAGE 127: left: William R. Thorsen house, Charles Sumner Greene Collection, Environmental Design Archives, University of California-Berkeley. right: Courtesy of The Gamble House, USC. Photo by David Mathias.

PAGE 128-129: upper: Saint Louis Art Museum, Friends Endowment, the Marjorie Wyman Endowment Fund, the Joseph H. and Elizabeth E. Bascom Trust, the Richard Brumbaugh Trust in memory of Richard Irving Brumbaugh and Grace Lischer Brumbaugh, funds given by an anonymous donor, and the Allen P. and Josephine B. Green Foundation. Photos by David Mathias.

PAGE 129: lower: Courtesy of The Gamble House, USC. Photo by David Mathias.

PAGE 130: Courtesy of The Gamble House, USC. Photo by David Mathias.

PAGE 131: left: Courtesy of Guardian Stewardship. Photo by David Mathias. right: Courtesy of Christie's. lower: Photo by David Mathias.

PAGE 132-133: Cordelia Culbertson house, Charles Sumner Greene Collection, Environmental Design Archives, University of California-Berkeley.

PAGE 134: Courtesy of the Detroit Institute of Arts. Photo by David Mathias.

PAGE 135: upper: Courtesy of The Gamble House, USC. Photos by David Mathias.

PAGE 136-137: William T. Bolton house, Charles Sumner Greene Collection, Environmental Design Archives, University of California-Berkeley.

PAGE 138: upper: Courtesy of Guardian Stewardship. lower: Photo by David Mathias.

PAGE 139: left: Courtesy of Sigma Phi. Right: Courtesy of The Gamble House, USC. Photos by David Mathias.

PAGE 140: Saint Louis Art Museum, Friends Endowment and funds given by the Marjorie Wyman Endowment Fund, the Joseph H. and Elizabeth Bascom Trust, the Richard Brumbaugh Trust in memory of Richard Irving Brumbaugh and Grace Lischer Brumbaugh, an anonymous donor, and the Allen P. and Josephine B. Green Foundation. Photo by David Mathias.

PAGE 141: upper: Geoffrey Diner Gallery. Photo courtesy of Sotheby's. lower: Photo by David Mathias.

PAGE 142-143: Mrs. L.G. and Miss Marion Porter house, Charles Sumner Greene Collection, Environmental Design Archives, University of California-Berkeley.

PAGE 144: Photo by David Mathias.

PAGE 145: Courtesy of The Gamble House, USC. Photo by David Mathias.

PAGE 146: Photo by David Mathias.

PAGE 147: Courtesy of The Gamble House, USC. Photo by David Mathias.

PAGE 148: David B. Gamble house, Charles Sumner Greene Collection, Environmental Design Archives, University of California-Berkeley.

PAGE 149: Courtesy of Sigma Phi. Photo by David Mathias.

PAGE 150: upper: Courtesy of Sigma Phi. right: Courtesy of The Gamble House, USC. Photos by David Mathias.

PAGE 151: Greene & Greene Archives, The Gamble House, USC.

PAGE 152-153: Courtesy of Warner Bros. Studios. Photos by David Mathias.

PAGE 154: upper: From the collection of Daniel Wolf. Photo courtesy of Sotheby's.

PAGE 154 (LOWER) & 155: Designed by Charles Sumner Greene (American, 1868-1957), executed by Peter Hall Manufacturing. Secretary, 1911. Mahogany with inlays of various woods, 208.3 x 137.8 x 61.0 cm. The Cleveland Museum of Art. Gift of Mrs. John A. Hadden 1981.76.

PAGE 156-157: Cordelia Culbertson house, Charles Sumner Greene Collection, Environmental Design Archives, University of California-Berkeley.

PAGE 158: inset: Photo by David Mathias. lower: Photograph by homeowner.

PAGE 159: Photograph by John Hamm.

PAGE 160: : upper: Photo by Richard McNamee. lower: Photo by Darrell Peart.

PAGE 161: Photos by Al Parrish.

PAGE 162: Photos by Jim and John Ipekjian.

PAGE 163: Courtesy of The Lodge at Torrey Pines. Photos by David Mathias.

PAGE 165: Photo by David Mathias.

BACK COVER: Photos by David Mathias.

Endnotes

GREENE & GREENE: AN INTRODUCTION

PG. 17 1. "A Special Citation to Henry Mather Greene and Charles Sumner Greene," *Journal of the American Institute of Architects*, 18 (July 1952), pp. 4-5.

2. Jean Murray Bangs, Greene & Greene, *Architectural Forum*, Vol. 89, No. 4, October 1948, p. 88.

PG. 19 3. M. H. Baillie Scott, *On the Choice of Simple Furniture*, The Studio, Vol. 10, No. 49, April 1897.

4. Jean Murray Bangs, *Greene & Greene, Architectural Forum*, Vol. 89, No. 4, October 1948, p. 86.

5. Henry Greene, quoted in "Domestic Architecture in the West", *The Craftsman*, Vol. 22, No. 5, August 1912, p. 536.

6. As quoted in Randell L. Makinson and Thomas A. Heinz, *Greene & Greene – Creating a Style*, Gibbs Smith, Salt Lake City, 2004, p. 25.

7. Anne Mallek, "The Beauty of a House: Charles Greene, the Morris Movement, and James Culbertson", in *A New and Native Beauty: The Art and Craft of Greene & Greene*, Merrell, London, 2008, pp. 32-35.

PG. 20 8. William Morris, "The Beauty of Life", Reprinted in *Hopes and Fears for Art*. Roberts Brothers, Boston, 1882, p. 108.

9. William Morris, "An Address Delivered in Support of the Society for the Protection of Ancient Buildings", London, 1882.

10. One should not assume that the attention to detail exhibited by Greene & Greene is the result of exposure to the writings of William Morris. It is likely that they arrived independently at the same conclusion.

11. According to *Brewer's Famous Quotations* (Nigel Rees, Sterling Publishing Company, Inc., 2006, p. 391), this quote is found nowhere is Ruskin's available writings. However, Ruskin's writings are certainly sympathetic with the sentiment.

12. "Domestic Architecture in the West", *The Craftsman*, Vol. 22, No. 5, August 1912, p. 547.

13. In a June 5, 1903, letter to Lucretia Garfield, Charles wrote, "The reason why the beams project from the gables is because they cast such beautiful shadows on the sides of the house in this bright atmosphere." In this case Charles referred to beams rather than rafters but the effect is certainly similar.

PG. 22 14. Anne Mallek, "The Beauty of a House: Charles Greene, the Morris Movement, and James Culbertson", in *A New and Native Beauty: The Art and Craft of Greene & Greene*, Merrell, London, 2008, p.29.

A BRIEF HISTORY

PG. 24 1. Much of this paragraph gleaned from: Edward R. Bosley, *Greene & Greene*, Phaidon Press Limited, London, 2000, pp. 8-10.

2. Supporters of the movement were many. Former President Rutherford B. Hayes, as a member of the Ohio State University Board of Trustees, proposed a Department of Manual Training for the university. The proposal was adopted though opposed, before and after the fact, by some faculty. Ross A. Norris, "The Cultured Mind the Skillful Hand: A Story About Art Education at the Ohio State University and Some Other Places", unpublished manuscript, pp. 83-84.

3. Calvin Milton Woodward, *The Manual Training School*, Ayer Publishing, Manchester, NH, 1969 (Reprint of 1887 edition).

PG. 25 4. The motto appears on numerous documents, including letterhead, pertaining to the Manual Training School. It was also engraved on a medal given each year to a top student.

5. Virginia Greene Hales and Bruce Smith, *Charles and Henry Greene, A New and Native Beauty: The Art and Craft of Greene & Greene*, Merrell, London, 2008, p. 42.

6. Manual Training School Prospectus, 1882-83, Washington University Archives, Washington University in St. Louis, St. Louis.

PG. 26 7. Woodward, *The Manual Training School*, pp. 38-49.

8. Bosley, *Greene & Greene*, pp. 14-18.

9. Kevin Starr, *Inventing the Dream — California Through the Progressive Era*, Oxford University Press, New York, 1985, pp. 54-55.

10. Bosley, *Greene & Greene*, p. 25.

11. Ibid. p. 26.

PG. 27 12. Thanks to Tom Moore for exploring this line of reasoning.

PG. 28 13. The Culbertson house is still lovely though very different — an heir had the second story removed and made other significant modifications. The changes, designed by architects Smith and Williams were at least sympathetic to the original.

14. Anne Mallek, "The Beauty of a House: Charles Greene, the Morris Movement, and James Culbertson", *A New and Native Beauty: The Art and Craft of Greene & Greene*, Merrell, London, 2008, pp. 18-24.

15. Thanks to Edward Bosley for clarifying the composition of the Darling house foundation.

16. Bosley, *Greene & Greene*, pp. 54-57. The drawing appeared in *Academy Architecture*, Vol. 24, 1903.

17. Ted Wells, "Greene & Greene in Long Beach: The Reeve-Townsend House," (Part 1 of 3), October 26, 2005. Podcast retrieved from twls.libsyn.com/index.php?post_year=2005&post_month=10.

18. Ted Wells, "Greene & Greene in Long Beach: The Adelaide Tichenor House," (Part 2 of 3), October 27, 2005. Podcast retrieved from twls.libsyn.com/index.php?post_year=2005&post_month=10.

PG. 29 19. Randell Makinson, "Greene & Greene: The Adelaide Tichenor House", *The Tabby*, Vol. 1, No. 3, July/August 1997, pp. 23-28.

PG. 30 20. The Greenes created furniture primarily for public areas of the house.

PG. 32 21. Bosley, *Greene & Greene*, p. 74.

22. 1½-inch scale details of desk and chair for living room, furniture drawing No. 4, Charles Millard Pratt house. Environmental Design Archives, College of Environmental Design, University of California at Berkeley. Thanks to Rich Muller for pointing out this detail.

PG. 34 23. Bosley, *Greene & Greene*, pp. 227-236.

PG. 36 24. *Merriam-Webster Online Dictionary*, 2008. www.merriam-webster.com/dictionary.

25. Arthur David (pseudonym for Herbert Croly) described a California bungalow as possessing these additional qualities: "Its whole purpose is to minimize the distinction which exists between being inside and outside four walls. The rooms of such a building should consequently be spacious, they should not be shut off any more than is necessary one from another, and they should be finished in wood simply designed and stained so as to keep so far as possible its natural texture and hue. The exterior on the other hand, should not be made to count very strongly in the landscape. It should sink, so far as possible, its architectural individuality and tend to disappear in its natural background."

Architectural Record, Vol. 20, October 1906, p. 310. David has overstated the extent to which a bungalow should forsake its identity but has captured a defining characteristic of Southern California homes. For further descriptions and discussion of bungalows, see Clay Lancaster, "The American Bungalow", *The Art Bulletin*, Vol. 40, No. 3, September 1958, pp. 239-253; M. H. Lazear, "The Evolution of the Bungalow", *House Beautiful*, Vol. 36, No. 1, June 1914, pp. 2-5; "The California Bungalow", *The Craftsman*, Vol. 13, No. 1, October 1907, pp. 68-80; Seymour E. Locke, Bungalows, "What They Really Are — The Frequent Misapplication of the Name", *House and Garden*, Vol. 12, No. 2, August 1907, pp. 45-53.

26. I am grateful to Bruce Smith for an informative discussion on this topic.

27. Randell Makinson, personal communication. With respect to Mr. Makinson, I continue use of the term here because it is well-recognized and expected.

PG. 37   28. Randell Makinson, Tom Heinz and Brad Pitt, *Greene & Greene: The Blacker House*, Gibbs Smith, Salt Lake City, 2000.

29. As originally built, the house's entry was two stories with a balcony ringing the interior at the second floor. The second story was later removed.

PG. 38   30. Sadly, the Thorsen furniture is no longer in the house. Happily, much of it is on display in the Scott Gallery of the Huntington Library, Art Collections and Botanical Gardens in San Marino, California.

PG. 39   31. The last three paragraphs are condensed from Bosley, *Greene & Greene*.

OF ENGLAND, NEW YORK, JAPAN AND CALIFORNIA

PG. 42   1. The marvelous James Culbertson house, for example, was shorn of its second story, its first story enlarged and otherwise altered. The addition is decidedly more modern than the original house. See, for example, Carolyn S. Murray, "A Great Old House Lives On", *House Beautiful*, Vol. 105, February 1962, pp. 118-123. One can argue that the renovation saved the house from demolition and was, therefore, beneficial.

PG. 43   2. Yost was not alone in his good fortune. Clay Lancaster noted, "Like the Gamble house, the Pratt house still contains much furniture designed and built by the Greene brothers." "The American Bungalow", *The Art Bulletin*, Vol. 40, No. 3, September 1958, p. 248. Jean Murray Bangs was more impressively privileged. She came to possess hundreds of original drawings of Greene & Greene works.

3. L. Morgan Yost, "Greene & Greene of Pasadena", *Journal of the Society of Architectural Historians*, Vol. 9, No. 1-2, March-May 1950, p. 11.

4. Chicago Architects Oral History Project, The Ernest R. Graham Study Center for Architectural Drawings, Department of Architecture, The Art Institute of Chicago, 1986 (Revised Edition Copyright 2000).

5. Ibid.

PG. 44   6. Ibid.

7. Yost, "Greene & Greene of Pasadena", p. 13.

8. Clay Lancaster, "The American Bungalow", *The Art Bulletin*, Vol. 40, No. 3, September 1958, p. 253.

PG. 45   9. Charles Sumner Greene, "California Home Making", *Pasadena Daily News*, Jan. 2, 1905, p. 26.

10. See for example, Charles Robert Ashbee, *A Few Chapters in Workshop Re-construction and Citizenship*, Guild and School of Handicraft, London, 1894. The second chapter has the wonderful title: On the need for the cultivation of the sense of Beauty and the questionable wisdom of looking for this from the British Middle Class.

PG. 46   11. Thorstein Veblen, "Arts and Crafts", *The Journal of Political Economy*, Vol. 11, No. 1, December 1902, p. 110. On the preceding page, Veblen prefaces the quoted conclusion thus: "Modern industry, in so far as it is characteristically modern, means the machine process; but according to the arts-and-crafts apprehension, only outside the machine process is there salvation. Since the machine process is indispensable to modern culture, both on business grounds and for reasons of economy, this limits the immediate scope of the arts-and-crafts salvation to those of higher levels of consumption where exigencies of business and economy are not decisive. The greater (90-99 per cent of the whole) range of industry must under present circumstances of business and household management remain untouched by any such proposed alteration of the character of the industrial process. The `industrial art' methods are too costly for general business purposes, and the `industrial art' products are (in point of fact) too expensive for general consumption; indeed it is of the essence of industrial art products, if they are to pass inspection by the adepts, that they must be sufficiently expensive to preclude their use by the vulgar."

12. Eileen Boris, *Arts and Labor — Ruskin, Morris and the Craftsman Ideal in America*, Temple University Press, Philadelphia, 1986, p. 9.

13. Ernest Batchelder, as quoted in ibid., p.29

PG. 47   14. Charles Robert Ashbee as quoted in ibid., p. 16. Ashbee reportedly wrote this when asked about the metalwork produced at an arts and crafts colony in New York.

15. Ibid, pp. 8-9.

16. Bosley, *Greene & Greene*, p. 38.

17. Gustav Stickley, "An Argument for Simplicity in Household Furnishings", *The Craftsman*, Vol. 1, No. 1, October 1901, p. iii.

PG. 48   18. Ibid, p. iii.

19. Charles Sumner Greene, "California Home Making", *Pasadena Daily News*, January 2, 1905, p. 26.

20. Charles Keeler, *The Simple Home*, Paul Elder, San Francisco, 1904, pp. 30-31.

21. Elmer Grey, "Style in Houses", *House Beautiful*, Vol. 7, March 1900, p. 199.

22. Henrietta P. Keith, "The Trail of Japanese Influence in our modern Domestic Architecture", *The Craftsman*, Vol. 12, No. 4, July 1907, p. 451.

PG. 49   23. Bosley, *Greene & Greene*, p. 39.

PG. 50   24. *House Beautiful*, Vol. 102, No. 8, August 1960.

25. Ralph Adams Cram, *Impressions of Japanese Architecture, Dover Press*, New York, 1966, pp. 30-31. The quoted edition is a reprint of the 1930 edition of the work, which was published originally in 1905. Cram was a devotee of Gothic forms, and thus his concession that even that form never achieved perfection is telling.

26. As quoted in *Japan-ness in Architecture*, Arata Isozaki, MIT Press, Cambridge MA, 2006, p. 36.

PG. 51   27. Curtis Besinger, "Lessons We are Learning from Japan", *House Beautiful*, Vol. 102, No. 9, September 1960, p. 193.

28. Ralph Adams Cram, Preface in *American Country Houses of Today*, Architectural Book Publishing Company, New York, 1913, p. v Cram wrote that, "The California style has Messrs. Greene & Greene and Mr. Mulgardt to set it forth…"

PG. 53   29. Wolf von Eckhardt, "The Just So of the Swerve and Line", *Time*, August 1, 1983.

30. David and Michiko Young, *Spontaneity in Japanese Art and Culture*, 2006, Chapter 3, http://japaneseaesthetics.com.

31. *House Beautiful*, Vol. 102, No. 8, August 1960, p. 120.

32. Ibid, p. 88.

33. The list is not nearly exhaustive as there are many other terms that express notions of beauty in Japanese aesthetics. Some others are Aware, Miyabi, and Wabi-sabi. See, for example, David and Michiko Young, *Spontaneity in Japanese Art and Culture*.

34. *House Beautiful*, August 1960.

35. Jiro Harada, *A Glimpse of Japanese Ideals*, Kokusai Bunka Shinkokai, Tokyo, 1937. As quoted in David and Michiko Young, *Spontaneity in Japanese Art and Culture*.

PG. 54   36. *House Beautiful*, August 1960, pp. 55-56.

37. The cloud scroll was likely brought to Japan by Buddhists. See John Dower, *The Elements of Japanese Design*, Weatherhill, Boston, 1971, p. 40.

PG. 55 38. Stanley Appelbaum, *The Chicago World's Fair of 1893: A Photographic Record — Photos from the Collections of the Avery Library of Columbia University and the Chicago Historical Society*, Courier Dover Publications, New York, 1980, p. 5.

39. Bruce Smith, *Greene & Greene and the Duncan-Irwin House: Developing a California Style*, Gibbs Smith, Salt Lake City, To appear. See also, Randell Makinson, *California Design 1910* (Timothy J. Anderson, Eudorah M. Moore and Robert W. Winter editors), Peregrine Smith, Inc., Salt Lake City, 1980, p. 98. (This is a reprint of the original 1974 edition by California Design Publications.)

40. Bosley, *Greene & Greene*, p. 67.

41. Letter from Adelaide Tichenor to Charles Greene, June 10, 1904. Environmental Design Archives, University of California at Berkeley.

42. Joe Sonderman & Mike Truax, *St. Louis: The 1904 World's Fair (Images of America)*, Arcadia Publishing, Mt. Pleasant, SC, 2008, p. 61.

43. The Main Hall of the Japanese pavilion is significantly smaller than the Shishin-den. Also, for some reason, the building at the fair includes a single gable on the roof on the front elevation. This is not present on the Shishin-den. The Shishin-den is the principle official building of the palace. It includes the throne room where enthronement ceremonies were conducted. See Tadashi Isikawa and Bin Takahashi, *Palaces of Kyoto*. Kodansha International, Tokyo, 1968.

PG. 56 44. Nonie Gadsden, "Greene & Greene: The Boston Years" (lecture), The Huntington Library, Art Collections and Botanical Gardens, San Marino, California, November 8, 2008.

45. Bosley, *Greene & Greene*, p. 42.

46. Randell Makinson notes that due to similarity in form it would appear that Imperial architecture, rather than temple architecture, was the primary influence. *California Design 1910* (Timothy J. Anderson, Eudorah M. Moore and Robert W. Winter editors), Peregrine Smith, Inc., Salt Lake City, 1980, p. 98.

47. Edward S. Morse, *Japanese Homes and Their Surroundings*, reprinted by Dover Publications, New York, 1961, p. 16. (Originally published by Ticknor and Company, 1886).

48. Sarah Handler, *Ming Furniture*. Ten Speed Press, Berkeley, California, 2005, p. 103.

PG. 57 49. Ibid, p. 103.

PG. 58 50. Ibid, p. 19.

51. Ibid, p. 20.

52. M.H. Baillie Scott, "On the Choice of Simple Furniture," *The Studio*, Vol. 10, No. 49, April 1897.

53. Charles Sumner Greene, "Bungalows", *Western Architect*, Vol. 12, July 1908, p. 3. By the time Charles wrote that, the "style of a house" had come to include the contents he had designed in addition to the structure.

PG. 59 54. Michael Cannell, *I.M. Pei Mandarin of Modernism*, Carol Southern Books, New York, 1995, p. 313.

55. "Parks for the People", *The Craftsman*, Vol. 22, No. 5, p. 523, 1912.

PG. 60 56. Alice Batchelder, as quoted in Robert W. Winter, *Arroyo Culture, California Design 1910*, Peregrine Smith, Salt Lake City, 1980 (reprint of 1974 original edition), p. 27.

57. For more on Charles Fletcher Lummis, see *Inventing the Dream* by Kevin Starr or *Charles F. Lummis: Crusader in Corduroy* by Dudley Gordon.

58. For more on George Wharton James, see *Inventing the Dream* by Kevin Starr. James is the author of numerous books on the Southwestern United States.

PG. 62 59. Charles S. Greene, "Bungalows", p. 4.

60. H.A. Reid, "Natural Arroyo Park Caught President's Fancy", *The Pasadena Daily News*, November 26, 1904, p. 10. This article is pasted in the scrap book that Charles and Henry kept beginning and during their time at MIT.

61. Theodore Roosevelt to Charles Fletcher Lummis, as quoted in Robert W. Winter, *Arroyo Culture*, p. 11. Lummis and Roosevelt attended Harvard together and remained friends.

62. "Parks for the People", p. 524.

PG. 63 63. Grace Ellery Channing, "The Meeting of Extremes", *Out West*, Vol. XIX, September 1903, p. 249.

64. Bosley, Greene & Greene, p. 58.

PG. 64 65. Helen Elliott Bandini, *History of California*, American Book Company, New York, 1908, p. 109.

66. According to Bosley, *Greene & Greene*, p. 227, the house cost $2,800. The firm had completed more expensive commissions as early as 1895, the second year of the practice.

67. Excerpt from quote by Elmer Grey in "The California Bungalow", *The Craftsman*, Vol. 13, No. 1, October 1907, p. 73.

PG. 65 68. Charles Keeler, *The Simple Home*, p. 18.

69. Victoria Kastner, "California Country Houses" (lecture), The Huntington Library, Art Collections and Botanical Gardens, San Marino, California, November 8, 2008.

70. Clive Aslet, *The American Country House*, Yale University Press, New Haven, 2004, p. 3.

71. Henry Greene owned a copy of *One Hundred Country Houses* by Aymar Embury (1909). In addition to showing many very grand country residences, the author discusses the Tichenor and Irwin houses in a chapter on Japanesque houses.

72. Florence Williams, "Bungalows of Southern California", *House Beautiful*, Vol. 36, No. 1, June 1914, p 16.

73. *American Country Houses of Today*, Architectural Book Publishing Company, New York, 1913.

74. John Galen Howard, Country House Architecture on the Pacific Coast, *Architectural Record*, Vol. 40, October 1917, pp. 323-355.

75. John Ruskin, Peace (The Eagle's Nest Lecture IX), Reprinted in *Little Masterpieces*, Bliss Perry editor, Doubleday Page & Company, New York, 1903, p. 190.

POEMS OF WOOD AND LIGHT

PG. 66 1. If the quote is accurate, it is unclear whether he originated the phrase. See, for example, Frank Schulze, *Mies Van Der Rohe: A Critical Biography*, University of Chicago Press, 1985, p. 281.

PG. 67 2. I.M. Pei's East Building of the National Gallery serves as an example of detail in modernist architecture. The angle of the triangular building is dictated by the adjacent streets: 19.5 degrees. Pei insisted on propagating that angle throughout the interior of the building even at the cost of convenience, despite the fact that few, if any, would ever notice. Designers in Pei's firm referred to this quality as "Miesian" in reference to the quote mentioned above. See Michael Cannell, *I.M. Pei: Mandarin of Modernism*, Carol Southern Books, New York, 1995, p. 260.

3. For a fascinating discussion on the relationship between Greene & Greene and modernism, see Edward R. Bosley, "Out of the Woods: Greene & Greene and the Modern American House", *A New and Native Beauty: The Art and Craft of Greene & Greene*, Merrell, London, 2008, pp. 230-257.

4. L. Morgan Yost, "Greene & Greene of Pasadena", *Journal of the Society of Architectural Historians*, Vol. 9, No. 1-2, March-May 1950, p. 13.

5. The Gamble House Centennial Exhibition provided a rare opportunity to observe this. When the Exhibition was at the Renwick Gallery in Washington, D.C., the Gamble chiffonier was displayed away from the wall, allowing a view of the back, which is exquisitely constructed and finished using the same materials as the rest of the piece.

PG. 70 6. L. Morgan Yost, "Greene & Greene of Pasadena", *Journal of the Society of Architectural Historians*, Vol. 9, No. 1-2, March-May 1950, p. 13.

7. Morgan Yost addressed this more eloquently than I: "Furniture was designed, not as stock pieces to be used in various houses, but individually. The characteristic details were repeated and carried through but in each case the furniture was thought out as an extension of the design of the house." See Yost, "Greene & Greene of Pasadena", p. 13.

8. John Ruskin, *The Poetry of Architecture: or The Architecture of the Nations of Europe Considered in its Association with Natural Scenery and National Character*, George Allen, London, 1893, pp. 5-6.

PG. 74 9. L. Morgan Yost, "Greene & Greene of Pasadena", p. 19.

PG. 75 10. Edward S. Cooke, Jr., "An International Studio: The Furniture Collaborations of the Greenes and Halls", *A New and Native Beauty: The Art and Craft of Greene & Greene*, Merrill, London, 1908, pp. 111-131.

11. Even after the appearance of the square ebony peg other materials were sometimes used for pegs. These include teak, mahogany and maple. Ebony was certainly the most common material for the characteristic square pegs. Thank you to Jim Ipekjian for sharing his considerable experience on this topic.

12. Darrell Peart, *Greene & Greene Design Elements for the Workshop*, Linden Publishing, Fresno, 2005, pp. 63-70.

PG. 76 13. In a typically Greene & Greene touch, shelves for case pieces in the Culbertson house are constructed with breadboards. These breadboards contain ebony pegs, likely concealing screws.

14. Work on the Blacker house began in 1907. Furniture design occurred early in the process though implementation trailed into 1909.

PG. 80 15. See Kazuko Koizumi, *Traditional Japanese Furniture*, Kodansha International, Tokyo, 1986.

16. There are numerous books about wabi-sabi. They range in topic from design to philosophy, religion and self-help.

PG. 84 17. See Bruce Smith, "Sunlight and Elsewhere", *A New and Native Beauty: The Art and Craft of Greene & Greene*, Merrill, London, 2008.

PG. 85 18. Wenjun Xing, "Social Gospel, Social Economics, and the YMCA: Sidney D. Gamble and Princeton-in-Peking", Ph.D. Dissertation, University of Massachusetts, 1992.

19. Many of Sidney Gamble's photographs were published in a retrospective after his death. See *Sidney D. Gamble's China 1917-1932 — Photographs of the Land and Its People*, Alvin Rosenbaum Projects, Chevy Chase, MD., 1989. His photographs are archived at Duke University.

PG. 86 20. Letter from Charles Greene to Mrs. Lucretia Garfield. Greene & Greene Archives.

21. Bruce Smith, "Sunlight and Elsewhere", *A New and Native Beauty: The Art and Craft of Greene & Greene*, Merrill, London, 2008, p. 83.

22. Clay Lancaster, *Japanese Influence in America*, Walton H. Rawls, New York, 1963, pp. 115-117.

23. Charles Keeler, *The Simple Home*, Paul Elder, San Francisco, 1904, p. 29.

24. Bruce Smith, *Greene & Greene Masterworks*, Chronicle Books, San Francisco, 1998, p. 144.

PG. 88 25. Ted Bosley points out that the most chalet-like of the Greenes' houses were not in Arroyo Terrace (Bosley, *Greene & Greene*, p. 93). The name stuck, however, likely due to the density of Greene & Greene houses in that neighborhood.

26. Charles Greene, correspondence, Environmental Design Archives, University of California-Berkeley.

27. For a wonderful discussion of the relationship between Swiss chalets, bungalows and Greene & Greene houses, see Bruno Giberti, "The Chalet as Archetype: The Bungalow, The Picturesque Tradition and Vernacular Form," *Traditional Dwellings and Settlements Review*, 3.1, 1991, pp. 54-64.

28. Early chalets were often constructed of logs, similar to an American log cabin. William S. B. Dana, *The Swiss Chalet Book*, William T. Comstock, Co., New York, 1913, p. 14.

29. Thank you to Ted Bosley for offering his opinion on the chalet influence.

30. See Dana, *The Swiss Chalet Book*, p. 19, 20, 31, 41, for examples.

31. Ibid. p. 127.

PG. 90 32. Ibid. p. 133.

PG. 91 33. Jean Murray Bangs, "Greene & Greene", *Architectural Forum*, Vol. 89, No. 4, October 1948, p. 88.

PG. 93 34. In many cases the term baluster doesn't apply in a traditional sense though the structure implemented serves that purpose. The Caroline DeForest house serves as an example.

PG. 95 35. Edward Cooke states that between 1907 and 1913, "…the Halls made about 400 pieces of furniture while working for the Greenes." This figure doesn't include Thorsen furniture which was made onsite. Edward S. Cooke, Jr., "Scandinavian Modern Furniture in the Arts and Crafts Period: The Collaboration of the Greenes and the Halls", in *American Furniture 1993*, Chipstone Foundation, 1993, p. 7.

36. This number does not include various additions, alterations and commercial projects. Several of the commissioned designs were never constructed.

PG. 102 37. Kazuo Nishi and Kazuo Hozumi (translated by H. Mack Horton), *What Is Japanese Architecture?: A Survey of Traditional Japanese Architecture*, Kodansha International, Tokyo, 1996, pp. 36-38.

38. Thanks to David Young for several useful exchanges on the finer points of this topic.

PG. 104 39. Early tsuba were quite plain. The ability to convey status came via intricacy and applied ornament in later examples. See Edward Dillon, *The Arts of Japan*, A.C. McClurg & Co., Chicago, 1910, pp. 126-138.

40. Captain F. Brinkley, *Japan: Its History, Arts and Literature*, Volume VII, J. B. Millet Company, Boston, 1902, pp. 265-266.

41. For much more on the components of Japanese swords see ibid., p. 210. For an amazingly detailed discussion of the chiseling of sword mounts and guards, see chapters 6-8 in the same work.

PG. 105 42. Clive Sinclair, *Samurai: The Weapons and Spirit of the Japanese Warrior*, Lyons Press, Guilford, CT, 2004 (originally published by Salamander Books, 2001), p. 83. Mokko-gata is translated as "four-arched outline" in Brinkley, *Japan: Its History, Arts and Literature*, p. 264.

43. Sconces for the Adelaide Tichenor house exhibit a mokko-gata form in the leaded glass, the first use of that feature in a Greene & Greene furnishing. Drawings in the Greene & Greene archives give dates of October 20, 1906, for the Robinson table and March 22, 1907, for the Bolton table.

44. Edward S. Cooke, Jr., *Scandinavian Modern Furniture in the Arts & Crafts Period: The Collaboration of the Greenes and the Halls*, Chipstone Foundation, 1993, p. 4.

PG. 108 45. As quoted in a eulogy by Richard Dawkins, September 17, 2001.

PG. 109 46. Edward S. Cooke, Jr., "Scandinavian Modern Furniture in the Arts and Crafts Period: The Collaboration of the Greenes and the Halls", in *American Furniture 1993*, Luke Beckerdite, ed., Chipstone, Milwaukee, 1993. This article is required reading for anyone interested in Greene & Greene furniture.

PG. 110 47. See Bob Lang's excellent book, which includes a discussion of this topic. *Shop Drawings for Greene & Greene Furniture*, Fox Chapel Publishing, East Petersburg, PA, 2006.

48. Special thanks to Jacqueline Dugas, The Huntington Library, Art Collections and Botanical Gardens, for her assistance in discovering details of the Thorsen sideboard.

PG. 114 49. Thanks to Nonie Gadsden, Museum Fine Arts, Boston, for confirming this number while the curio cabinet was on display there as part of the Gamble house centennial exhibition: A New and Native Beauty: The Art and Craft of Greene & Greene.

PG. 115 50. The golden ratio, denoted , is defined as follows. Consider a rectangle with side lengths in the ratio 1:x. Now break the rectangle into a unit square and the new rectangle that results is the unique value for x such that this new rectangle also has sides with the ratio 1:x. This value is, or about 1.618. Thank you to Tom Moore and Tom Volz for exploring this topic.

PG. 116 51. "Joints are emphasized and used as pattern." L. Morgan Yost, "Greene & Greene of Pasadena", *Journal of the Society of Architectural Historians*, Vol. 9, No. 1-2, March-May 1950, p. 18.

PG. 117 52. See, for example, the dining room of the Laurabelle Robinson house.

53. For a detailed discussion, see Jack A. Sobon, *Historic American Timber Joinery: A Graphic Guide*, The Timber Framers Guild, Becket, MA, 2002, pp. 46-51.

54. Edward R. Bosley, *Greene & Greene*, Phaidon Press Limited, London, 2000, p. 94.

55. Okkake daisentsugi resemble the stop-splayed joints in American timber construction.

56. For informative discussions of many Japanese architectural details, see JAANUS, the Japanese Architecture and Art Net Users System at www.aisf.or.jp/~jaanus.

PG. 118 57. Finger joints are also a form of open mortise and tenon. They are sometimes referred to as such by docents of the Gamble House during tours. Woodworkers have been known to scoff at the description only to learn later that the docent was, in fact, correct in the use of the term.

PG. 120 58. This author believes that the Laurabelle A. Robinson house should be included in the set of Ultimates. Constructed beginning in 1905, the Robinson house would then be the first Ultimate Bungalow. See Chapter 2 for further discussion of this topic.

59. Randall L. Makinson, Thomas A. Heinz and Brad Pitt, *Greene & Greene: The Blacker House, Gibbs Smith*, Salt Lake City, 2000. This book wonderfully chronicles the decline and restoration of the house.

60. Morgan Yost writes of visiting the Blacker house with Henry Greene in 1946 and reports that Mrs. Blacker died the next year. These two statements are slightly out of sync with respect to timing. Thus, the visit may have occurred in either 1945 or 1946.

61. "The inside of the house is perfect yet; apparently not a scar or shrinkage or blemish. Quite a number of years ago I had Savage go over all the woodwork and furniture; and so it looks and is as smooth as velvet yet…" As quoted in Makinson, et al., p. 103.

PG. 121 62. For a more detailed discussion of this topic, see Makinson, et al., pp. 18-19, 41-56.

PG. 130 63. Edward Bosley as quoted in: Ted Wells, *Greene & Greene in Long Beach: The Adelaide Tichenor House* (Part 2 of 3), October 27, 2005. Podcast retrieved from twls.libsyn.com/index.php?post_year=2005&post_month=10.

PG. 134 64. Unfortunately, the pins were not always re-stowed before the arms were retracted. Scars on the table's breadboard ends attest to multiple occurrences.

65. For a discussion of the mechanism on this table, see Alan Marks, "Greene & Greene: A Study in Functional Design," *Fine Woodworking*, No. 12, September 1978, pp. 43-44.

PG. 135 66. Ibid, pp. 43-44.

67. The mechanism on the Robinson dining table is similar but that on the Gamble table is more refined.

PG. 140 68. Cutouts in the sconces are echoed by a similar detail on the tabouret.

69. One detail approaching a constant is the use of leather straps to hang lighting fixtures.

70. See, for example, the Daibutsuden at Todaiji (the Great Eastern Temple) in Nara, Japan.

71. I was unable to include a photo of the table lamp. See *A New and Native Beauty: The Art and Craft of Greene & Greene*, Merrell, London, 2008, p. 258.

PG. 144 72. See the section on Lighting for additional examples of Greene & Greene art glass.

PG. 146 73. Edward R. Bosley, *Greene & Greene*, Phaidon Press Limited, London, 2000, p. 116.

74. Thanks to Tom Moore for sharing the recent developments on this topic.

PG. 147 75. Thank you to John Hamm for sharing his experience with this topic.

PG. 149 76. An escutcheon is, in this context, a small protective plate around a keyhole.

PG. 152 77. This house is often referred to as the Cordelia Culbertson house.

PG. 153 78. Ralph Adams Cram, Preface in *American Country Houses of Today*, Architectural Book Publishing Company, New York, 1913, p. V.

79. The piece was almost certainly sold at the Prentiss estate sale (Elisabeth Allen purchased the house from the Culbertson sisters prior to marrying Francis Prentiss). What became of it between that time and its arrival at Warner Bros. is a mystery. Thanks to Ted Bosley for sharing his thoughts about this.

Index

Ideas. Instruction. Inspiration.

These and other great Popular Woodworking products are available at your local bookstore, woodworking store or online supplier.

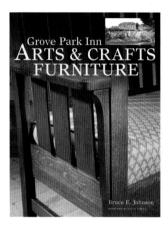

GROVE PARK INN
ARTS & CRAFTS FURNITURE
by Bruce E. Johnson
The Grove Park Inn opened in 1913, decorated with Arts & Crafts furniture. The Inn has retained many of the original pieces and has acquired a large and rare collection of original Arts & Crafts furniture. You'll find measured drawings for many of these pieces, making this a wonderful collection for history buffs and woodworkers alike.

ISBN 13: 978-1-55870-8495
hardcover • 176 pages • Z2279

THE PERFECT EDGE
by Ron Hock
The mystery of the elusive sharp edge is solved. This book covers all the different sharpening methods so you can improve your sharpening techniques.

ISBN 13: 978-1-55870-858-7
hardcover • 224 pages • Z2676

POPULAR WOODWORKING
MAGAZINE
Whether learning a new hobby or perfecting your craft, *Popular Woodworking Magazine* has expert information to teach the skill, not just the project. Find the latest issue on newsstands, or order online at www.popularwoodworking.com.

BOX MAKING BONANZA
DVD-ROM
Boxes are an excellent opportunity to learn, practice and master many of the techniques and joinery used in all woodworking projects.

ISBN 13: 978-1-55870-864-5

This disc includes the full book content from: *Box by Box, Creating Beautiful Boxes with Inlay Techniques, Simply Beautiful Boxes*
DVD-ROM • Z4824

Visit **www.popularwoodworking.com** for articles, videos and to join our community.

Recent Articles	Featured Product	Note from the Editor
Read the five most recent articles from Popular Woodworking Books. • Kitchen Makeovers - Pull-Out Pantry Design & Construction • Woodshop Lust Tom Rosati's Woodshop • Woodshop Lust David Thiel's Woodshop • Wood Finishing Simplified Strictly, Stickley Oak • Wood Finishing Simplified In a Pickle (Whitewash on Oak or Pine)	**Made By Hand** $21.95 *Made By Hand* takes you right to the bench and shows you how to start building furniture using hand tools. By working through the six projects in this book, you'll learn the basics of hand-tool woodworking and how to use the tools effectively and efficiently, then	**Welcome to Books & More** We've got the latest reviews and free sample excerpts from our favorite woodworking books, plus news on the newest releases. Check out the savings at our **Woodworker's Book Shop**, and don't miss out on building your Wish List for the holidays. If you missed our newsletter's **"Print Is Dead" poll results**, check them here, and subscribe (below) to our newsletter to receive special sale items and book reviews not found anywhere else. *– David Baker-Thiel, Executive Editor* *Popular Woodworking Books*

A woodworking education can come in many forms, including books, magazines, videos and community feedback. At Popular Woodworking we've got them all. Visit our website at www.popularwoodworking.com to follow our blogs, read about the newest tools and books and join our community. We want to know what you're building.

Sign up to receive our weekly newsletter at http://popularwoodworking.com/newsletters/